Career Potentials
in Physical Activity

Career Potentials in Physical Activity

Bryant J. Cratty, Ed.D.

Professor of Physical Education
UNIVERSITY OF CALIFORNIA, LOS ANGELES

PRENTICE-HALL, INC.
ENGLEWOOD CLIFFS, NEW JERSEY

© 1971
by Prentice-Hall, Inc.
Englewood Cliffs, New Jersey

13–114710–2

Library of Congress Catalog Card Number: 79–136631

Printed in the United States of America

Current Printing (last digit):

10 9 8 7 6 5 4 3 2 1

PRENTICE-HALL INTERNATIONAL, INC.   London
PRENTICE-HALL OF AUSTRALIA, PTY. LTD.   Sydney
PRENTICE-HALL OF CANADA, LTD.   Toronto
PRENTICE-HALL OF INDIA PRIVATE LIMITED   New Delhi
PRENTICE-HALL OF JAPAN, INC.   Tokyo

This book is dedicated to my students.

Preface

My purpose in writing *Career Potentials in Physical Activity* is twofold: to provide fledgling students in physical education and associated major fields with an idea of how broad their career opportunities are and to expose these students to some of the subject matter areas which, if explored more deeply, will lead them toward more effective performance in their chosen profession.

Perhaps to some readers occasional statements in the text may seem too glib, too controversial, or downright false. I have tried to learn from those students to whom I have been exposed at the University of California during the past years, as I was admonished to do by a professor of education whose identity is now obscured in my memory. One important lesson I have learned from today's students is to "tell it like it is!" I have tried at least to tell it like I *think* it is.

In my attempt to veer away from the usual evangelical approach to athletics, physical movement, and so on, often seen in this type of orientation text and indeed in most literature of the profession, I have found it necessary to take a more critical look at some of the practices in careers which somehow use physical activity purportedly to help people. Athletics, physical education, and similar services, if not properly applied and presented to children and youth, are as likely to cause consternation, emotional trauma, and at times physical problems as they are likely to uplift, improve, and revitalize. One of the best ways to improve the service of any group of professional workers is to engage in critical, scientific, and objective evaluation of the services extended to people and, in turn, of their response to these services. This process of evaluation is as true in medicine and law as it is in teaching, if the members of these professions are truly to be called professionals.

There are several threads running through the text which might be called more explicitly to the reader's attention. For example, I have intimated that teachers of physical education and athletic coaches might show kindness to children and youth entering their spheres of influence. The use of psychological punishments to exorcise negative feelings about activity and to encourage vigorous participation is as unsound as the not uncommon practice of making children run laps (as a demonstration that running is a punishment to be avoided) when a child shows reluctance to participate in a physical education class.

The opportunities for recent graduates of physical education programs to serve in a broad spectrum of occupations are indeed present as we enter the 1970s and proceed into the 1980s. The only limitations upon career choice rest in the limitations within the students themselves. Some universities send a surprising number of their graduates in physical education to medical schools; other graduates enter special education, educational psychology, human factors laboratories, and similar fields. However, there are even more opportunities to serve children and youth, opportunities which at times are overlooked by those starting out in physical education programs. Hopefully, the student will be exposed to some of these career channels as he reviews the contents of this book and will hence seek practical work experiences as an undergraduate.

In this text I have tried to encourage students to examine their motives and abilities, and if they feel unqualified, to change their major to one in which they do not deal with people in situations permeated by vigorous physical activity, since participation in athletics and the other various forms of physical education virtually never results in a neutral experience for those involved. A child leaves the gymnasium or athletic field with either a negative or a positive feeling about himself and about the activity in which he has just participated. The psyches of children associated with college graduates in physical education who have sound academic backgrounds and are also sensitive to feelings about others will be uplifted instead of trampled.

My sincere thanks to members of the staff here at UCLA who reviewed portions of the manuscript for technical flaws. My sagging but brave secretarial staff composed of Misses Sara Dobbins, Barbara Goen, and Dianne Jue worked in their usual diligent and competent manner to translate my, at times, incomprehensible typing into acceptable English. My thanks also to my wife and daughter who continue to inspire me by their very presence and by their health, good humor, and encouragement.

I cannot, however, place the blame for the inaccuracies and distortions which undoubtedly remain in the manuscript upon my family, my clerical staff, or my tolerant colleagues. For these I am solely responsible.

BJC

Contents

CHAPTER
NINETEEN **Historical Perspectives** 191

CHAPTER
TWENTY **Mechanics of Movement** 203

CHAPTER
TWENTY-ONE **Testing and Measurement** 213

Career Potentials
in Physical Activity

PART ONE

Introduction

CHAPTER ONE

Introduction

There are many possible directions and careers an individual might take when working within the field broadly defined as physical education. Some of these careers are: teacher educator and researcher at a university, physical education teacher at the elementary, secondary, or college level, curriculum supervisor within a school district, and teacher of physical education to the physically, emotionally, or mentally handicapped. In addition, many with an undergraduate background in physical education find themselves working after graduation as classroom teachers or as recreation workers.

In general, however, the jobs classified as physical education have several common characteristics:

1. The job entails some kind of service to some group of people or to an individual.
2. The position usually requires the professional worker to deal in the medium of motor activity when rendering the service.
3. Some type of purportedly beneficial change is the objective of the application of a program of movement tasks. This change might include increased competencies in movement itself, for example, improved muscular fitness or skill development. On the other hand, the objectives might be concerned with the improvement of other facets of the personality, such as better emotional, social, or even academic functioning.

4. The physical educator usually has in his possession some type of academic credentials gained from course work taken after high school involving both theory and practice.

A great deal has been written by both physical educators and those in other fields about just what criteria should be applied before one can attach the label "profession" to a certain field. There are some who would not regard the practice of physical education as a profession, while others believe that it is. It is often difficult to identify a field of endeavor as a profession, differentiated from a vocation. Usually the former term is a more prestigious one, while the latter denotes somewhat less stature.

A number of criteria have been suggested for defining a profession. The student may attempt to decide for himself, following a review of the book, and perhaps following his course of study at college, whether in truth physical education as presently constituted should be termed a profession or a vocation. These criteria include:

1. A profession provides a service to people or to societal institutions.
2. Membership in a profession requires academic credentials of a rather high level.
3. Professions constantly seek to improve the capacities of their members, and continually engage in self-examination and evaluation.
4. Practices carried out within a profession are based upon a valid body of knowledge which has been established as the result of scientifically sound research programs.

One may evaluate the quality of a field of endeavor such as physical education by either of two means. On one hand, the general supports of the field might be examined by assessing the quality of undergraduate preparation to which students are exposed or the quality of literature in the field. On the other hand, a more valid approach, the quality of performance of practitioners in the field may be measured against some of the criteria outlined above. For example, one might ask: Does the physical education teacher *act* as if he has been exposed to a body of knowledge which is scientifically based? Does the physical educator seem to seek, and be amenable to, efforts at self-improvement? Perhaps most important: Just what *is* the *quality* of the service purportedly rendered to children and youth by the physical educator?

Despite the efforts of some physical educators at the university level somehow to cloak all within the career field under consideration with a protective mantle of professionalism, there are physical educators rendering a quality of service to youth so poor as to give lie to the label, "a professional person." One of the threads within the materials which follows involves the elaboration of just what professional behavior consists of, and how the undergraduate student may learn to function at a true professional level after graduation.

Several other objectives have been incorporated into the chapters which follow. This introductory section hopefully will help the undergraduate student to understand what is involved in becoming both a scholar and a practitioner of physical education while still in college. It not only attempts to orient the student toward reasonably sound study habits and professional relationships while still an undergraduate but tries at the same time to delineate just how the student may begin to think and perform as a professional person. This first section also contains guidelines which the student might keep in mind when relating to his fellow students, professors, and instructors at the college or university he is attending.

Part Two of the text contains an overview of some of the courses the student is likely to encounter while majoring in physical education. The exact classes and contents, of course, are different in each college and university in the land. At the same time most curriculums in the country are beginning to incorporate most of the subject matter areas outlined in Part Two. Perhaps if some of this content is not included in your major program, and if you feel it may be relevant to your needs following graduation, you might, before graduation, together with a student-faculty committee, help to institute additional meaningful courses. It has not been attempted to present penetrating discourses on the various content fields within the usual physical education curriculum. The chapters are little more than expanded course outlines. Each chapter is followed by a bibliography which the enterprising student might consult for additional insights into an area of interest.

Part Three contains discussions within its chapters (15-23) which will aid the student to perceive the broad expanse of career opportunities opened by a major in physical education. Again the treatment of these subjects is not exhaustive, but merely sketches the various ways in which a physical educator might be expected to function after graduation.

Part Four outlines ways in which the student may obtain helpful work experience both during and following graduation. Again human relationships are emphasized, for above all, a physical educator generally works with people in some way, and unless the student is able to work well with people, his or her effectiveness will surely be hampered.

Part Five contains a chapter which attempts to look ahead and predict the directions which physical education may be taking during the next twenty years.

The last objective, which it is hoped will be to some measure achieved by reference to the material in this text, involves aiding and encouraging the student to engage in a reasonably accurate self-assessment of his or her motives, competencies, and skills. The college years are usually looked upon as a period of self-improvement, and guidelines for improvement may best be initiated with an enumeration of both the talents and deficiencies the student possesses.

Why Physical Education?

A prospective physical education teacher should initially consider just why he or she has chosen to become a physical education major student. Generally, physical education students at a university mention three primary reasons:

1. They have found satisfaction in participating in physical activities and wish to share their gratification with others.
2. They wish to serve children and/or youth through the media of various physical activities.
3. They have received personal rewards in high school sports and wish to remain in a field in which they achieved, matured, and were reinforced.

All beginning physical education majors, particularly the males, should ask themselves, whether their primary purpose for entering the field is to continue to gain the *personal* gratification they knew as high school and perhaps as college athletes; or whether they really see themselves in a *service* role after graduation from college.

While it is to be expected that most individuals in the various professions function under the influence of both selfish and altruistic motives, the physical educator should primarily be moved to perform well not for personal aggrandizement, but for the satisfactions he may obtain while having some part in the improvement of the youth he serves.

A second related question, to which the student should offer at least a tentative answer, concerns why he or she has selected to major in physical education as opposed to other available college majors. If the major has been chosen or selected for him because of the belief that it represents a "snap" course of study, he may be in for disappointment; for within recent years many curricula within colleges and universities have undergone marked revisions and have incorporated increased amounts of work in the basic biological, physical, and behavioral sciences, particularly during the first two years of study. At the same time, if the student has been counseled into the physical education major as an easy way to get through college, and perhaps to serve the needs of the athletic department, then he is being exploited to a marked degree.

A student who spends four or more years of his life attending classes which will later be irrelevant to him and to his life's goals is deluding himself, and when this occurs it is pathetic to behold.

A third concept which the student should come to terms with is the fact that most 17-, 18-, and 19-year-olds possessing the capacity to engage in university- and college-level work are likely to perform well later in a number of careers. The supposition that there is just one best occupation for an individual is as fallacious as the hypothesis that there is only one perfect mate waiting somewhere in the world for you to come in contact![1] On the other hand, there are certain characteristics of various occupations and professions which may be roughly paired with individual personality traits, needs, and competencies. It is desirable for many freshmen and sophomore students whose career goals are only vaguely defined to obtain sound vocational counseling based upon the scores derived from various vocational aptitude, personality, and occupational interest tests. Pursuing an unsatisfactory major course of study for a prolonged period of time is not sound. Refusing to change majors in order to facilitate graduation, even though one dislikes the career toward which one's major leads, is also unwise.

A fourth main consideration is that within each career field, with physical education no exception, there are innumerable different functions an individual might perform. The recreation director, the physical education teacher in a school for the blind, and the university researcher dealing with cellular level problems of exercise carry out daily tasks which are quite different from one another. Within the field of physical education, the student might begin to consider just what facet of the field holds potential interest for him.

A fifth major factor in the assessment of just why people enter physical education, or any college major for that matter, revolves around the manner in which individual motives change from day to day and from year to year. Within a given week an athlete, for example, is surrounded by a constellation of motives, reasons he may perceive for performing well, any one of which (or combination of which) may impinge upon him at a given point in time. Within a longer time span the same holds true. Things which "turn on" a student entering college simply may not matter when that same student is a senior; while motives which are important to the senior may not be relevant when that same individual is entering his 40s and 50s! Thus, if at all possible, the student contemplating majoring in physical education should attempt to see himself five, ten, or even 20 years removed from college. The student should ask himself if he will still be motivated to perform

[1]If this were true, the likelihood of the two ever meeting would be extremely slight.

well as a teacher, using physical activity as a tool, when he is 40 and 50 years old, long after the approval of the crowd he may have heard as a high school athlete has faded into the distance. Students should attempt to determine just what intrinsic value they see for themselves and for others in engaging in physical education activities.

Similar to the evolvement of the importance of various motives which certainly occurs from the nineteenth year to the fiftieth year of life is the metamorphosis of behavior and values which occurs during the college years themselves. It is often found that the college freshman enters the institution of higher learning "bright-eyed" and slightly in awe of college and university professors, the institution of higher learning itself, and the various societal subsystems to which he is exposed. During the sophomore year the student frequently encounters a provocative professor or two who helpfully encourage him to become critical of "absolute truths," institutions, and indeed of the professors and instructors themselves! The student at this point becomes hypercritical and often stumbles over himself in his eagerness to criticize those in authority positions in his home and at the campus. This critical attitude, which at times may simply be a type of protective mechanism, continues until about the beginning of the fourth year of university work, at which time a third and final phase may prevail. The senior often finds himself in a state of panic as he begins to come to grips with the realization of how *little* he really knows. He may find himself with the appalling feeling that he really does not know much of anything, and may ask himself the question, Just why should anyone hire me with my limited background?

In truth, however, this final stage is perhaps the sign of at least the beginnings of an educated person. For the freshman might be likened to a lighted match whose knowledge is represented by a small circumference of light, and whose ignorance is represented by the corresponding small circle of darkness. At this point he is unaware of really how much there is to know and is thus happily unaware of his ignorance. By the time the student has reached the senior year, however, the circle of enlightenment has significantly increased, and with it the corresponding circle of darkness and ignorance. The student has become aware of all there is to know, and of all the potential background there is yet to be acquired. Hopefully this awareness of ignorance is not accompanied by a total feeling of incompetence, but rather by a feeling that: "I shall attempt to do my best using the tools I have acquired, within the limitations of which I am aware."

An arrogant, know-it-all attitude at graduation is as unproductive as is a feeling of helplessness and confusion. The major course in physical education should impart to students participating in it three important tools: (a) meaningful ways to teach various physical activities and sports skills, (b) an awareness of reasons why people move, learn, and teach as they do, and finally (c) a sound philosophy within which the fledgling student-teacher may grow professionally and render appropriate and meaningful service to those in his charge. The extent to which these objectives are reached may be better assessed during the final stages of the senior year.

Overview

It is important for students who contemplate entering physical education to attempt not only to evaluate their own feelings, abilities, and present and future motive systems, but also to try to assess accurately some of the more measurable advantages and possible disadvantages of the field they have chosen to enter.

For example, one might list as possible disadvantages to working in physical education and athletics: (a) the possibly low salary scale when compared with other nonteaching professions, and the possibility of a fixed salary which would not reflect inflationary trends; (b) the low status accorded some physical education and athletic departments by their more "academic" colleagues on high school and college faculties; (c) the inordinate amount of extracurricular work which sometimes falls to the physical educator, which often takes the form of extrasupervisory functions, responsibilities for campus discipline, and other work best left to the police; (d) the great amount of physical work entailed in coaching, moving equipment, and otherwise working with and around individuals engaged in physical activities and athletics; (e) the pressure to win in athletics, which is sometimes a primary criterion for the retention of athletic and physical education personnel.

On the other hand, there are possibly an equal number of positive factors associated with careers in physical education and athletics which should be considered. For example: (a) It is usual to find that a coach and physical education teacher possesses a remarkable amount of rapport with students. He is in a position to elicit positive changes in students' outlooks and in their behavior, because of the status he may have in their eyes as a result of his association with athletics. (b) Often coaching and other ancillary duties are compensated financially, so that a career in physical education may be reasonably well rewarded. (c) High prestige and favorable status are accorded many coaches and physical education teachers by their school communities and by the town in which they work. (d) The opportunity to work with a community's youth in the dynamic activities which abound in physical education and athletic programs is reward enough for many who place high value upon service to mankind.

Thus, the student must weigh both the good and bad points in the field he proposes to enter and to be educated toward. No sales talk from a professor or instructor should be allowed inordinately to sway his opinion. Parental values, while worth considering, similarly should not be the total basis upon which to evaluate the worth of the vocation for which he is preparing. Rather, he must examine himself, his motives and capabilities, and then evaluate the pros and cons of physical education as well as other lines of endeavor he might be suited to undertake. Only after this type of introspection plus job evaluation has taken place can a happy match be made.

Student Activities and Discussion Questions

1. What personality traits would seem best to suit one for entering the field of physical education?
2. What personality tests and vocational aptitude and interest tests are offered in your school's counseling service? How predictive are these of later professional success? What are the procedures one must go through to take these tests. How long do they take? What followup counseling procedures are engaged in by the staff administering them at your college or university? If no such counseling is available at your college, to what community or governmental agency might you go for similar advice?
3. Interview a male and a female physical education teacher in your community. Ask them to outline the drawbacks and advantages of their chosen careers as they see them. Which of the factors they mention are likely to be unique to their situations? Which of the factors they mention are likely to be found in the responses of a large number of physical education teachers?
4. What books can you find which contain guidelines for the selection of a vocation and/or a profession? Can you apply these guidelines to yourself in your selection of physical education?
5. In what ways might your value system change during the next five, ten, 30 years? What changes in your life might elicit these differences in how you feel about things?
6. Interview a winning and a losing coach at the end of the sports season. Attempt to determine what they see as advantages and disadvantages in their chosen occupations.
7. Discuss possible similarities and differences between the roles of physical education teacher and athletic coach in a high school.
8. What traits do you have which should contribute to your positive performance as a physical education teacher and/or an athletic coach?

Consider your appearance, physical structure, performance in sports, personality, as well as intellectual endowments.

9. Consider what traits you might possess which could potentially detract from your performance as a physical education teacher or athletic coach. How might you rectify these shortcomings during the years you are an undergraduate?

References

Books

Johnson, Granville B., *Your Career in Physical Education: An Introduction to the Profession for Young Men and Women.* New York: Harper & Row, Publishers, 1957.

Nash, Jay B., *Opportunities in Physical Education and Health Education.* New York: Vocational Guidance Manual, Inc., 1960.

Pope, Laurence A., *A Professional Career in Physical Education.* Englewood Cliffs, New Jersey: Prentice-Hall, Inc., 1962.

Periodicals

College Student Personnel. Washington, D. C.: 1607 New Hampshire Avenue, N. W.

CHAPTER TWO

Your Physical Education Major

The teachers of physical education during the early part of the 1800s were interested faculty members in either a college or a high school. At times the upperclassmen led the younger boys and girls in exercises usually based upon some European system of gymnastics. The first formal teacher-training program for physical education instructors was established in 1861 in Rochester, New York, by the North American Turnerbund, an organization founded on the principles of the German *Turnverein* (literally, *turning place*). This school quickly closed, however, because of the onset of the Civil War, and did not reopen until after the war.

It is believed by most authorities that the first true physical education training institute was established by Dio Lewis in Boston in 1861, and was called "A Normal Institute for Physical Education." The first graduating class consisted of 13 students who were taught to administer gymnastic exercises. Their course consisted of nine weeks, and the students studied from six to 12 hours per day. This school lasted seven years, and during that period graduated about 250 students. Following the closure of Dio Lewis' school, the only teacher-training institute open was one started by the Turners in New York in 1866, called the "College of the American Gymnastic Union." This school moved to Indianapolis where it became permanently located.

During the latter part of the 1800s, majors in physical education were established in a few colleges and universities in the country as it began to be recognized that formal teacher education was needed. Dudley Sargent, at Harvard University, established summer workshops in the early 1880s for prospective teachers, but it was not until 1892 that a regular two-year course was instituted by Sargent. Sargent emphasized both theory and practice, and focused on a program which emphasized balanced physical development through the use of various pulleys and gymnastic equipment.

A number of other physical educators opened private teacher-training schools in the latter part of the nineteenth century. However, it was not until 1900 that many colleges began to include a professional curriculum in physical education into their courses of study. The University of California, the University of Nebraska, Oberlin College, and the University of Missouri were among the first to offer such courses.

During the 1920s and 1930s, physical education courses proliferated in the various universities in the country for several reasons. In some cases there was an increased emphasis on teacher education in general, and thus physical education was aided by this trend. Some of the major programs during this period were instituted at places in which the less academically able athletes could be "harbored" so that athletic teams would be well manned.

Research courses and laboratories began to appear in other teacher-training institutions during the 1930s and 1940s. An emphasis upon scientific measurement, together with a research trend in general education, began to prompt the departments in some institutions to emphasize a balance of theory and practice in their curriculums.

At the present time, departments of physical education which train teachers may be characterized in a number of ways. The "personalities" of these departments depend upon many factors, including the number and background of their instructors and professors, their geographical location, the specific demands for trained personnel made by the community surrounding them, their stated or implied philosophical orientations, the administrative framework in which they reside, as well as the internal constitution of the department itself.

One of the first tasks of a physical education major student should be, with or without the aid of a course instructor, to become familiar with the unique characteristics of the physical education department in which you find yourself. Some of the things you might look for in this type of survey include the following:

1. Is the department's philosophy stated in some document you are able to obtain? How was this stated philosophy derived? In what way does it reflect the individual philosophies of the department members? Does it conflict with or complement any of your personal commitments?

2. If such a philosophy does not appear in printed form, just what is the general feeling the department and/or individual faculty members have about the goals and objectives of the major program, and about the place of physical education in general education?

3. How many faculty members make up the department? How might they be classified (i.e., men, women, researchers, teachers of applied courses, etc.)? What are their main interests and backgrounds? Which members of your faculty have interests which correspond roughly to your own? How might you work with professors with interests common to your own during your undergraduate years?

4. What courses are you required to take during the next years of college? Which, if any, are optional? What is written about these courses? What is *said* about them by other students who have taken them?

5. What is the relative emphasis upon theory versus practice? Which of the courses involve primarily lecture versus activity and physical participation? How do these courses relate?

6. What courses are required outside the physical education department? How do these integrate with courses taught within your physical education department?

7. What courses, if any, provide you with teaching experience with children? During what years are these courses required?

8. What physical skills will you need to participate in the various activity courses? In which physical skills do you feel deficient? Do courses in skill improvement integrate with courses in teaching methodology?

   Obtaining information concerning some of the points in numbers 1 through 8 above should better prepare you for the years ahead. Following a survey of your own academic and physical attributes, you should be able to pinpoint the places within the curriculum for which you can begin to prepare yourself. At the same time a survey of the curriculum and staff in your major department might also prompt you to work for possible change in the content of various courses, and perhaps even to suggest the addition or deletion of present courses through the proper channels. The second part of the text contains chapters which delve into the possible content of various courses often found in physical education major curriculums.

Types of Major Programs Presently
Found in the United States

The classification of physical education major curriculums in the various colleges and universities within the United States is a somewhat difficult undertaking, for there are many types of departments influenced by the factors previously outlined (staff makeup, geographical location, administrative characteristics, etc.). At the same time it might be helpful, as a beginning student, to outline briefly just how various programs might be classified, and the types of focuses and administrative environments which may be found. In this way you may compare what you find within your own program with various other possibilities of which you might now be unaware. The classification system presented below attempts to look at the various curriculums from several standpoints, including the emphasis upon theory versus practice, the nature of the staff, as well as the various ways in which a department may be organized and may reside within the total college or university hierarchy.

Theory and Practice

In the education of teachers one cannot often find a department of physical education whose courses contain information which may be categorized as entirely theory or, on the other hand, whose courses contain solely the "practical" or the "applied." The majority of departments offer both theoretical courses as well as courses with content more applicable to the teaching of specific sports and recreational skills. At the same time it is possible to characterize most curriculums as emphasizing either the theoretical underpinnings of motor activity, or composed primarily of courses emphasizing suggestions which can immediately be applied to coaching and/or teaching situations.

A theory is a reasonably general statement which either categorizes or attempts in some way to predict some phenomena, thus trying to create order out of potential scientific chaos. One may either build or consult theories of various degrees of magnitude. Thus, a theory may be one which is rather universal in nature, as exemplified by Einstein's theory of relativity; or in the case of a theory pertaining to human behavior, one of the more comprehensive personality theories. Lower level theories encompass somewhat narrower ranges of human behavior or of the physical universe. Examples of these could include some of the more restrictive learning theories, motor learning theories, or perhaps a theory of motivation. The term "model" is sometimes employed to designate a potential theory which may not be well delineated because of the lack of supporting data.

The validity or worth of a theory can be assessed by examining the quality of the scientific data upon which it purportedly rests, as well as by evaluating the quality and quantity of the research which it has seemed to inspire. Theories are helpful guidelines for the formulation and evaluation of new practices in physical education. And while theories are often difficult to interpret, translating the tenets of a theory into practice is often a helpful experience which may stimulate the intellectual growth of the student majoring in physical education.

Thus, a curriculum which to a large degree rests upon theory contains many courses which may not offer exact guidelines for practice, but instead attempt to illuminate knowledge about various relevant facets of human motor behavior. There is a deemphasis in such curricula upon courses which show in exact ways how one should teach all the various sports skills. Instead, more general guidelines are offered concerning, for example, how skills may develop from infancy to maturity and how individuals learn motor skills, how the physiological systems and cellular mechanisms accommodate and change as a result of exercises, and what laws of physics should be considered when evaluating and examining the human in action.

Those spearheading this type of curriculum have often suggested that physical education practices should refer to and rest upon a basic discipline which they have termed "kinesiology" (the study of movement), human movement, or some similar label. It is advanced that if one learns about, explores, and understands the scientific bases of movement itself, one should be able to plan and carry out applied programs of a number of types; including not only traditional physical education practiced in the secondary schools, but also systems of physical rehabilitation for the handicapped, activities intended to improve the efficiency of the industrial worker, indeed any program in which human action in some way plays a part.

A more thorough discussion of the content of the types of courses which are often found in such a curriculum is found in Chapters Fifteen through Twenty-three. The evolution and emergence of these curriculums, often seen at larger universities, form one of the more fascinating chapters of recent trends in physical education in the country. At times their evolution has been hastened by pressures from educational policy committees within universities, who seem constantly to be striving to uncover the major theoretical base for all programs within their purview. Had physical educators within such environments declared themselves to be concerned *only* with the practical and applied business of training teachers they might have found themselves excluded entirely from university programs in which they had resided for a number of years.

Some of these curricula were also inspired by several sagacious leaders who have attempted to formulate sound theoretical bases for programs of physical education at these institutions. These leaders seemed to be dissatisfied with the emphasis only on how to do things *to* people, and began during the late 1940s, the 1950s, and the 1960s to examine the whys of doing things *with* people.

At times, however, these so-called "theoretically-based programs" are not as sound as they may seem. They sometimes contain courses taught in the traditional ways and containing the usual content, overgrown with a canopy of jargon which has little meaning except to those formulating it. Real changes in course content and in the capabilities of teacher educators do not always keep pace with the proliferating models or theories of human movement which appear on the pages of various journals in our profession.

At the same time there have been serious attempts by many within the physical education field to instill real content into various of the theory courses traditionally taught, as well as to institute new courses of study covering subject matter which was not previously considered in a very penetrating way within physical education curriculums. Particular emphasis within recent years has been placed on the addition of courses based upon data obtained from the behavioral sciences, including psychology, sociology, as well as physical and cultural anthropology. These subject-matter areas are covered in Chapters Seventeen and Eighteen.

When designating any coherent course of study, or modifying a curriculum, one should ask: Just what is the nature of the student "product" which one hopes will emerge? Evaluating a curriculum in which there is a marked emphasis upon the theoretical and scientific bases of motor activity in essence requires one to evaluate the nature of the student which it will potentially spawn. Although courses of this nature have not been with us a long time in this country (perhaps for little over 10 years at this printing), there are some indications as to their advantages and drawbacks. These may be ascertained by inspecting the apparent capabilities and blind spots of the students who march from the portals of the various universities which have been in the forefront of this relatively new "movement" movement.

In general, it seems that students whose backgrounds in physical education (kinesiology, or whatever) have been highly theoretical in nature may be better equipped to do several things upon graduation:

1. They are often motivated to, and highly capable of, participating in graduate training at the master's and doctoral level. They often stand a better chance of later becoming university researchers and possibly teacher educators.[1]

2. They are usually able to evaluate new practices which might be instituted at their schools. They are more likely to change their own behavior when working with students at the elementary or secondary levels, as they hopefully are more capable of assessing, and either accepting or rejecting, various new theories and practices which appear often in educational journals and in the popular press.

3. They appear more likely to accommodate to individual differences in their students. For example, they may prove more tolerant and understanding of the clumsy child in their class, perhaps attributing his ineptitude to minimal neurological impairment, because they have learned about the nature of the nervous system as undergraduates. They may be more sensitive to the activity needs of various ethnic groups in their charge, as they have been exposed to courses dealing with the sociology of sport and physical activity when in college. They are perhaps focused more upon the teaching of *youth*, rather than upon the teaching of a *course*.

4. Many students obtaining this type of theoretical background find themselves in supervisory roles in which they must devise curriculums, formulate guidelines for student assessment, and the like.

An inordinate emphasis upon theory versus practice in these courses of study, however, does not always produce a superlative graduate. For example, I have seen many students subjected to this type of program who seem only capable of writing excellent term papers, but who are almost oblivious to even simple principles of leading a class in physical activities. Some are not capable in physical skills, and some students from the curriculums of this type began to feel during their senior year, and rightly so, that they did not have enough sharply honed "teaching tools" to serve them during their imminent entry into teaching. They may know the whys but are unacquainted with the hows of physical activity. And it is obvious to most that good teachers must *do* things with and to students, and not be merely capable of engaging in highly academic discussions with their own colleagues and major professors.

Like the curriculums emphasizing theory, the more applied curriculums also may produce graduates with mixed patterns of attributes. Generally these courses of study contain content which is highly practical. Coaching courses are taught during the final two years, often con-

[1]In some ways it is an unfortunate trend seen on some university and college faculties that some of the newer members exposed to prospective secondary teachers have indeed never taught secondary school themselves.

ducted by coaches of the major and minor varsity sports at the institutions. These men are pragmatic and tend, in practical terms, to "tell it like it is," an attribute not to be demeaned in this day and age.

During the first several years in a curriculum of this second kind, the students are exposed to many hours of gymnasium and field work. They are often encouraged, indeed prodded, to improve their own movement capacities in a number of team and individual sports. This prodding usually results in a helpful expansion of their capabilities, which may not have fully developed because of prolonged participation in only one or two sports during their high school careers. These sports skills are many times tested during the senior year, with successful performance a criterion for graduation.

Students emerging from such curriculums are usually self-confident when confronting classes. Often they are permitted actual teaching experiences early in their college careers. They can "operate," they can demonstrate, they know progressions of gymnastic skills, they can conduct tennis drills, and they are aware of considerations prior to, during, and following a basketball season to insure success.

At the same time the students exposed to an inordinate number of hours of practicing, with less emphasis upon the theoretical whys, may have certain chinks in their professional armour. For example, they may be *too* certain of the value of the practices, exercises, and drills they have obtained from their major professors. They may not evaluate the real worth of what has been handed them to do in college, and may find themselves teaching with the same methods 20 years after graduation as they were equipped with upon initially emerging from their teacher-training program.

Such curriculums are often found in smaller colleges in which there is no administrative division between the physical education and athletic departments. This arrangement may often weaken the standards in the former program, as few coaches can be found who will jeopardize the athletic eligibility of the athletes on their own teams by awarding low grades to these same individuals when teaching them in their major classes.

Taken together, these two types of curriculums are, as was mentioned, unlikely to appear in the somewhat simplistic and pure form as outlined in the previous paragraphs. Rather, a given curriculum may be discerned as leaning toward one emphasis (the academic-theoretical), or the other (the applied-practical, "how-to-do-it"). And indeed this is the healthier situation. For it is believed by most sound training teachers that a student taking a major or minor course in physical education should be exposed to *both* theory and practice. For a prospective teacher to know *why* and not to know *how*, is as unsound as it is simply to be able to operate without being aware of the causes of the techniques he uses, and about the varieties of student behavior he may encourage.

If you find yourself in a program which you feel places too much emphasis on one direction (the practical) or the other (the scientific), you may have to provide an adjustment yourself to achieve the balance you should hopefully have. You may have to engage in a program of skill improvement on your own, by taking activity classes not required within the major. Conversely, you may visit the library in an effort to formulate for yourself the theoretical underpinnings for some of the absolutes handed to you in the more pragmatic curriculum.

There are several other trends seen in various curriculums in physical education throughout the country which may be reflected in your own. For example, there are an increasing number of students engaging in a physical education minor, who are taking courses which would permit them to teach physical education in the schools, while preparing themselves in more depth in another major area of study. Indeed several colleges in the country have instituted a coaching minor, designed for men and women who wish to coach a sport at the high school or college level, but who wish to take the majority of their work in another academic field.

There are several important administrative trends which reflect important philosophical metamorphoses. For example, some physical education departments seem to be attempting to strengthen themselves by incorporating increasingly more subdivisions of study within their confines. A student, for example, may major in dance, health education, recreation, special education and physical education, or a number of other special emphases within departments of physical education.

In contrast, several departments, to better justify physical education as possessing a unique and "pure" subject matter area, are divesting themselves of ancillary submajors of the type enumerated in the previous paragraph. The dance divisions have often left the departments to join other colleges within the university (usually the college of fine arts). The health education divisions may emigrate to the department of public health, while the recreation division may find itself also detached from its "mother department."

There is another shift of the philosophical pendulum within departments which purportedly emphasize a highly academic approach. Some of these are now beginning to emphasize teacher training to a greater degree, as opposed to training university researchers and the like. Some have started a master's program emphasizing teaching methodology, while others have again begun to admit that the main job channels for their graduates, despite their pronouncement to the contrary, are indeed high school and elementary teaching. This realization in turn has prompted them to focus upon teaching methodology to a greater extent than they did a few years ago.

Summary

This chapter has attempted to aid the student to sort out the nature of the physical education major or minor program upon which he is embarking. Many times a student arrives at a college and the curriculum that confronts him is almost dazzling to behold, outlined with highly optimistic pronouncements in speeches by the department chairman, while at the same time the actual courses and their contents are only dimly perceived. The student starting to major or minor in physical education should be given, and/or should obtain for himself, not only a clear understanding of the details of what lies ahead, but at the same time a reasonably coherent understanding of the broad emphasis and basic philosophical directions currently ascribed to by the department in which he finds himself. Some of the guidelines delineated in the previous paragraphs should aid the prospective student of physical education to carry out this type of analysis.

References

Downey, R. J., *Exploring Physical Education*. Belmont, Calif.: Wadsworth Publishing Company, 1962.

Jenny, J. H., *Physical Education, Health Education and Recreation; Introduction to Professional Preparation for Leadership*. New York: The Macmillan Company, 1961.

Zeigler, Earle, *Philosophical Foundations for Physical, Health, and Recreational Education*. Englewood Cliffs, New Jersey: Prentice-Hall, Inc., 1964.

CHAPTER THREE

Becoming a Scholar

All students upon enrolling at a college or university are officially termed "student," but few of these students earn the honor of being called "scholar." There are many ways of graduating without really taking advantage of the opportunities for intellectual improvement offered by university and college communities. Students who do strive to become more than mere grade collectors terminate their college careers with far greater feelings of accomplishment than do those who did not so strive; and at the same time the former stand a better chance of making valuable contributions to themselves and to others as a result of their exposure to higher education.

There are three types of experiences which can contribute to the personal, social, and intellectual growth of a student: (a) the interaction in informal ways with other students and with instructors and professors in the institution; (b) taking advantage of the written materials in the library and the lecturers who visit the campus; (c) gaining deep and meaningful understandings by participating in formal course offerings.

In addition, there are mechanical, operational procedures which, if carried out well, should contribute to academic success at your college or university. These include selecting appropriate ways to study, obtaining information from your lectures in an efficient manner, and arranging your daily schedule to permit yourself to assimilate the learning experiences to which you are exposed.

To proclaim the single most efficient way to carry out some of these operations would be presumptuous. Students differ in their capacity for study, in the manner in which they listen to lectures, and in their ability to discipline themselves during their time at college. There are, however, some general and reasonably sound guidelines which some readers may find appropriate for their growth as students. Some of these are outlined in the paragraphs which follow.

Learn Things and Learn How to Learn

Students often decry the necessity to learn "facts." Rather, they lament, they should be exposed to profound ideas and from these they should be encouraged to generate even more erudite concepts. While there is a great deal of truth in the assumption that concepts are more important than minutiae, in order to think one must consider about specific things, or facts.

As a student you should attempt not only to acquire general guidelines, principles, and concepts; but also to obtain information from the several disciplines which contribute to knowledge about physical activity and physical education.

Scholars attempting to define creative thinking have suggested that this type of high-level theorizing involves bringing together, the synthesis of, hitherto unrelated facts and/or ideas. It would thus seem that to be creative one must have at one's disposal a number of facts which potentially may be merged. With an increase in the number of things known there is a parallel increase in the potential for original thinking.

Particularly during the early college years, students are faced with the necessity for acquiring a great deal of information, despite their possible yearnings for really important ideas. Chemical formulas and concepts must be acquired and memorized; the names of muscles, their attachments, actions, and their place of insertion into various bones must be learned in beginning courses so that students can later analyze the manner in which the human anatomy functions when engaged in various athletic movements. Thus, most freshmen and sophomores at the university are faced with the necessity of memorizing large groups of facts.

The research on learning contains several important guidelines which should help you to better retain the information to which you are exposed. Some of the more important ones are as follows:

1. Gradually attempt to acquire a large amount of information. Space your efforts to learn and to retain over a period of time. A student who

tries to cram the contents of a course into his "memory store" during the final part of the semester is likely to perform poorly on the final examination. Attempts should be made from the first day of a class to acquire the information contained in the course.

2. Immediately review information to which you have just been exposed. It has been found that information (such as a series of numbers) which is not mentally rehearsed within a minute or two after being given to people may not be retained. Ten minutes taken immediately after a class to review class notes is time well spent.

3. Be conscious of the number of available channels through which you may absorb information; but do not overload yourself by trying to use too many channels at once while striving initially to take in new information. Two examples may clarify what is meant by these two related principles.

In the process of learning a body of facts you may fully utilize your learning capacities by tape recording the information, listening to it, and then attempting to repeat it either in writing and/or verbally. The act of outlining the information constitutes one exposure during which your vision and motor capacities are being employed in the act of writing. Reading the information into the tape recorder constitutes a second exposure to the information, using verbalization as a learning tool; and at this time you also hear yourself say the material. You then may listen to the tape recorder while at the same time reading your outline, which constitutes a simultaneous visual and auditory exposure to the information. This type of information-acquisition process may continue as you attempt to predict what will be heard on the tape. Turn off the tape, write out what you feel will follow, and turn on the tape; then compare what has been written with what was spoken on the tape. Increasingly larger sections of the tape may be predicted and verified in this way, and the outcome of such practice is likely to be the acquisition of a great deal of information.

An example of what may occur if a student tries to use too many channels of incoming information at the same time may be found by considering the circumstances surrounding the lecture class. During such a class the student is usually attempting to listen to a professor and at the same time to write notes on what is being said. Both acts, the writing and listening, cannot be carried out at exactly the same time; so the student is forced first to listen, and then to attempt to turn off the lecturer's words while writing a sentence or two, and then to resume listening. In this manner the student may proceed through the hour, alternately listening and writing. It is obvious that when the student is writing, some important part of the lecture may be missed. Also, the act of writing requires concentration which can detract from the student's ability to do anything more than listen for words, rather than spending time to consider relationships and meanings within the lecture's content.

There are several ways in which a student may alleviate this overloading of his channels for gaining information. He may, for example, take a tape recorder to class,[2] so that he can not only devote his full attention to what is being said, but also review the information at a later convenient time. This process is, of course, somewhat expensive, especially if the tapes are retained. It also may prove time-consuming, and technical difficulties may interfere with the taping of the lecture.

Another method of acquiring information in lectures without the necessity for daily note-taking utilizes the help of several fellow students. A group of four or more students may arrange to take notes alternately. Thus, only one of the group is occupied in a given day in the task of note-taking. The note-taker is then obligated to make his notes available to his fellow students by reproducing several copies. There are several obvious drawbacks to even this method, however. For example, the note-taker's ability must be trusted by the other members of the group, and the time and expense needed to reproduce the material may be troublesome. At the same time, however, most of the members of the group are left free to listen to both content and meanings in the lecture presented. So this method might be attempted with reasonable success within many situations.

4. Attempt to relate information to other information you have acquired in the past. Structure, outline, and integrate information in your mind and on paper. It is extremely difficult to memorize facts which somehow seem to float in the air without being tied down to previously known information or to some kind of practical or theoretical reality. As you acquire a body of knowledge about motor learning, sports skills, anatomy, or the mechanics of movement, you are likely to find that the acquisition of additional data becomes easier. You will have formed a mosaic of ideas into which you can more easily insert new ideas. The problems of forming initial conceptual frameworks that may be faced when first exploring a field of knowledge will be reduced with increased exposure to the same or to similar material.

5. During your early months at college, attempt to search out ways in which you can gain practical experience with children and/or youth of the age you eventually wish to confront as a teacher. Although more detailed discussions of this aspect of your program are found in other chapters (e.g., Ch. 25), it is important to mention here the fact that when one gains experience he may be better able to understand the

---

[2]With the permission of the instructor.

need for information obtained in classes. Conversely, after seeing children in action one often feels the need to search out information to explain the behavior observed.

There are other operational and conceptual techniques which may be employed to advantage by the college student attempting to improve his scholarship. For example, a student should endeavor to improve upon various personal techniques of transcribing information. Typing skill is an invaluable aid to a student at any level. Not only are papers "turned out" more neatly, but coherence of thought is often enhanced when typing rapidly. Shorthand skills, not too difficult to obtain, are an obvious aid to note-taking.

It is difficult to find a text dealing with the improvement of study habits and scholarship which does not suggest that a weekly schedule be composed, in which time for study, play, and work is carefully outlined. And indeed this is a sound practice. However, when working under this type of schedule keep two primary points in mind. (a) The schedule should be reasonably flexible. There may be weeks or days in which less demands to study are made upon you, and you may devote more time to other interests. (b) The schedule should be reasonably well filled. If you leave too much free time within your weekly schedule, you may find yourself relatively less productive. It is a common finding among college athletes that their grades are higher during their competitive seasons. They seem to have their schedules so crowded during these weeks of the semester that they have little time for random "horse play." To survive academically they *must* move from class, to practice, to study, in a reasonably organized manner. If there is something productive scheduled for most of their time, there is always something they *must* do to remain in college.

Other operational means can be employed by college students to deal better with the demands within the courses they are taking. The laws of transfer of training tell us that transfer of skills between two tasks will occur to the extent to which rather exact preparation is made for the second task by practicing a reasonably similar first task. With this axiom in mind, tests of various kinds should be most effectively dealt with if the student prepares in a rather precise way for the type of examination he is to face. Students habitually practice for written tests only by reading the material upon which they are to be examined; whereas sound practice would include the formulating of written tests and then taking them. If the expected tests are to be one-hour essay tests, then practice for them should also be in the form of one-hour written exercises in which practice in responding to hypothetical questions is gained.

During the past several years in my undergraduate and graduate classes, I have required my students to take a half-hour oral examination. I doubt whether any of these students, judging from their usually less-than-relaxed and able performances in the verbal exercise, have practiced the type of test for which they were later responsible. Oral test-taking, for best results, should be preceded by practicing oral responses to questions. Written tests, in a similar way, should be practiced in ways which exactly duplicate the nature of the expected examination.

Other means for retaining and learning should be applied by the enterprising college student. Retention, for example, is enhanced by overlearning and by chaining comparable information together in meaningful ways. Overlearning implies that the learning has exceeded some minimum criterion. If it is desired to list on a test all the larger muscles of the body, without omissions, then preparation for this type of examination should consist of being able to repeat perfectly *more* than one written and/or oral run-through of names of the various muscles of the body.

A successful college student learns how to use the library at his institution early in his career. Students should take advantage of the library orientation programs which most universities provide. When visiting the library, you should become aware of materials at the reference desks, which are surveys of large sections of the literature in which you may be interested. At the same time, during your initial sojourns through this part of college you should explore the various periodicals and books dealing with the subjects in which you are interested. Several of the chapters which follow contain lists of the research journals which provide information pertinent to the study of man in action.

Becoming a successful scholar involves more than merely executing certain correct mechanics of studying and of test-taking. Many students withdraw before graduation because of emotional, financial, and/or family difficulties rather than because of academic incompetence. Success in college entails somehow achieving a harmonious relationship within your total environment, including your fellow students, your family, your instructors, and usually at least one member of the opposite sex.

Some of the chapters which follow contain principles which suggest how you may interact best with others in the college community. At the same time, learning how to learn and how to remember does form an important part of the base upon which some of your emotional stability and security may rest. Some of the techniques outlined on the preceding pages should prove helpful to you.

Student Activities and Discussion Questions

1. What facilities on your campus are available to students who feel that they need counseling for personal or emotional problems? Just how can you contact these services? What are their costs?
2. Obtain a research article dealing with the retention of written information. Review its contents, and determine just how its findings might apply to you as a college student attempting to retain information of various kinds. You might try the *Journal of Educational Psychology, Journal of Psychology, Journal of Verbal Behavior,* and *Perceptual and Motor Skills.*
3. Can you find information which relates the retention of verbal-written information to the retention of motor skills? How are written information and motor skills comparable with regard to learning and retention? How are they different?
4. Design an "ideal" weekly schedule for a college freshman or sophomore majoring in physical education, including a 24-hour day and a 7-day week. How much time should be allotted to study, work, recreation, etc. within such a schedule?
5. How, why, and when should you interpolate physical activity within the schedule devised in 4 above?
6. Discuss how you might use a tape recorder in the collection of information presented to you during a lecture class. What are the advantages and drawbacks in the use of such a tool?

References

Allen, C., *Passing Examinations.* New York: The Macmillan Company, 1963.

Cole, Luella, *Student's Guide to Efficient Study.* New York: Holt, Rinehart and Winston, Inc., 1961.

Einstein, B. W., *Guide to Success in College.* New York: Grosset & Dunlap, Inc., Publishers, 1967.

Elliot, H. C., *The Effective Student: A Constructive Method of Study.* New York: Harper & Row, Publishers, 1966.

Froe, O. D., *How to Become a Successful Student.* New York: Arco Publishing Company, 1959.

Mace, C. A., *The Psychology of Study.* Baltimore: Penguin Books, 1968.

Pauk, W., *How to Study in College.* Boston: Houghton Mifflin Company, 1962.

Wasserman, E. R., *The Random House Guide to Graduate Study.* New York: Random House, Inc., 1967.

Boade, A. W., ed., *Academic Freedom: The Scholar's Place in Modern Society.* New York: Oceana Publishers, 1964.

CHAPTER FOUR

Personal Relationships
with Classmates
and Instructors

A job in physical education, athletics, or one of the innumerable associated fields involves working with people, with children of various ages and at times with adults. It is important during your undergraduate years to examine the manner in which you relate to others with whom you come in contact. This type of self-examination may come about in an informal way or in some more structured manner. You may, for example, merely engage in silent introspective self-evaluation of your social competencies, needs, and abilities to relate to others. On the other hand, you may acquire rather structured counseling containing advice based upon some type of objective personality assessment.

Other relatively structured techniques which purport to heighten self-awareness, social sensitivity, and the like may be engaged in. For example, some form of the popular, and sometimes misused, sensitivity training can often be helpful to you as an undergraduate student. Sensitivity training is related to the concept of "positive psychiatry" which emerged in the 1950s. It is based upon the concept that not only may disturbed people engage in productive self-assessment procedures, but also individuals who are reasonably healthy psychologically might improve their effectiveness through group therapy. This type of experience generally has several goals in mind: the improvement of interpersonal communication techniques, the enhancement of the ability to listen to others, and the acquisition of information from others through which your personal impact may be assessed. A most important outcome of this type of group experience is a more accurate grasp of just how other people feel about things. Hopefully during this process participants can begin to determine more accurately how their own personalities are viewed by others.

Group processes of this type are best accomplished if a well-qualified leader is available; indeed, they may even be harmful if not adequately guided. At the same time, the group's interactions should not be overdirected by the trainer. Generally the main business of sensitivity training, or whatever it may be called, is the evaluation of group and individual reactions themselves, without seeking a more concrete objective. It may be the first, and last, time that the participants will have the opportunity to communicate their true feelings to other people. It may also be the first time that most of the participants have had the "truth" about their personal impact related to them in reasonably objective terms.[1]

A number of realizations useful in teaching physical activities might emerge from either formal or informal assessment of the ways others interact socially, with each other and with you. For example, the marked differences between males and females in feelings about physical activity may become illuminated in helpful ways during the early undergraduate years if young men and women in the major program come together in classes, engage in programs together, and also have frank group discussions. As a result of this type of conversation the young women might gain an appreciation of why the men have chosen to become physical education teachers and coaches, and of how deeply they may feel about the role of athletics in the life of youngsters. On the other hand, the young men who really listen to their female classmates might also come to appreciate just how strongly the latter feel about such matters as the emotional and aesthetic values of participation in dance.

Differences of objectives and values among males and females taking part in a physical education major program can also be explored in discussions during the early years of college. Such discussions may explore why or, more specifically, discover just what experiences prompted each member to undertake a course of study which would lead toward a leadership role dealing with vigorous physical activity.

Several types of personal strengths and/or weaknesses similarly may be explored in precise or informal ways during these early years of col-

---

[1]This type of participation, of course, can be traumatic for some who are less stable. In some cases the group's comments can quickly "peel away" protective psychological "armor" upon which some are dependent for stable and productive day-to-day behavior.

lege. For example, it might be interesting to find in others, or in yourself, whether motives to enter physical education are based upon needs for continued achievement in physical activity and sport, or upon needs to serve and to improve others. You may find that some have based their decision to enter coaching on the need to experience athletic success vicariously, success which had *never* been enjoyed by the prospective teacher of sports!

Another major social dimension which might be evaluated objectively (most major personality test profiles contain this item) is whether the potential physical educator is outgoing or withdrawn; or to use more technical terms, is introverted or extroverted. It is usually considered desirable for those who enter physical education or one of the associated fields to be rather outgoing and sociable, to relate easily with others, and to be able to talk to others without an undue amount of social strain.[2] If you find that you are being rated by your classmates, or by those who constructed personality tests, as somewhat introverted, you might examine yourself, and perhaps decide to take some alternative professional direction or devise ways of improving your social skills. It often helps to take part in some type of organized group activity, or to work with children in situations which are not likely to be pressure-laden and in which your initial efforts are not likely to be strictly assessed and monitored.

Other basic personal social competencies which can be assessed, explored, and possibly improved at college are the abilities to (a) quickly and accurately assess your own impact upon groups with which you are confronted; and, stemming from this, to (b) modify the approach you use with individuals and groups in reasonably rapid and desirable ways. Whenever you confront an individual or group, you will have an effect whether or not you speak. The ability to evaluate the nature of the impression you make by your gestures and voice (its tone as well as the content of what you say) is one of the most important skills you can possess as a teacher and as a coach. Associated with this first ability is a second: the ability to modify your communication behavior on the basis of your assessment of the class reactions to *you*. More detailed discussions of your relations to students later to be in your charge are found in Chapters Six and Twenty-five. However, an important early indication of just how you affect others socially can be

[2]This is not to infer, as was often done in literature in the 1930s and 1940s, that the introvert, if social withdrawal is not extreme, is somehow not well-adjusted, or is evincing some kind of maladjusted behavior. In truth, at times the child who is too socially active may be evincing signs of emotional instability, and that the relatively quiet child or adult may indeed be an extremely stable individual, one who just does not prefer frequently to voice opinions and relate socially to others. It is often difficult for some relatively outgoing physical education teachers and coaches to relate well to the quiet child, because of this kind of personality difference.

gained from discussions and feedback from your student colleagues within the physical education major.

You might examine your social relationships with your fellow students from several angles: (a) How are you assessed by them as a prospective teacher, as a friend, and as a professional colleague? (b) How do you find yourself relating to them? Can you understand and communicate only with those who have interests and professional goals similar to yours? After classes are over, do you find yourself solely with a collection of athletes and future coaches, with dancers, with women, men students; or are you willing and able to communicate at various times with all types of individuals? In what way may your preferences for company within the physical education major color your relationships with your colleagues when you find yourself teaching in a school after graduation? (c) What seems to be the *quality* of your personal impact on others? Are people seemingly influenced by you in positive ways? Do they ignore you? What does the nature of this impact upon others predict for your future teaching or coaching success? How might you increase the likelihood of a favorable impact on others?

In addition to relationships between and among students within the physical education major, you should be aware of the potential quality of student-to-student relationships within the total college population. What do the students on your campus think of physical education majors? Are stereotypes formed by them? Is there some justification for negative stereotypes being constructed by others within the campus community?

Most physical education major and minor students are aware of the various positive and negative pictures that are painted of those associated with physical activity. The big, dumb male athlete and the overly masculine-appearing girl in the physical education major are stereotypes prevalent and painful, yet which may be truly descriptive of some in our field.

A stereotype is usually based upon some evidence, and is shaped by the particular prejudices of the one voicing it or expanding upon it. The big, dumb athlete may indeed be large, and an athlete; but he may not be as dumb as he is painted by the narrow-shouldered academician who may have had unpleasant experiences in physical education or athletics while in high school. By this type of ridicule the latter may seek to perpetuate an unwholesome image of those who experienced success in activities in which he failed. The too-masculine-appearing girl does at times crop up at athletic contests or within physical education major classes; but she also may be seen elsewhere, and may not be as overpowering as she is painted by unkind observers who have some bone to pick with physical education or athletes.

Physical education major students can dispel the somewhat unhappy images which some on the college campus may hold of them by individually striving to correct the unwholesome impressions outlined above. Both men and women in physical education should strive doubly hard to improve their appearance. It is perhaps unfortunate, but nevertheless true, that you are seen by far more people than those who talk to you and really learn what you are like. A girl who is vigorous and active, skilled in a number of sports, may through her participation gain two important social and personal advantages. Her abilities make her a desirable and exciting companion for men who are likewise engaged in sports in which both may participate. Secondly, her participation, if vigorous and extensive, is likely to "streamline" her figure, also a socially desirable outcome. However, if the girl cannot adjust her behavior and appearance to conform to reasonably accepted standards of femininity, her impact upon the youth she is later to serve, as well as the somewhat unwholesome image she presents of herself and of others in the physical education major, should prompt her to find another field of endeavor or to obtain help in the form of psychological counseling.

In my opinion, and in the opinion of many men, an active woman is sexually desirable because of her very vigor. She need not lessen or obliterate her feminine impact by assuming inappropriate mannerisms and standards of dress. Young women interested in physical activity should and can exhibit a range of movement behaviors, from the direct and vigorous motions needed in their favorite activities to the more feminine movements exhibited as they walk, gesture, and take part in currently popular social dances. I feel that the hiring of female physical education teachers who exhibit less than a wholesome feminine image is a disservice to the youth for whom they should be models of behavior, appearance, and performance.

The male major similarly should take stock of the impression he may be making, as an individual, upon the rest of the undergraduate student body. There is no need to be an athlete-bum; athlete-scholars abound.

Unfortunately, many college and university athletes find themselves both exploited and punished by various portions of the academic community in which they find themselves. The athletic department, or the coach who has recruited them, expects, indeed demands, that they spend an inordinate amount of time in their sport. Many football players during the season must spend from 3 p.m. to 8 p.m. each day being whirlpooled, taped, placed in darkrooms with film, and training-tabled. The football weekend may extend from Thursday or Friday at noon, depending on how far away the game happens to be, until late Sunday night when the projectionist finally falls asleep.

After the coach takes his "pound of flesh" (or often, his ton) each week, the professor takes his shots. Striving hard to maintain "high academic standards," he may proceed to talk, scream, rant, spell out, explain, outline, discuss, counsel, test, and then fail the athlete. Professors in all departments actually take various attitudes toward athletes, depending upon how emotionally involved the professors are in the athlete's sport. It is the strategy of most athletes in larger universities, together with a specialist who is often hired by the athletic office, to winnow out just who on the campus conducts the "Mickey" courses.[3] Some professors may simply flunk athletes without a hearing. Others will fall all over themselves in their eagerness to pass athletes, permitting more years of eligibility and athletic fame reflecting upon them and upon Old Siwash University, with which they may be closely tied emotionally.

It is of course not always found that male physical education majors are athletes subjected to the stresses outlined previously. Still, many find themselves in this situation and may take several courses of action, some of which are beneficial neither to them nor to the student colleagues they are in some ways representing. The athlete may in a constructive way seek to improve himself academically by taking courses in a variety of departments, attempting to see past the three or four years of college athletics he is currently enjoying. He may additionally "buckle down" and get the most he can, within his time and energy limits, from the physical education major courses to which he is exposed. Both courses of action are more desirable than simply giving up and presenting an attitude on the campus which both by speech and appearance, is less than professional and academic.

A male physical education student may at times find that the major he has selected will work to his advantage when in other departments in the college and university. Perhaps familiar with the usual "dumb," etc., stereotype often foisted upon those training to be P. E. teachers, the professors dealing with other subjects may be pleasantly surprised when P. E. students demonstrate that they indeed wish to try hard, and have the mental equipment to deal effectively within a subject matter area other than athletics.

A final way you as a student in the physical education major should relate to your student colleagues in other departments is to attempt to understand what issues they are championing. You should seek to understand and to dissect the issues which, on your campus, may cause student and faculty unrest and irritation. This is not to say that you should take part in disruptive and violent tactics which are increasingly practiced only by an identifiable minority of radical students on each campus; but at the same time one of the privileges you have in the 1970s is to be among students who care about important political and

---

[3]"Mickey," or "Mickey Mouse": simple, stupid, easy grade.

social issues, who voice their concern, and who at times act in constructive ways about those conditions which disturb them. As a physical education major you not only should immerse yourself in your own subject matter, but should view yourself as a member of a total academic community whose issues and concerns become your issues and concerns.

Your Professors and Instructors

A third important group of people with whom you must deal when studying physical education are your instructors. You are exposed to one another for many hours a week, and your mutual abilities, idiosyncracies, and personality traits are the focus of innumerable discussions lasting many hours, both in faculty lounges and in student dormitories. Students spend as much time in classes studying the professor as they do studying the subject matter.

Like students, college instructors come in a variety of types and sizes, and possess a remarkably wide range of abilities and opinions. Their backgrounds are varied, and they range from the instructors who are primarily concerned with the teaching or coaching of various sports skills, to those who always seem submerged in their research laboratories. Your instructors holding professional ranks may have a doctor's degree obtained after from three to ten years of postgraduate study, often encompassing courses in psychology, physiology, education, research design, and language. The assistant professor, who has perhaps recently entered your school, may be more subject-matter oriented, having just acquired his Ph.D. He may be less secure in his new position than his older colleagues, and may be trying a little harder, imposing high standards, and generally putting forth his maximum effort. The associate professor generally has been in college teaching longer, and has what is termed "tenure" or permanence in his position. The full professors are usually the older members of the faculty. They have purportedly exhibited superior abilities in working with students, researching, writing, and perhaps contributing to community efforts, so that their colleagues have promoted them to the highest professorial rank.[4]

The quality of college and university professors and instructors is shaped by their unique personal characteristics, by their personal

[4]Promotion is usually carried out by committees whose composition is not known by the one considered for promotion; they rate his writings, evidence of teaching competence, and other indications of professional ability, including university and community service.

values and philosophies governing their concepts of adequate conduct as faculty members, and by the unique backgrounds of experience they bring to their classrooms.

As a student you may be confronted by individuals whose teaching performance you find inadequate. Their performance may be poor in reality, or you may imagine it to be so. For example, your instructor may lack information to impart to you, or he may be unable to communicate what information he does possess. The instructor may be unable to organize information, one of the vital jobs of a college teacher. The classroom performance of your inept instructor may suffer from the fact that he attempts to teach in a too authoritative manner, allowing little or no time for student expression or consistently showing disrespect for student opinions. On the other hand, your least-preferred instructor may simply conduct student-directed discussions with little or no effort made on his part to bring what experience and background *he* may have to the class members' attention.

However, you may be misevaluating your instructor's abilities. He may be attempting to impart general principles and theory to you, and you may lack the ability and/or experience to translate these into practical solutions. You may simply lack the capacity to understand the complexities of the information extended to you and be reluctant to engage in the extra study which would make the course content more comprehensible. Whether you as an individual have some personal problem preventing you from taking advantage of the instructor's presentation, or whether the teacher has a real deficiency, may be partly determined by consulting other class members concerning your feelings.

You may be faced with what, if anything, you might do if you find that your instructor is less than adequate. There are different courses of action open to you. You might make the best of the situation by using the lecture periods for studying other course content, attempting to supplement the fragmentary material you obtain in class, engaging in library research, or merely being tolerant of your instructor and hoping for more effective stimulation in other classes.

On the other hand, you might take action to *do* something about weak or inappropriate instruction to which you are exposed. This can take the form of collecting data from class members, perhaps through a questionnaire, concerning their evaluation of the course, and then presenting this information to the instructor himself, to the department chairman, and perhaps to the dean of the school in which the department resides. (An example of such a questionnaire appears in the appendix, formulated by students for just such a purpose.) Student-faculty seminars can in some ways aid instructors to perceive the fact that they might improve their instructional content or methods.

Your instructors, as individuals or as a group, may, in your opinion, be excellent teachers. Those primarily interested in theory and research may present their information well, and the information they present may be highly relevant because they themselves have collected it. The teachers of methods courses also may communicate well and present information which you know will be helpful in your later work as teachers and coaches.

Just as you as students, and prior to that time as children at your parents' knees, appreciate praise when you do something well, so do your instructors. Student appreciation and praise, unsolicited by the instructor, presented in writing and representing individual or group opinion, is a potent way to reward your instructors and professors. This type of evidence is important to faculty committees which rate and promote deserving faculty members at your college and university. You can usually exert a positive effect upon the promotion of instructors you feel are competent by proceeding in the manner discussed above.

Your department chairman may meet with you alone, or with a group of students, when you reach your senior year. During this meeting you could outline in an organized way just what you felt were the strong points and weak points of the curriculum to which you had been exposed. Your department chairman should not ignore your suggestions and observations.

One of the important ways in which you can interact with your instructors and professors is in conferences outside class. Some students and instructors seem to have marked needs for an inordinate number of meetings during the school year. On the other hand, professors should keep regular announced office hours during which their students can consult with them concerning problems students are encountering in the course. Many students need a small number of these conferences during their college careers, while others seem to require many.

One thing to remember is that the professor has problems of his own. He may be seeking to complete work other than that dealing with teaching; work upon which his promotion, and thus his professional future, may be based. The professor also may have personal problems which are equal in magnitude to those you as a student might wish to discuss with him. Often the student will gain more help with personal problems by consulting with those whose jobs are directed toward that end (i.e., the university psychological counseling staff) rather than seeking to unburden himself to his departmental instructors.

At the same time, some of the most important contacts and associations you may form during your college career are those with instructors you respect. These same instructors welcome a closer relationship and deeper understanding of you as a student than can be gained in a classroom. Conferences with professors often lead toward productive individual projects of a service or research nature which you might engage in as an undergraduate or graduate student; and you should make your interests known particularly to professors whose interests parallel yours. Finally, professors cannot write letters of recommendation which are needed upon graduation in a very meaningful way unless they come to know you better through relatively frequent meetings scheduled formally or informally.

Summary

You as a physical education major student should constantly be sensitive to the quality of your relationships with other major students, with students within other departments on the campus, and with your instructors and professors. Seeking to expand your knowledge of the values, abilities, and goals of fellow physical education major and minor students should form a base from which meaningful professional relationships may grow following graduation. Physical education majors must often, because of preconceived stereotypes, take special pains through their dress, speech, and academic performance to dispel potentially unwholesome and unfavorable opinions others within the college and university community might form about them. All college students, in the 1970s and 1980s should welcome the opportunities to engage in controversial discussions which may lead toward social, economic, political, and moral betterment. Physical education major students should not withdraw or ignore campus controversies, because upon graduation as coaches and physical education teachers they may find themselves holding a sensitive role in the midst of these same controversies within the communities and schools they hope to serve.

One's professors should not be looked upon as potential supermen, nor as hopeless incompetents, but as individuals whose lives have been dedicated to youth and whose abilities and opinions span an extensive range. The student may choose to attempt to aid the incompetent instructor to improve his offerings, and to relate better his teaching to the needs of the students by seeking specific ways to improve instructor-student communication. At the same time, the student should attempt to come to know his more valued instructors as individuals, so that through association he may gain more than can be offered in the classroom. Capable instructors and professors can be rewarded in valuable and concrete ways by students who transmit to the departmental superiors written evidence of their feelings.

References

Lepp, I., *The Ways of Friendship*. New York: The Macmillan Company, 1966.

Leuba, C. J., *Personality, Interpersonal Relations, and Self-Understanding*. Columbus, Ohio: Charles E. Merrill Books, Inc., 1962.

Reilly, W. J., *Successful Human Relations*. New York: Harper & Row, Publishers, 1952.

Wallace, W. L., *Student Culture: Social Structure and Continuity in a Liberal Arts College*. Chicago: Aldine Publishing Company, 1966.

Zaleznik, A., *The Dynamics of Interpersonal Behavior*. New York: John Wiley & Sons, Inc., 1964.

CHAPTER FIVE

Professional Organizations

In addition to the informal relationships you may achieve with your fellow students and with various faculty members, there are various types of more organized groups which you may help to form or become associated with during your undergraduate years. These associations may serve you in various ways both during your graduate years and also in your teaching and coaching years following graduation.

At the national, state, and local institutional levels there are several organizations with which new physical education majors and minors should become acquainted. Nationally, the American Association of Health, Physical Education and Recreation (AAHPER), within the National Education Association, forms a type of cover organization with which several groups more specific in focus are associated. Founded in 1885 as the American Association for the Advancement of Physical Education, its early organizers were primarily college physical educators who held the M. D. degree. In 1903 its title was changed to the American Physical Education Association, and in the middle 1930s the words "Health" and "Recreation" were added to the title. A recent trend is to examine the all-encompassing nature of the title and thus the composition of the organization; and future developments may again lead to more fragmented and manageable organizations focused specifically upon physical education, health education, or dance, recreation, athletics, scientific research, and the like. The National Association is organized as follows:

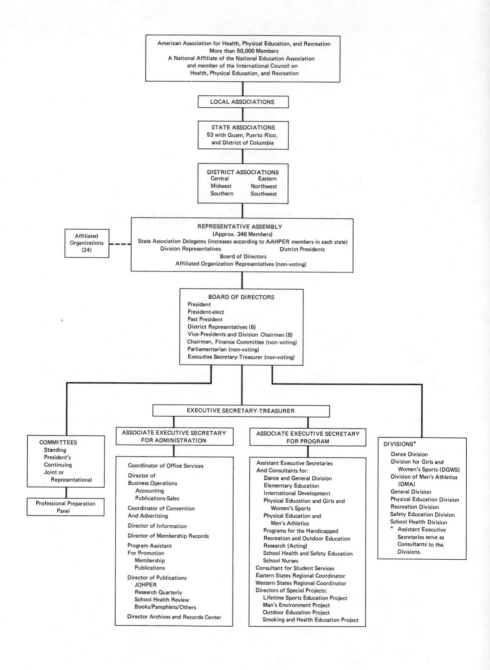

American Association for Health, Physical Education, and Recreation
More than 50,000 Members
A National Affiliate of the National Education Association
and member of the International Council on
Health, Physical Education, and Recreation

LOCAL ASSOCIATIONS

STATE ASSOCIATIONS
53 with Guam, Puerto Rico,
and District of Columbia

DISTRICT ASSOCIATIONS
Central   Eastern
Midwest   Northwest
Southern   Southwest

Affiliated Organizations (24)

REPRESENTATIVE ASSEMBLY
(Approx. 346 Members)
State Association Delegates (increases according to AAHPER members in each state)
Division Representatives   District Presidents
Board of Directors
Affiliated Organization Representatives (non-voting)

BOARD OF DIRECTORS
President
President-elect
Past President
District Representatives (6)
Vice-Presidents and Division Chairmen (8)
Chairman, Finance Committee (non-voting)
Parliamentarian (non-voting)
Executive Secretary-Treasurer (non-voting)

EXECUTIVE SECRETARY-TREASURER

ASSOCIATE EXECUTIVE SECRETARY
FOR ADMINISTRATION

ASSOCIATE EXECUTIVE SECRETARY
FOR PROGRAM

DIVISIONS*

COMMITTEES
Standing
President's
Continuing
Joint or
    Representational

Professional Preparation
Panel

Coordinator of Office Services
Director of
Business Operations
    Accounting
    Publications-Sales
Coordinator of Convention
And Advertising
Director of Information
Director of Membership Records
Program Assistant
For Promotion
    Membership
    Publications
Director of Publications
    JOHPER
    Research Quarterly
    School Health Review
    Books/Pamphlets/Others
Director Archives and Records Center

Assistant Executive Secretaries
And Consultants for:
    Dance and General Division
    Elementary Education
    International Development
    Physical Education and Girls and
        Women's Sports
    Physical Education and
        Men's Athletics
    Programs for the Handicapped
    Recreation and Outdoor Education
    Research (Acting)
    School Health and Safety Education
    School Nurses
Consultant for Student Services
Eastern States Regional Coordinator
Western States Regional Coordinator
Directors of Special Projects:
    Lifetime Sports Education Project
    Man's Environment Project
    Outdoor Education Project
    Smoking and Health Education Project

Dance Division
Division for Girls and
    Women's Sports (DGWS)
Division of Men's Athletics
    (DMA)
General Division
Physical Education Division
Recreation Division
Safety Education Division
School Health Division
*   Assistant Executive
    Secretaries serve as
    Consultants to the
    Divisions.

Most states in the U. S. contain AAHPER-affiliated state organizations. In addition, there are other national and local organizations composed of coaches, recreational workers, health educators, and the like which will be discussed in the subsequent chapters.

Two types of clubs to which physical education major students may belong are found on many college campuses. There is a men's physical education fraternity called Phi Epsilon Kappa. Many campuses also have student major clubs which operate relatively independently, or in conjunction with the national AAHPER or state organizations.

In common with other professional groups, these organizations are concerned with the propagation of goals and improvement of the personnel in the profession. Standards for personnel and programs are often prescribed by subgroups at the state and national levels. Communication between members is facilitated through their various publications, including the *Journal of Health, Physical Education and Recreation*, and other newsletters and research publications such as *The Research Quarterly*, published by AAHPER; *The Physical Educator* put out by Phi Epsilon Kappa; as well as newsletters and magazines published by many of the state organizations.

Effective legislation influencing programs in health, recreation, and physical education is often the goal of many of the state organizations. At the national level rather extensive and helpful research efforts are mounted to improve practices within the teacher education institutions and high schools throughout the country. For example, in the 1960s research was carried out by AAHPER dealing with the formulation of adequate norms for the evaluation of skill, as well as several projects dealing with the fitness of youth. Studies of health attitudes and knowledge as well as information concerning recreational facilities and needs have been compiled by various subgroups within the national organization during the past ten years.

Physical educators have formed groups at the local levels, or have organized professional groups representing a portion of a state or a county. This fragmentation is found, for example, in the State of California, and in many of the other larger states, including Texas and New York. Most of these local organizations hold professional meetings monthly or quarterly, while the state organizations and sections of the national organization, as well as AAHPER itself, conduct yearly conventions which students may attend. You should find out just which meetings and conventions are being held in your area this year, so that you might attend programs that interest you in the months ahead.

The College Physical Education Association and the College Women's Physical Education Association, both concerned with college teaching, are examples of other groups with special interests which have been formed throughout the country. Your instructor might bring others to your attention. Additional organizations will be discussed in some of the chapters which follow.

Student Benefits from Participation

Participation in a professional organization while an undergraduate may be potentially valuable to you in several ways. For example, you might make professional contacts which could help you find a position following graduation. Exposure to ideas and speakers at conventions and meetings may stimulate you intellectually, and the demonstrations and workshops which often accompany conventions and meetings usually contain teaching and coaching techniques which will later become helpful. Experienced teachers are usually found taking part in these workshops, and observation of the general methodologies they employ may provide cues which you may later use to your advantage.

The formation of and participation in a student organization within your school may be even more useful to you, as the program content can be geared toward meeting specific student interests and needs. For example, outstanding physical educators can be brought in as speakers, workshops in which students may deal with coaching techniques can be held and methods of teaching gymnastics or the dance may be covered in various sessions. Group trips to conventions, athletic contests, dance symposiums, health conferences, and the like might be arranged. Group projects dealing with community problems can be instigated and carried out. Recreational programs and athletic programs in culturally deprived areas can be staffed with student volunteers, for example, providing for productive experiences for the children involved as well as for the participating college students.

On the other hand, participation in, or formation of, a student physical education major group may not be desirable for several reasons. The demands upon student time, coupled with the necessity on the part of many to work their way through college, may leave little time for additional meetings, whatever their potential value. So-called "streetcar colleges," to which the majority of the student body must travel each day from distant homes, may not prove to be an environment in which a student major organization can prosper. Organizations should serve their members' needs, and if the needs to meet the necessary academic demands of the college and the financial necessities of life are too great, little energy will be left over for participation in a student organization.

For students majoring in physical education who are able and interested under the conditions mentioned above, student professional organizations within the department of education might provide an outlet for their energies and enhance their futures as teachers.

Summary

The student should attempt to match his own professional goals and the immediate demands placed upon him with the possible advantages of membership in a student-professional organization. While such an organization can provide a place for personal and academic growth, organizational demands upon his time may prove incompatible with other academic and financial demands.

The activities potentially found within student professional organizations can be extremely helpful from a number of standpoints. Introduction to the programs of other post-graduate professional organizations, obtaining stimulation from invited speakers, as well as observing and adopting helpful practices presented in workshops and demonstrations, are only some of the activities in which a professional organization can engage.

Student Activities and Discussion Questions

1. Draw an organization chart of the National AAHPER Organization. Show subdivisions, councils, and special groups affiliated with AAHPER at this time.
2. Outline and explain the organization of the group in your state concerned with physical education, health, and recreation. What are its current projects and goals? When and where will be its next meetings? What are the contents of these meetings to be? Who are its current officers?
3. Write a brief paper dealing with the history of a state or national organization. Discuss trends, philosophy, and leaders throughout the years.
4. If no professional student organization is to be found within your department, discuss the problems and principles which should be kept in mind if one is to be organized.
5. What would you include in a questionnaire to all major and minor students on your campus from which to decide just what procedures you might go through to organize a professional group. Include items on the questionnaire which might guide you in future professional program planning should such a group be organized.

6. Discuss reasons for and against fragmenting organizations dealing with health, physical education, recreation, physical therapy, dance, classroom teaching, etc., on your campus or in the nation as a whole. Should separate clubs interested in dance, health, coaching, physical education, teaching, or for male physical educators, female physical educators, etc., be formed on your campus; or would such subdivisions be in some ways undesirable? In what ways?

PART TWO

Career Channels

CHAPTER SIX

Secondary
Physical Education

The majority of the physical education curriculums in the United States focus on the preparation of the high school and junior high school teacher. Most of the graduates of these programs, if they enter teaching at all, find themselves in a secondary school.

Most states require a B. S. degree before you may teach in a secondary school. Many require an additional year of schooling following the acquisition of this degree, during which you must usually take additional education courses. In addition, you must engage in practice-teaching experiences for one or more semesters under the direction of a master teacher in a school near the university or college you are attending during this fifth year.

Many secondary teachers possess an M. A. degree, and most have acquired college units past the B. S. degree. Most school districts require their teachers to gain some kind of professional units yearly, by attendance at formal classes, workshops, etc., to be eligible for a regular salary increment.

It is usual to find that teachers of physical education are qualified, because of their college minor, to teach other courses in the school; and many do so. In addition to teaching physical education classes, you may find yourself teaching courses in health, life science, history, and the like, depending upon your background. This type of combination can be enjoyable as you gain experience in two different types of teaching situations during a single work day.

Most college students have had recent experience as secondary school students themselves; thus a detailed recital of just what high school physical educators do, or do not do, may be unnecessary. At the same time, the college students may have been exposed to high school programs which were limited in their scope and which may not have provided a good model to copy.

Devising a Good Physical Education Program

Good high school programs are comprehensive and flexible in their offerings. They provide opportunities for students to engage in the usual team sports in season, and afford specific teaching in the skills of these sports. But they should not consist solely of a yearly repetition of the usual football for eight weeks, basketball for eight weeks, and baseball for eight weeks, as is sometimes the case, but should also contain opportunities for students to learn activities which will serve them as young adults emerging from the schools. If possible, tennis, swimming, and the like should also be offered.

An adequate high school or junior high school program should contain classes in which students may pursue individual interests and expand their abilities to engage in German gymnastics, rhythmic gymnastics, modern dance, and the like. Furthermore, a good physical education program at the secondary level should provide for chances to engage in various activities in which both sexes may participate by introducing individual sports such as badminton and tennis as well as recreational activities involving folk and social dance.

Programs of secondary physical education should also contain classes which permit accommodation for individual differences in physical and emotional needs. Fitness classes, courses to remedy special motor problems, as well as courses which permit the flexibility needed by youth evidencing cardiovascular problems, asthma, and other disabilities, should be found in a well-rounded curriculum of high school and junior high school physical education.

Some secondary programs of physical education contain courses in which health knowledge is extended, while in others driver training classes, drill teams, and the like occupy the time of physical educators. While many would disagree that these latter classes should take time from what might be considered regular physical education, at the same time these classes often become the responsibility of physical education teachers.

There is more than enough content in the activities considered to belong in a physical education program to occupy five periods a week for the six years of secondary school without including health teachings and the numerous other encroachments which often appear in the curriculum and are thrust upon the physical education teacher. In an adequate program, time should be allotted to teaching individual and team sports, evaluating the outcomes of these courses, providing tasks which are intended to promote physical fitness, and providing the students with a sufficient background into the *whys* of the various activities in which they are engaging.

There are several basic principles that should be followed when devising a good secondary physical education program:

1. The program should be broad and comprehensive in its offerings, accommodating to individual differences in interests and in physical capacities.
2. The program should be coherent and integrated from the seventh grade through the twelfth grade. There should be a gradual progression of activities introduced from the more simple to the more complex. Lead-up drills incorporating basketball should precede playing the total basketball game, simple field games should precede football, less difficult batting games should precede softball. Rhythmic gymnastics and floor work should come before introducing the heavy German apparatus (such as beams or bars), while less strenuous tasks requiring the development of strength and endurance should be placed before those more taxing in nature.
3. Provision should be made for time to evaluate the goals of the program.
4. The students should be permitted, at least during their final three years, to select from a number of activities rather than given no alternatives.

In addition to teaching the formal classes in physical education, the secondary teacher may be asked to coordinate various other ancillary programs within the school. In many high schools there are rather well-developed programs of intramural sports in which various school organizations compete. Numerous after-school programs are often the responsibility of physical education teachers, including recreation programs of various kinds, girls' athletic associations, drill teams, etc.

It may seem to some, after this brief description of what *should* and may take place within a secondary school program, that a physical education teacher must be a kind of all-encompassing athlete-teacher, capable of effectively instructing from ten to 15 activities. However, it is unrealistic to expect anyone to be proficient in performing, interested in teaching, and capable of ably instructing more than four or five activities. To some professionals this statement may be somewhat shocking. Many curriculums in physical education in our country terminate with the exposure of the senior student to a large number of proficiency tests, which if not passed may result in withholding the student's degree, or at least holding up his opportunity to work for a credential.

The research evidence that has been available for the past 15 years, however, suggests that it is unrealistic to expect even a select population of people that are likely to major in physical education to evidence outstanding proficiencies in a large number of sports activities. Majors in physical education *can* learn the mechanics of various sports skills and the rules and strategies of various games; however, high levels of performance proficiency which will serve them well during their teaching careers may reasonably be expected in only four or five different sports. A physical education major should attempt to gain above-average competence in one or more field sports or basketball; in some kind of rhythmic or developmental activity such as gymnastics, modern dance, or rhythmic gymnastics; and in combatives (in the case of males).

A physical education major student should also be familiar with aquatics, and possess the ability to teach beginning swimming. He or she should furthermore be equipped to teach at least one sport, such as tennis, golf, badminton, or archery.

As important as the gaining of ability to teach various activities to high school youth is, so is the acquiring of information concerning the nature of the adolescent. You will be better able to accommodate to individual differences when teaching specific sports skills, and to plan more flexible programs, if you have as thorough an understanding as possible about the characteristics of adolescents. A thorough discussion of adolescent characteristics may be found in several recent texts, some of which are listed at the end of the chapter. In addition, you should obtain information concerning the adolescent in various courses within the physical education and education departments. The following paragraphs will acquaint you with some of the major considerations to keep in mind when working with the adolescent in the secondary school.

The adolescent entering secondary school, usually a junior high school, is between 13 and 15 years old. The girls at this age are usually physically and emotionally more mature than the boys, but the physical prowess of the boys is beginning to surpass that of their female classmates. Both boys and girls, may be beset with a number of problems, while the various physical and societal forces impinging upon them may be creating personality changes.

Marked differences in physical maturity within a group of adolescents may be seen at this age. The early-maturing boys will be about twice as strong as their later-maturing friends. Some girls will be physically quite advanced while some of their classmates will appear immature in comparison.

Both early- and late-maturing youngsters of these ages (13 to 15) will have problems of various kinds which may be either alleviated or compounded in a physical education class. The late-maturing boys will have a great deal of difficulty competing with their early-maturing friends. The latter will run faster, be considerably stronger, and possess impressive physiques compared to their physically younger classmates.

The late- and early-maturing adolescent girls in junior high school will not usually evidence such marked performance differences as their male counterparts. While the early-maturing girl *could* outperform her less-mature peer, she may *choose not* to do so. Her earlier maturity is likely to turn her interest to the opposite sex, rather than to sustain her in performance efforts needed in sports and games. While reasonably high correlations between physical capacity measures (strength and endurance) and physical performance in various motor tasks are obtained by testing boys, this high correlation does not appear when contrasting the scores of adolescent girls. Girls during this age period do not always work up to their capacities, a tendency which may cause their physical education teachers some degree of consternation. Adolescent girls in our society are often difficult to motivate toward exerting reasonable effort in hard physical tasks; they are more concerned about their appearance and other social skills than about proficiency in a game.

Adolescent boys, both during junior and senior high school years, also are often difficult to work with. Many, particularly the early-maturing ones, are highly motivated, work hard, and do well. Others, particularly during the high school years, have found out that they are not good performers after hundreds of encounters with physical activity, and have a poor feeling about how they perform physically.

These poor performers, if given opportunities to engage in activities in which they may experience and record improvement in their *own* performance scores, may begin to work harder in your classes. Recently, several writers discussing the importance of sport and physical efficiency to the young man have commented that the pursuit and achievement of excellence is of vital importance to many people at all ages and in many lines of endeavor. They further point out that one of the few ways in which a young man may achieve excellence is in physical activities. It may be your job as a physical educator in a high school to aid those who are less than excellent to achieve success in physical tasks, by providing them with ways in which they may improve upon their own endeavors.

You may provide regular training experiences which will enable adolescent boys, for example, to run farther and faster, rather than only giving them infrequent tests in the 100-yard dash or half-mile run, as is sometimes done. You may rate the boys in your classes on the percent of personal improvement, rather than comparing them against norms or against the performance of their peers.

The adolescent girl may be motivated to perform better in your classes in several ways. You may, for example, capitalize upon the fact that she places a high value upon her physical appearance; and demonstrate to her how a good physical condition may aid in achieving a better bearing while moving, and in gaining an improved figure.

Both boys and girls may be aided in your classes by providing them with skills in social dance, and with increased proficiencies in individual and team sports which they can play together. In this manner the clumsy overtures between the sexes often observed in early and middle adolescence may be transformed into happy and comfortable experiences.

Peer group judgments of the society to which they are exposed become increasingly influential in the formation of values during the adolescent period. The physical educator, to work effectively with youth in this age period, should (a) be aware of the adolescent values important within the particular school in which he or she is working, and (b) attempt when possible to blend and incorporate these values into his program when it is reasonable to do so. For example, teaching a coeducational class of sixteen-year-olds the schottish may not be as appropriate as introducing them to more modern social dance forms similar to those with which they perhaps have already experimented.

It is to be expected that the adolescent of the 1970s and 1980s will not blindly accept, and participate vigorously in, any aspect of the school curriculum that he does not deem important. The young individual of this age, exposed to the cynicism, problems, and trying experiences of the 1960s, may be expected to be extremely critical of what will happen to him in school and what his teachers expect to do. Driving children through activities, a ploy which may have worked in the 1960s and earlier, is not likely to be as effective with the adolescent of the 1970s and 1980s. I believe that this is a healthy state of affairs.

The adolescent of the 1970s will want to know *why* he is engaging in specific activities, to become aware of the basic principles underlying exercise, and in other ways become intellectually involved with planning his own program. If scorned, he will likely, as did many adolescents during the early part of the twentieth century, merely tolerate and subtly resist a high school physical educator who attempts to push, drive, and otherwise mold him with what to him are meaningless tasks; then upon graduating he may either start out again on his own to learn recreational skills, or give up vigorous physical activity entirely.

Your Rapport with Your Future Students

One of the underlying concerns and perhaps fears most undergraduates taking physical education courses have is whether they will relate well to the youth they will later teach and, conversely, whether the youth will be "turned on" by them. There are a number of conditions which are likely to produce either friction or rapport between an adolescent and his physical education teacher.

1. If the physical educator is seen by his pupils to worry too much about being accepted, he is likely to be considered insecure, and thus not worthy of their respect. During your early attempts at teaching, at least try to appear to know what you are about. This leads to the second consideration.

2. Confront your classes well-prepared for the lessons of the day, and also well-prepared by your background to answer questions and to deal with situations as they may arise during the class period. There is no substitute either in coaching or in teaching for knowing in detail all aspects of what you are trying to get across. The lack of background will immediately become apparent to even the most disinterested student, who may attempt to capitalize upon your apparent ineptitude.

3. Realize that not all students you confront will like you, and that you will not like all of them. However, liking is not an imperative; rather, you must deal with all youth in a professional manner independent of your basic feelings. You should demand respect from students who apparently detest you, and in turn offer your professional guidance and services to students whose demeanor you find undesirable. It is likely that you will find in your classes students who idolize you without question; perhaps you may represent all good things to them, or they may be unusually happy about physical activity. There will also be a large group of students who accept you without either undue adulation or rejection. You will also find a group of students in every large class who, upon your first confrontation with them, will not appear to like you or what you are "selling" very well at all! Undue worry about how any of these three groups feel about you may detract from your professional conduct. If you break your own arm patting yourself on the back when you begin to feel the warm glow from those who revere you, you are as foolish as if you spend an undue amount of time worrying about those who reject you. Do your job, and you will be surprised at the respect directed your way.

4. Concentrate on earning the respect of your students by your professional appearance and behavior. Self-respect usually precedes

gaining respect from others. If yours is flagging, attempt to resolve this type of personal problem before entering teaching, or the students you find there will pick it up and perhaps dent your ego further.

5. Get close to your students by encouraging communication; but not too close. They may attempt frequently to bring you down to their level in numerous ways; resist their attempts, they really would rather not see this happen. They would like you to remain as you are, their teacher and example, and not be one of the boys (or girls). You are older, you are in many ways different from them. Try to understand and guide them, to sponsor their organizations; but don't join their clubs.

6. In situations which you feel demand discipline, first take a deep breath, smile, and think before acting. When you do act, be decisive and make your actions appropriate to the transgression. Do not overreact. If possible, deal privately with a class member to be disciplined. Embarrassing him in front of a class, as he may have tried to do with you, not only lowers you to his (or her) level, but also gives the transgressor no way to turn—he must defend himself in front of his peers or lose all status.

An interesting phenomenon usually occurs when a student in front of a class engages in some inappropriate behavior which may require a reprimand. The class members first enjoy the "show" of the misbehavior occurring; however, they will usually feel more comfortable if you as the instructor indicate that you are capable of handling it in a reasonably efficient fashion. No reaction on your part, when one is obviously called for, is likely to worry the rest of the class; they may ask themselves: "Is there a chance for complete chaos here; can anyone get away with anything?" When the incident is handled well they usually are more secure and feel the teacher is really in charge when things may become upset. Too severe a "bawling out" of an individual student in front of other class members may have the immediate effect of subduing a problem, as perhaps the students may temporarily ask themselves: "Could that severe censure happen to me!" At the same time too marked a public reaction from a teacher, directed toward one youth, may have long-term effects which may be later manifested in subtle and overt hostility directed toward the instructor.

As you gain experience in secondary school teaching, you will begin to do several things better when disciplining students. (a) You will not hear so much in the way of negative comments directed your way; and upon hearing less, fewer are likely to be launched. (b) You are likely, after your first year of teaching, to be able to react in a stern manner when appropriate and not really upset yourself at the visceral level. (c) You will begin to employ increasingly effective means of dealing with situations which arise.

A further factor which may either help or hinder your efforts to work with students and to impose discipline when necessary is the building up of a "folklore" in the school about what you stand for, or perhaps what you do not stand for, in the way of behavior. Despite the fact that the students become aware of your expectations, you will need to continue to maintain your image as a fair, competent teacher during each class period of each of the years you remain a physical education teacher.

Your Colleagues and Administrators

You have a number of obligations as a physical education teacher to your colleagues and to your superiors in the secondary school. You should attempt in every way possible to let them know that you feel a part of the school in which you are teaching, by attending meetings and by dressing in appropriate ways (doffing your gymnasium clothes) when you arrive. You should let them know when the opportunity arises about the content of your classes, although classes in physical education are the most easily observed of any in the high school or junior high school. Moreover, word will get around about what you are doing in your classes faster than you will believe.

You should feel obligated to become aware of the policies which govern your behavior, and in other ways attempt to integrate your efforts with others in the school. There will be evenings during which parents may be invited to speak with you about the progress, or lack of it, evidenced by their children in your classes. On these occasions in particular you should be prepared to represent your portion of the curriculum in an effective manner. It is to be expected, however, that parent participation in such programs will diminish to some degree in the latter years of high school.

A most important colleague with whom you should attempt to work closely and in harmony is the educator of the other sex who teaches the girls (or boys). You have the same goals, and are much of the time employing similar means to reach these objectives. Male physical educators are not inherently lazy, as many women in the field suggest; they may be trying to conserve their energy to get through a total school day which involves three or four hours of strenuous coaching.[1] As a matter of fact, there are probably as many incompetent female physical educators as there are incompetent male physical educators.

---

[1]Thus, the cause of their behavior lies in the administrative arrangement in which they work, not solely in their attitude toward the average child. Further discussion and possible accommodations which may be helpful are in Chapter Ten.

Some young physical educators of both sexes are not as capable as the older ones; however, the reverse may also be true.

Women physical educators in the secondary school may prove difficult to work with because they are frequently and inexcusably relegated to fewer and poorer-quality facilities than are allotted to the boys' program. There is no justification for this type of facility apportionment either from an educational or a philosophical viewpoint; yet this too frequently is the case.

Summary

Your work in secondary physical education will be with adolescents, teaching them various kinds of motor activities. *You should enter the schools* prepared to participate within a comprehensive and flexible program suited to the needs and interests of all. More important, you should be equipped by your background to justify the type of program to which you subject the students; as they may not blindly accept the ten minutes of exercises, a lap, and "throw out the ball" type of program which was too frequently offered to youth in the 1960s.

You should also be prepared to work as a professional educator in a total educational environment. You should be ready to assume the obligations placed on all the teachers of your school, and to conduct yourself in as professional a manner as possible.

Your dealings with students should be impartial and reflect your competence. You should be prepared to deal with disciplinary problems in a manner which will not be likely to engender more of these. You should deal with your teaching colleagues of the opposite sex as professional partners, not as opponents in a kind of contest in which the youth you both serve are likely to be the losers.

References

Books

American Association of Health, Physical Education and Recreation. *Physical Education for High School Students.* Washington, D. C.: American Association of Health, Physical Education and Recreation, 1955.

American Association of Health, Physical Education and Recreation. *Physical Education for High School Students.* Washington, D. C.: American Association of Health, Physical Education and Recreation, revised 1960.

Bookwalter, K. W., *Physical Education in the Secondary Schools.* Washington, D. C.: Washington Center for Applied Research in Education, 1964.

Bucher, C. A., *Methods and Materials for Secondary School Education.* St. Louis: Mosby Publishing Co., 1965.

Cassidy, Rosalind F., *Counseling in the Physical Education Program*. New York: Appleton-Century-Crofts, 1959.

Cowell, Charles L., *Curriculum Design in Physical Education*. Englewood Cliffs, New Jersey: Prentice-Hall, Inc., 1955.

Cratty, Bryant J., *Psychology and Physical Activity*. Englewood Cliffs, New Jersey: Prentice-Hall, Inc., 1968.

Mohr, D. R., *Teachers Guide for Physical Education for High School Students*. Washington, D. C.: American Association for Health, Physical Education, and Recreation, 1963.

Thiller, A. G., *A Dynamic Concept of Physical Education for Secondary Schools*. Englewood Cliffs, New Jersey: Prentice-Hall, Inc., 1963.

Periodicals

High School Journal. Chapel Hill, North Carolina: University of North Carolina Press, School of Education.

CHAPTER SEVEN

Elementary
Physical Education

Perhaps one of the most neglected aspects of the physical education program in the United States is the services rendered to elementary school children. In most of the so-called civilized countries of the world which have educational systems comparable to ours, the quality of the program to which their young children are exposed is superior to that found in this country. And yet during no other period in life, except possibly the preschool years, will physical activity have a more profound effect upon the general emotional, social, and physical development of the child.

Some behavioral scientists have postulated that the amount of personality change which can be achieved through education is greatest during the time of life that a given aspect of the personality is normally in a state of flux. If this is true, then it should follow that during the 0-8 years when motor development occurs fastest, a well-conceived physical education program is likely to have the most beneficial effect upon children and youth. During these early years of life children are relatively unsophisticated, and are interested in activity and in learning how they can improve their movement capacities. Sportsmanship becomes a topic of serious consideration when presented well, while learning the rules of football similarly receives their concerted effort.

Despite the apathy toward developing programs of physical education for elementary school children in the 1950s, during the middle of the 1960s a great deal of interest was focused on the supposition advanced by some that motor activities applied in the correct amounts to young children would produce increases in academic proficiencies of various kinds.[1] This impetus is partly responsible for the apparent increase in interest accorded physical education for younger children toward the latter part of the 1960s and early years of the 1970s.

In the larger school districts in the United States, programs for elementary school children sometimes exist only on paper. Curriculum guides are available to teachers, containing activities of various degrees of relevance and usefulness. There are usually one or more supervisors of physical education, some of whom are primarily responsible for elementary school programs. At the same time the services offered *directly* to the child through the efforts of his classroom teacher or some specialist in physical education are virtually absent. It is usually up to the classroom teacher to engage in some physical education program, a decision which is largely dependent upon his interest and his perceptions of his ability to teach this potentially tiring subject.

In other school districts, some of which are among the more heavily financed, specialists are assigned to one or several schools, and work in helpful ways with the children. At times the outcome of even this kind of potentially well-functioning program suffers because of the lack of consistent and prolonged student-teacher contact throughout a given week.

Despite the conditions described in this perhaps gloomy introduction to elementary physical education, the opportunities for positions and for serving children are expanding. Children of these years are delightful to work with, highly motivated, and activity oriented. These children are younger and less sophisticated than those in secondary school; the former are not afraid to mess up their hair and will participate vigorously, unlike their older sisters in high school. The boys have not yet found out which are good or bad at athletics, and all usually participate without the self-consciousness often seen in inept adolescents. Children of these ages like movement and, when receiving responsible adult direction in their efforts, usually respond in positive ways, a quality of response which in turn is rewarding to their teacher.

Another positive trend is the fact that more and more men are entering elementary physical education programs. Their presence may provide a great deal of help for the boys in elementary schools, who are perhaps too often confronted with female authority figures both at home and at school.

[1] I have dealt with these ideas in numerous texts written during the 1960s and 1970s, some of which are listed at the conclusion of this chapter.

Preparation for the elementary physical education teacher should consist of the acquisition of two primary areas of information. They should learn about general child development, particularly motor development. Some of the guidelines for structuring this body of information are found in Chapter Twenty-two. A second type of competency which should be developed deals with the analysis and teaching of physical skills.

The elementary physical educator, to be maximally effective, should attempt to acquire background in several subject matter areas. At the same time, several other types of skills should be developed while an undergraduate:

1. Competencies should be developed in the area of tests and measurements, so that the motor efficiencies of children during the early, middle, and late elementary school years may accurately be assessed. The skills needed are those which involve not only giving and interpreting test scores, but also the ability to construct valid test batteries incorporating a broad range of motor tests.

2. The ability to formulate curriculum should be learned. Many of the positions in elementary school physical education involve little or no direct contact with children, but require the writing of meaningful curriculum guides helpful to the classroom teacher. The ability to write well, coupled with an awareness of appropriate activities for children of both sexes and of all ages, are requisites for the formulation of a sound curriculum.

3. Elementary school teachers should know a lot of things to do. Some of your courses should offer the opportunity to experiment with various activities and games, and to observe children formulating their own games and attempting games which have been devised by teachers. Without a variety of activities available, the teachers find that the students in their charge may quickly tire of the sameness of frequently-relied-upon motor tasks. One of the primary ways in which all children are motivated to perform any kind of task is by making it novel and of optimum complexity. Activities should not be too difficult or prove threatening, nor should they be too easy, thus insulting to the children's self-concept.

4. Theoretical knowledge concerning the basic elements of motor performance should be mastered; including a knowledge of mechanical principles, the neurological bases for movement, the physiological changes occurring during vigorous exercise, as well as information pertaining to the emotional and social development of children. Without this basic information, a teacher or supervisor of elementary school physical education cannot be expected to deal with individual differ-

ences in children, nor to select sound programs of activities. Additionally, a teacher who merely relies upon instinct rather than background when working with children and formulating programs may do more harm than good. A teacher well-equipped professionally may not only deal better with children, but is also able to evaluate new practices with some degree of expertise, a function often needed in school districts. Particular help is needed in the assessment of various perceptual-motor theories which will purportedly enhance intellectual development, and which are advanced at reasonably frequent intervals.

The physical education teacher within an elementary school in some ways helps to maintain the daily tempo of individual children and of groups of children. One of the primary sources of negative feelings about physical education voiced by elementary school teachers concerns the fact that physical education periods seem to overstimulate children, and when they return to classrooms they are often unable to "settle down" to their schoolwork. The elementary school physical education teacher should be aware of individual differences in the activation levels of various children in his school, and employ ways to calm them down following physical education.

Quiet periods following physical education and recess periods may be instituted to lower children's levels of arousal from the high levels they need, and which they maintain on the school ground, to the lower levels of activation suited to effective classroom functioning. Several books dating from 1938 contain methods of relaxation training appropriate to children, methods which will help some children calm down and perform better in classrooms. The use of slower music, and various activities in which the children learn to change the rate and tempo of their movements following vigorous activity, should be helpful to most younger children in elementary school and to certain older children who may have difficulties calming themselves down when it is appropriate to do so.

A number of interesting research findings should be considered when deciding how often to have recess during a school day, how long recesses should be, and how they should be placed within various academic exercises. The evidence indicates the complexity of the problem of truly integrating motor activities in helpful ways with the practice of more academic operations. For example, evidence dating from the 1930s indicates that there is an optimum level of activation which may be produced by muscular activity—squeezing hand grips one-half maximum or running a treadmill at about 50 percent maximum— which will enhance memorizing word lists and doing mathematics problems. There are also indications that confining fit children with high activity needs for too long a period within a restrictive classroom environment is likely to result in a lowering of the effort they bring to their schoolwork; while conversely, less fit children may continue to work well academically for prolonged periods of time when restrained in classrooms. Another interesting line of investigation, using both humans and rodents as subjects, has produced findings that suggest that vigorous exercise applied immediately after initial learning of something new is likely to result in partial or complete obliteration of the "memory traces" laid down by the new material in the nervous system.

Taken together, these findings indicate that recesses and periods of physical education should take place at relatively frequent intervals through the school day, particularly in the case of the more active and fit children; while these should probably not occur immediately following a lesson which is likely to be intellectually difficult for them. The sensitive physical education teacher, in cooperation with school administrators, classroom teachers, and school psychologists, should attempt (within the existing state laws governing the duration of school days, recesses, physical education period length, etc.) to plan an elementary school day which varies to meet the individual needs of children in the school evidencing various levels of habitual activation and needs for activity. At the same time, they should make sure that classroom periods are not too prolonged, and that opportunities for vigorous action do not immediately follow difficult reading or mathematics lessons.

Learning Games

Several researchers in the country have within recent years experimented with the manner in which various learning games might aid certain classroom operations. The data emanating from these investigations have been highly encouraging, and indicate that some children learn best when their total body is in action during the learning process. This approach is different from merely permitting a child to let off steam in the playground and then return to the relatively passive classroom environment to really do his work. Rather, the children in these studies, and in numerous school districts around the country which have heeded the data, perform physically while at the same time engaging in various academic exercises. The sequence of activities which has been developed started with a variety of activities designed to calm down children, and to focus their attention for increased periods of time. Activities asking the children to move in various ways "as slowly as you can," as well as the previously mentioned relaxation training, are found in this initial phase.

The second phase involves games pointed toward helping the children gain an awareness of the qualities of various geometric patterns. Large triangles, semicircles, rectangles, and similar figures are painted on playgrounds, besides the usual circles and squares previously found there. The children run around these figures, play games on them and, most important, observe and discuss their properties (i.e., "a triangle really does have three sides and three angles wherever it is found"). They are being prepared to discriminate the differences between the 26 letters of the alphabet. Recognition of numbers constitutes the next step in this progression.

As the children acquire the ability to recognize letters and numbers, they are introduced to what we have found to be a highly motivating activity designed to enhance serial memory ability. The ability in children to remember a series of actions is correlated with the manner in which they can remember a series of pictures, letters, and numbers. This movement type of serial memory practice, among other activities, may require a child to perform several actions on various geometric configurations, and then watch while another child tries to duplicate the actions in the correct order.

Number games, mathematics problems, counting, as well as spelling problems are engaged in by jumping and hopping in various squares containing either letters or numbers. At times squares containing these figures are carried around in various relay contests. The number of games which may be played are limitless. Children in the third and fourth grades who have been exposed to them continue to be interested in them, and to evidence improvement for a considerable period of time.

The sequence continues and involves at the more advanced levels various problem-solving tasks, in which children engage in choice behavior ("How many ways can you jump into the circle?") as well as the development of new games.

The evidence we have at this point indicates that these learning games are highly motivating for children with learning problems, for immature normals (kindergarten through second grade), and for older retarded children. Our data tell us that children taught in the manner described above learn as much as, or more than, they learn from extra tutoring in small classroom groups. Furthermore, the evidence we have collected tells us that it is not merely that we give children a chance to play and to be active in these games, but that activity coupled with thought and practice in classroom skills will, in this combination, prove helpful to many children.

Practice in these learning games is not considered to be an adequate substitute for a good physical education program at the elementary school level. Nor should learning games in all cases replace the usual learning methods employed in classroom such as looking, hearing, speaking, and similar activities.

These learning games have proven at the elementary school level to be a valuable addition to many school programs, and the prospective elementary school physical education teacher might learn about their underlying rationale. References at the completion of the chapter contain further information about these interesting new activities.

Basic Movements Versus Sports and Recreation Skills

For many years in England and other countries, as well as in some places in the United States, there has emerged what might be termed the "Movement" Movement. This movement is in many ways an extremely constructive program; for in essence it includes a number of experiences which permit children to enjoy their motor capabilities, and encourages them to engage in a wide variety of experiences. Various creative activities may be contained in a program of movement education, including exploratory actions on the grass, in which children are given a minimal amount of cues and are asked to move as they feel a particular animal or perhaps the wind might move. Various apparatuses are often employed. Hoops and balls are popular. The children may be asked to see how many ways they can place the hoops in relationship to each other, and then to demonstrate how they can move among them. Such programs usually give children maximum freedom for creative effort, and at the same time encourage a great deal of vigorous exploratory activity. The basic rationale underlying such programs is that these activities prepare the child for whatever movement requirements will confront him, and provide a sound base for later adolescent and adult activities, including social dancing, sports skills, and the like.

Despite the apparent value of this type of program, there are those who are somewhat skeptical of the claims made by the proponents of movement education. These individuals claim, for example, that the transfer from early exploratory movement experiences to specific sports skills required later in life may not truly happen, and point out that there is no experimental evidence substantiating that transfer will actually occur. These scientifically-minded critics of the value of movement education point out that to acquire specific skills one must practice these skills rather than hope for transfer from previously practiced and often dissimilar activities.

However, with the evidence that is presently available, a sound course of action might be to encourage general developmental movement experiences similar to those proposed within movement education curriculums during the early years of elementary school; and as the child approaches the third and fourth grades, to phase gradually into the program an increasing number of specific sports skills which he will later require to carry out socially—prized, recreational, and athletic activities. This type of approach may be depicted as follows:

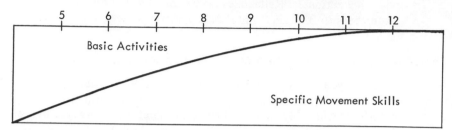

Figure 7-1. Approximate percent of time which may be spent on basic movement activities versus practice in sports skills at various ages.

A number of criteria may be applied to determine how much of an elementary school child's physical education program might consist of various basic developmental movement tasks (balance, agility, and the like) versus games and sports skills. For example, children with movement problems who appear clumsy, and those who perform considerably below norms on motor tests to which they are exposed, should engage in basic developmental activities for a more prolonged period of time during their elementary school careers before being exposed to the more complex game skills, than should children who do not evidence any measurable or observable movement deficits. Girls, by the nature of games socially approved for them (hopscotch and the like), generally spend more time than do boys in basic activities before attempting to deal with the complexities inherent in ball games. But at the same time, the younger boys in elementary school, as a group, are usually not as neurologically mature as are the girls of the same chronological age; and thus the boys may need basic activities for a relatively prolonged period of time.[2]

The elementary school teacher of physical education should be reluctant to embark too quickly on adopting new and magical movement cures for a variety of academic ills, without a thorough and penetrating examination of the rationale underlying the theory. Often such conceptual rafts are composed of termite-ridden logs which may tend to sink

[2]There is a trend seen in some parts of the country to place six-year-old boys with five-year-old girls in both physical education and indoor classes; thus while their chronological ages are not matched, their "maturational ages" are more congruent. I believe that in some cases this type of matching by developmental level, rather than by chronological age, is sound.

before reaching the end of the educational river upon which they have been launched. (See References for Chapters Nine and Eleven.)

In the 1970s the teacher of young children, using movement as a modality, should attempt to involve the children intellectually as often as he can. The theory for teaching methodology conceived by Mosston and reviewed more thoroughly in Chapter Twenty-three, offers a great deal of promise. Children of today usually seek games which in some way parallel the attributes they will need to succeed as adults. Relatively few of today's adults depend upon muscle for success. The skill, ingenuity, and strategy which seem to serve young children better are reflected in the manner in which they are beginning to construct games, if left to their own devices. Just as the young Australian aborigine learns at an early age to use his hands in making the simple but necessary implements, so does the young child in our "modern" culture seek in his games the intellectual "ingredients" which will later serve him to good advantage.

The elementary school physical educator should be sensitive to the various problem children he may observe while at play, or withdrawing from play. The boy who seems to be playing too often with the girls and enjoying their companionship too much is likely to pick up their gesture patterns and suffer rather severe social censure from the boys on the playground. A youth of this type should usually be referred for a thorough psychological screening. The boy or girl who withdraws too much from play companions may also be the cause for some concern. The child, usually a male, who is more clumsy than his peers should elicit the special attention of the physical education teacher.

These children, composing from 15 to 20 percent of the so-called normal population, may need special help in basic motor activities in classes specifically designed for them. These children should be identified as early in the elementary school years as possible. The first day they enter school is an appropriate time, and remedial help should be given to them during the first months. This aid can be extended in special classes meeting two to three times a week, in which tasks leading toward better control of the larger muscles are introduced to them. At other times during the school week, if necessary, they might be afforded special practice in the writing and printing behaviors they need every school day.

If they are not given this help, these children are likely to become the troublemakers within the classroom and around the schoolyard. The frustration they will experience if unable to play well and to perform various classroom functions adequately will be apparent, and will manifest itself in various other ways usually deemed inappropriate by their teachers. On the playground, for example, they may exhibit several types of behavior, including withdrawal from games and overly aggressive attitudes toward their peers. A kind of "court jester" behavior, which is marked by a joking and silly approach to all physical activities as a way of avoiding them, is also often seen in these children.

Summary

The elementary school physical education teacher should be technically competent, as well as a sensitive observer of the behavior of children. He should be able to integrate his efforts with the others at the school who have the total welfare of the children at heart.

He should be equipped professionally with a theoretical background in physiology, psychology, child development, and mechanics of movement—a background which will enable him accurately to assess new practices, to evaluate individual differences, and to accommodate to these differences when planning curriculums.

The practices he brings with him to the children in his charge should include numerous games and activities appropriate to various age levels and to both sexes. At the same time he should possess the personality to be able to establish the rapport with children which will permit him to transmit these activities effectively.

The elementary school teacher should be sensitive to a number of ways in which movement activities may either contribute to or detract from the total educational program. He should be sensitive to the fact that children overly stimulated in physical activity may be returned to classrooms too activated to work well; and he might become familiar with special ways to adjust this level of activation at the termination of the physical education period. His background should permit him to incorporate in direct ways various classroom skills with various motor activities.

The physical education teacher of elementary school children should be able to measure and to observe atypical movement behavior in children, as well as other types of personality problems which may manifest themselves in children at play. He should seek to refer these children, if their problem is obvious, to other professional members of the school staff for evaluation and possible remediation. At the same time the physical education teacher should take upon herself more often the problem of remedying the problems of children who evidence minor motor difficulties.

The student in training should seek several different types of experiences with young children during his college career. The opportunity to work directly with children, supported by theoretical knowledge gained in the classroom, is a better total experience for an undergraduate than either theory or experience taken alone.

References

Ainsworth, D. S., *Basic Rhythms: A Study of Movement*. New York: Chartwell House Publishers, 1955.

Anderson, M. H., and Elliot, M. E., *Play with a Purpose*. New York: Harper & Row, Publishers, 1966.

Blake, O. W., and Volpe, A. M., *Lead-Up Games to Team Sports*. Englewood Cliffs, New Jersey: Prentice-Hall, Inc., 1964.

Corbin, C. B., *Becoming Physically Educated in the Elementary Schools*. Philadelphia: Lea & Febiger, 1969.

Cratty, Bryant J., *Developmental Games for Physically Handicapped Children*. Palo Alto, California: Peek Publications, 1969.

————, *Developmental Sequences of Perceptual-Motor Tasks for Neurologically Handicapped and Retarded Children*. Freeport, Long Island: Educational Activities, 1967.

————, Martin, S. M. M., Jennett, C., Ikeda, N., and Morris, M., *Movement Activities, Motor Ability and the Education of Children*. Springfield, Illinois: Charles C. Thomas, Publisher, 1970.

————, *Active Learning*. Englewood Cliffs, New Jersey: Prentice-Hall, Inc., 1971.

————, *Perceptual-Motor Behavior and Educational Processes*. Springfield, Illinois: Charles C. Thomas, Publisher, 1969.

————, and Martin, S. M. M., *Perceptual-Motor Efficiency in Children, The Measurement and Improvement of Movement Attributes*. Philadelphia: Lea & Febiger, 1969.

————, *Some Educational Implications of Movement Experiences*. Seattle: Special Child Publications, 1970.

Hackett, L. C., and Jenson, R. G., *A Guide to Movement Exploration*. Palo Alto, California: Peek Publications, 1966.

Ilg, F. L., and Ames, L, B., *School Readiness: Behavior Tests Used at the Gesell Institute*. New York: Harper & Row, Publishers, 1964-65.

Kirchner, G., *Physical Education for Elementary Children*. Dubuque, Iowa: N. C. Brown Company, 1966.

Murray, R. L., *Dance in Elementary Education*. New York: Harper & Row, Publishers, 1963.

Pearson, C. E., *A Classroom Teacher's Guide to Physical Education*. New York: Bureau of Publications, Teachers College, Columbia University, 1962.

Schurr, E. L., *Movement Experiences for Children: Curriculum and Methods for Elementary School Physical Education*. New York: Appleton-Century-Crofts, 1967.

Smalley, J. E., *Physical Education Activities for the Elementary School.* Palo Alto, California: National Press, 1956.

Vagel, C., *Methods Guidebook in Physical Education and Recreation for the Elementary Classroom Teacher.* Palo Alto, California: National Press, 1966.

Wallis, Earl, and Logan, Gene, *Exercise for Children.* Englewood Cliffs, New Jersey: Prentice-Hall, Inc., 1966.

Young H. L., *A Manual Workbook of Physical Education for Elementary Teachers.* New York: The Macmillan Company, 1963.

CHAPTER EIGHT

Administration and Supervision

In some way, all physical educators and coaches are administrators. Taking roll in a physical education class is an administrative function. Overseeing a game involves an aspect of supervision and administration. Ordering equipment for a team prior to the season also is an administrative exercise.

Yet some physical educators, and those dealing with competitive athletics, have jobs whose titles denote the fact that they are *primarily* administrators or supervisors of some kind. Athletic director, curriculum consultant, supervisor of physical education, recreation specialist, and similar job-title descriptions involve duties which are primarily those having to do with the organization of things and people for the solution of various kinds of educational problems involving physical activity.

Many undergraduate curriculums have courses concerned primarily with outlining sound administrative procedures and functions connected with athletics and physical education. Several of the coaching courses you will take may have a portion of the time devoted to specific administrative problems connected with sports.

At times, these courses deal with administrative functions in some detail: making out a departmental or team budget, ordering equipment, specifying legal responsibilities of teachers and administrators, organizing teams and individuals for competitions of various kinds (tournaments and the like), gaining publicity for various phases of the athletic and physical education program, and similar functions.

At other times, these courses also concentrate upon general administrative concepts and principles of supervision. In this somewhat broader context, such topics as enhancing interpersonal communication, encouraging democratic interaction among group members, supervisor-centered versus subordinate-centered decision making, and perhaps the personality qualities of effective administrators and supervisors may be discussed and examined.

The administration of physical education and athletic programs may evolve into dull routine functions or be highly creative, depending, in part, upon the administrator's approach to the problems he will face. Similarly, supervising people can be either creative or oppressive, both to the supervisor as well as to those being supervised.

In general, a supervisor within a school district is likely to be an individual with the job of recommending, providing materials, and encouraging better teaching by conducting workshops and providing similar services to teachers. Usually, he has little or no direct authority over the hiring and firing of instructors, but works more like a master teacher.

Within a reasonably large school district, there may be several types of supervisors connected with physical education, recreation, and athletic programs. There may be a supervisor of secondary physical education; sometimes two: one whose responsibilities are primarily directed toward the girls' curriculum, the other with jurisdiction over the boys' program. Some larger school districts have a supervisor of boys' athletics. Most school districts containing six or more elementary schools usually employ at least one individual whose efforts are focused upon the elementary school physical education program.

A large school district will contain a number of administrators, individuals with responsibility and authority over the day-to-day operation of the schools, their personnel, business functions, special services (e.g., health, transportation, special education), and similar functions. Additionally, within each secondary and elementary school there are likely to be from one to five individuals who have administrative functions at least part of the school day.

In general, both administrators and supervisors have ascended to their positions after demonstrating superior teaching abilities as classroom teachers, and also by improving themselves in courses and workshops during their first years of teaching. They usually must obtain special state credentials or certificates which require the acquisition of additional college degrees past the Bachelor of Science.

Individuals selected as administrators usually have demonstrated a little extra initiative. They have probably at some time devised and carried out some innovative teaching procedure, or perhaps organized workshops for the improvement of themselves and their fellow teachers. They may have taken a special interest in some extracurricular aspect of the school program, or in some other way indicated to their superiors that they might bring a little extra to the job if permitted to move into a role in which they could assume formal leadership of some kind.

Sometimes administrators and supervisors are promoted from within a district. At other times, particularly in the case of higher-echelon personnel, they may be brought in from other school districts in which they have evidenced promising performance.

Young teachers, upon entering their first classroom, may tell themselves, and perhaps others who are willing to listen, that they are headed toward administration. They sometimes infer that they are truly destined for greater things than "mere" classroom teaching or physical education teaching, and it is only a matter of time before their expertise as potential supervisors and/or administrators will be recognized. Such individuals generally do not proceed very far. It is believed that the first step toward administration or supervision is effective performance when working directly with children and youth. Supervisors and administrators are usually at least one person removed from the actual child served, and if they have not engaged in a meaningful way in this service role prior to assuming their administrative positions, they are unlikely later to be truly effective within the administrative structure.

This general overview of the nature of administration and supervision, the positions available and formal titles, as well as a description of the several channels one might follow to reach such positions, does not contain the administrative and supervisory functions and processes which you are going to be responsible for when entering your first few years of teaching. As pointed out, however, there are a great many supervisory and administrative functions you will be confronted with as a physical education teacher and athletic coach during your first months and years on the job. Some of these, together with interrelated problems, are discussed on the following pages. These and other functions may be considered in greater detail in your course on the subject contained in your undergraduate curriculum.

Administration Functions

Some of your administrative jobs will be purely operational, and some will be more subtle and revolve around the manner in which you work with the youth and adults with whom you will be associated. Among the administrative functions with which you must deal in your first teaching experience are:

Legal Aspects of Teaching

You should be thoroughly acquainted with the nature of the legal conditions which govern your behavior and the behavior of the students in your classes. You should know the answer to such questions as the type of punishment you may employ as a teacher, the degree of legal liability assigned to you as a teacher in your district, and the insurance available to cover you in the event a negligence suit is brought against you. In addition, you should be thoroughly familiar with the nature of the contract you sign with the district; and if help is needed in its interpretation, you should seek the advice of an attorney.

Administrative and Supervisory Structure

You should be aware of the exact nature of the supervisors and administrators who have jurisdiction over you. You will want to know to whom you can go with various problems related to teaching; who is in a position to officially commend, or to condemn, your efforts; and whose judgment will be considered when you are retained or not retained as a teacher in a district. Help in finding out the answers to administrative questions may be obtained by requesting or constructing an organization chart, indicating the individuals who have direct authority over you, as well as those who assume a supervisory role over your activities. Such a chart might well look like that of Figure 8-1, with the solid lines indicating direct lines of authority, and the dotted lines indicating those who can recommend and assist you but purportedly can exert no direct influence over your career.

It might be useful at this point to contact a teacher holding a job similar to the one you are considering, to determine whether the manner in which an administrative unit is set up on paper is truly the manner in which it operates. Within most organizations there are official as well as unofficial lines of communication and authority, both of which should be carefully studied and considered. The unofficial administrative channels indicate who is really telling whom what to do, and may be more important to study than the official ones.

Supervision of Whom and What

You should gain a clear understanding of the manner in which you are to function as a supervisor in situations other than your classroom. It is common practice to have teachers supervise special events at the school (dances, athletic contests, etc.), as well as assume supervisory roles

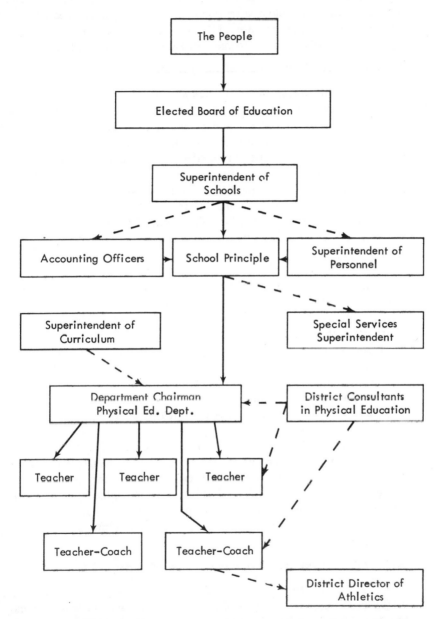

Figure 8-1. Typical administrative arrangement within which a physical education teacher may function.

during the school day (lunch periods and the like). These functions should require your close attention and, at times, may necessitate a different approach than that used in your class teaching or team coaching situations, where you exert more direct authority and influence.

Administrative Duties within the Department

Some physical education departments involve all their members in decisions dealing with the developing of curriculum, the hiring of new members, the ordering of equipment, and similar functions. Thus, you should be prepared to justify what equipment items or facilities you request, be able to voice criteria for effective teachers of physical education, and be able to make constructive suggestions concerning curriculum content and the placement of the activities you recommend within the school calendar. You should be aware of deadline dates for the submission of items for a yearly budget, and of other policies relevant to the administrative duties which you may share.

Policies of the Department

A physical education department or athletic department simply should not operate without policies concerning the scheduling of games, the hiring of personnel, the formulating of a budget, and similar matters. More often than not, however, these policies are stored in someone's head, and are not formally stated for all to read. There are two ways to become familiar with the policies confronting you as you enter teaching: (a) to engage in prolonged conversation with those who are seemingly in positions of authority, or (b) to offer to write down a policy statement of your department. Although this latter course of action might be viewed as presumptuous by your superiors, it might aid in the clarification of matters to a considerable degree. The writing of a department policy statement should begin by consulting existing written school board policies and school policies which in any way might influence the program in physical education and athletics. From this beginning you might then start to formulate a concise statement of just what your department is about, and how various administrative functions will be carried out.

Special Administrative Assignments That May Be Available

There are a number of special administrative jobs with which you might find yourself confronted during your first years of teaching and coaching. For example, it may be your turn to hold the conference track meet or swimming meet (it usually is, when a new coach enters a league!). The number of administrative details you will face, relative to preparing entry blanks, hiring officials, gaining publicity, and similar functions, will be beyond belief and should be planned for carefully. At the same time such procedures should be accompanied by frequent consultations with older and wiser "heads" within the school and league.

You may wish to run a tournament involving a single or double elimination of the individuals or teams composing it. You should be thoroughly aware of the manner in which teams (or individuals) are "seeded" and are placed in such tournaments. For example, these are usually arranged so that the "top-seeded" teams meet last in the tournament, and also so that the highly-favored teams play the fewest games.

You should be familiar with the setting up of round-robin tournaments, for interschool competitions, and for providing interesting competitive arrangements for the members of your physical education classes.

Daily Administrative Duties

One of the most appalling things seen in American physical education at the secondary level is the fact that usually about half of the available time in a class period of one hour (or 50 minutes) is taken up with functions other than physical activity.[1] It is believed essential that the physical education teacher become proficient in carrying out such administrative functions as taking roll and the like with as little time taken from class as possible. For example, most teachers, after a few days (or weeks), should be able to identify all class members by sight; thus, roll may be taken while the students are in action in games or in other activities, rather than having them stand passively for a long portion of the class period while identifying themselves.

Equipment should be made readily available for each class prior to the class meeting. Dressing facilities should permit easy and quick access to the play areas; and in other ways the physical education teacher should attempt to maximize the activity time available.

Supervising Students

In addition to administrative functions you may have to perform as a coach and physical educator there are a number of less exact techniques

[1]One of the most constructive suggestions to circumvent this problem is to have physical education for an hour and a half at a time two or three days a week, instead of every day. Thus a greater percent of the time each week may be devoted to activity, while a smaller percent of time will be taken up with dressing and undressing for competition (three showers, etc., per week, instead of five). The total time purportedly devoted to physical education remains relatively the same (about four and one half to five hours). This arrangement would, of course, often necessitate the reorganization of the school curriculum in other ways.

of dealing with the students and others with whom you might come in contact. You are literally a supervisor of students in your classes, students in extracurricular activities, and athletes on your teams. The manner in which you supervise will, to a large degree, influence the manner in which these students will react to and work with and for you; thus, to a large measure the manner in which you deal with students will determine your success as a teacher and coach in your school community. Some of these principles are briefly described below. Others will perhaps become apparent to you as you interact with people with whom you will be working.

Understanding Individuality

One of the first principles you might consider is the fact that people are different, from each other and from you. They may not have the same backgrounds, the same positive feelings about physical activity, and the same health standards as you feel are necessary. While your standards and values might be superior in some way, it may prove less than helpful to all concerned to attempt radically to change, within a short period of time, the standards and values of students with whom you come in contact.

Those you supervise in classes and on teams should first be considered as valuable people, independently of their backgrounds. Second, you might consider why they are different from you, rather than simply imposing your demands and standards on them because the local board of education has somehow given you the legal jurisdiction over several hundred students.

The apparently inept overweight boys in your classes may be obese because they eat too much and/or exercise too little, or because they have emotional problems from which they are attempting to "eat their way out." On the other hand, they may be overweight (and the psychiatric literature supports this observation) because they have mothers who are acting in a subtly hostile way by overfeeding them! You do not aid these boys by pointing out that they are fat (they know this), or by imposing impossible performance demands without the proper conditioning procedures and dietary counseling.

Facilitating Interpersonal Communication

You should, if possible, leave channels of communication open between you, your colleagues, and students whom you supervise. Severely embarrassing admonishment of an individual student, in front of a class, serves to block rather than to facilitate communication; by such behavior on your part you have left him no way to turn, except against you in either obvious or subtle ways.

When listening to students, really listen! Their parents may never have done so; they are paying you the compliment of suggesting that you might; so do! You may, for example, attempt to repeat at regular intervals what they have just said to you, so that you truly understand what it is they are trying to say. Listen not only to words, but attempt to grasp shades of meaning by evaluating the manner in which they communicate, their facial expressions, the words they select, and the emphasis given to various things they tell you.

Understanding Group Tensions, Needs, and Communication Patterns

Remain alert to tensions your classes and teams may evidence as they face you en masse. What do their faces say? They may reveal more than students are willing to risk voicing to you in direct ways. Realize that they are interacting among themselves, out of your earshot, about you and about your class (or team). What do you expect these interactions to consist of?

Why are these youth placing themselves under your supervision? Have they no choice? Are they simply assigned to your class? Have they chosen your team? Are they participating in spite of you or because of you?

Who are the natural leaders in the groups confronting you? How were they selected by their peers? Would you select the same boys or girls to lead? Why? How might you use these leaders effectively? How are they using *you*? How might you bring out leadership qualities in boys and girls by providing them with opportunities to direct the efforts of their classmates or team members?

The research indicates that on athletic teams there may exist an optimum amount of group tension relative to winning and performing well, which may at times be reflected in hostility evidenced between group members. Teams which are too happy with each other, particularly with inept members, may not care enough about winning. At the same time, teams and physical education classes which evidence an inordinate amount of intragroup conflict may in some way be "sick" and performing less than adequately. As an effective supervisor (coach or teacher), you should be able to assess the degree of tension in groups, and attempt to resolve inappropriate feelings which individuals in your charge have about each other.

Deciding Who Directs

One of the critical questions when working with people in groups concerns the degree to which decisions should be made by the group, or by those officially supervising them. The gradual passing of decisions to class members and to team athletes has been discussed in other chapters. Additional guidelines are found in the literature dealing with business administration. Two industrial psychologists have evolved a framework for determining the degree to which decisions may be made by the supervisor (manager), or by those he supervises. Essentially, they have suggested that the manner in which decisions are made may fluctuate from situation to situation, and from time to time. Guidelines for deciding who makes a decision about the group efforts (the group or the manager) should come from an attempt to assess accurately what they term "the forces" in the group, those qualities the manager brings to the situation, as well as the factors inherent in the situation itself.

Supervisors of physical activities should be well aware, if these guidelines are valid, of the forces he brings to the situation (his background, his needs for authority, and his competencies); and of the needs, backgrounds, and competencies possessed by the members of the group he is supervising. The physical education teacher and coach similarly should become able to modify his approach and the degree of authority he exerts as situations change within his team or physical education class. As the students in his charge become more adept at making decisions concerning various facets of the class operation or team strategy, it would seem appropriate to let them do so.

There are innumerable other technical aspects of supervision and administration, as well as human factors inherent in working with people, which have not been touched upon in these pages. The student is referred to texts dealing with industrial psychology and the sociology of work groups, as well as material directed specifically toward outlining administrative procedures. In general, one of the paramount rules one must be aware of when given administrative responsibilities is that appropriate authority must accompany this increase in responsibility. When one accepts or seeks additional responsibilities within an educational environment (or in any environment, for that matter), he should also be given the authority to carry out the additional responsibilities. In briefer terms, responsibility should accompany authority, and the acceptance of responsibility should be undergirded by basic knowledge about people and of administrative operations.

Summary

A number of administrative and supervisory functions is inherent in the teaching and coaching of physical activities. Additionally, other formal positions within the school hierarchy may be filled by physical education personnel, and people holding these positions exert direct or indirect influence upon coaches and physical education teachers. The new teacher should thus know who in a supervisory role will be acting upon him in various ways, and in turn be aware of the ways in which he may at present, or in the future, carry out an administrative and/or supervisory function within the school hierarchy.

Administration involves carrying out rather direct operations, such as budgeting, planning, evaluating of personnel and program, hiring of teachers, and carrying out public relations of various kinds. Supervision within the school district and the school itself usually involves behavior which is more supportive than dictatorial, more advisory than authoritarian.

Student Activities and Discussion Questions

1. Interview an administrator in a medium-sized school district. Attempt to ascertain the overall administrative plan of the district, and obtain an organizational chart if possible. Decide just who does what in relation to, and with, physical educators and coaches.
2. Find out the requirements in your state for the assumption of formal administrative duties in the school districts. What credential or credentials are needed; how are these obtained; what teaching experience is required?
3. Discuss with an athletic director of a high school just what administrative functions he assumes. Does he have a written athletic policy to guide his actions? What overall school policies, written or implied, regulate his conduct?
4. Study the literature dealing with group interactions in industry. What problems and tensions do people have in work groups which may also be found in groups working for curriculum changes, in groups discussing athletic policy, or in departments of physical education in a high school?

References

Forsythe, C. E., *Administration of High School Athletics*. Englewood Cliffs, New Jersey: Prentice-Hall, Inc., 1962.

George, J. F., *School Athletic Administration*. New York: Harper & Row, Publishers, 1966.

Grieve, A. W., *Directing High School Athletics*. Englewood Cliffs, New Jersey: Prentice-Hall, Inc., 1963.

Hughes, W. L., *The Administration of Physical Education for Schools and Colleges*. New York: Barnes Publishers, 1954.

Irwin, L. W., *Principles and Techniques of Supervision in Physical Education.* Dubuque, Iowa: W. C. Brown Company, 1960.

Voltmer, E. F., *The Organization and Administration of Physical Education.* New York: Appleton-Century-Crofts, 1967.

CHAPTER NINE

College and University
Education and Research

An introductory course may seem to be an inappropriate time to discuss the possibilities of your entering college or university teaching. At the same time, preparation for teaching and research at this level may be based, to a large degree, upon what you do as an undergraduate. Your undergraduate years will pass more quickly than you think; thus, the formulation of long-range career goals may be wise. Furthermore, while at this point in your career you cannot envision yourself as a college or university teacher or researcher, your values and goals may change after teaching at the secondary or elementary level for a few years.

Generally, however, from a financial standpoint your decision to prepare to join a university or college faculty should be made within a year or so after graduating from college with a B.S. degree. Too long a delay in making this decision will often result in a college salary markedly lower than what you would be making after five or more years in an elementary or secondary school.

The type of position you may fill on a college or university faculty depends upon your interests, qualifications, and background. There are an unusually large number of ways you might spend your time. For example, you may be engaged in teaching courses primarily designed to upgrade the physical fitness and skill standards of the average college student in the various individual and group games and sports. Usually, people in this role are also concerned with improving these same qualities in physical education majors during their first two years in the teacher-preparation curriculum. If the physical education departments and athletic programs are administratively connected, people teaching lower-division skill classes and physical education major classes are often connected in some way to the intercollegiate sports programs. They may be assistant or head coaches in the various competitive sports, in addition to teaching "service" classes of various kinds.

Individuals hired to teach classes of this nature may be half-time teaching assistants or graduate students who are working for higher degrees within the physical education department. Usually the requirements these individuals must meet are a B.S. degree and undergraduate grades which qualify them for graduate school. Additionally, they must prove to the satisfaction of the department chairman, or the coordinator of the program, that they possess the abilities to demonstrate and to teach the skills in which they are assigned.

Others who work in the activity program, or who teach the classes in which the performance competencies of the major students are improved, are full-time regular members of the physical education faculty. These individuals usually have at least a B.S. degree and have also demonstrated that they possess unusual skill in teaching various activities. They may also be able to teach physical education majors the methods to be employed when instructing various skills. Some may have a master's degree, although others may have been hired without any degree at all simply because they possess unusual skill in teaching specific activities.

The salary scale roughly parallels that of public school teachers; however, like others in college or university work, they are usually not required to possess any type of secondary or elementary teaching credential issued by the state in which they teach. Often, particularly in smaller physical education departments, people teaching activity classes are also on the professorial faculty, and conduct theory courses or even graduate-level seminars. Within departments of average or above-average size, however, there is usually a separation, with respect to duties, of the professorial staff and those teaching activity courses. However, there are many departments with the policy that all members of their staffs teach at least one activity course each semester.

Another group of people within a university or college department of physical education is engaged more in classroom teaching, conducting courses in which theoretical information is presented. Members of this latter group are more likely to possess a doctor's degree, and may also be engaged in research of various kinds. They have received usually either a Ph.D. degree (Doctorate of Philosophy), a degree in which research skills are emphasized, or an Ed.D. (Doctorate of Education), a professional degree. Generally, the Ph.D. degree requires the student to take more work in research design, plus demonstrating competencies in one or more foreign languages. The Ed.D. degree, on the other hand, does not usually require language competencies, and there may be less emphasis upon statistics and research design. Both degrees require three or more years' work after the master's degree (which usually takes at least one year), and both degrees usually require the individual to complete an original research study supervised by a committee of professors.

The individual, after completing the doctorate, usually takes a position at a university other than that at which the degree was earned. The starting job title is usually "assistant professor." During these first years he must demonstrate his ability to teach well, to engage in creative work (including writing and research), as well as to work effectively within the university community and in the community at large. After a period of from four to eight years, a committee of professors (whose composition is usually unknown to him) collects information about his competencies—including comments from students regarding his teaching, his writings, and letters from those in and outside the university who know of his work—and considers him for promotion to the next level, associate professor. This second step gives him what is called "tenure," or permanency within the university community. Tenure is usually reached after three years of secondary teaching, if the instructor's performance has been satisfactory.

It is often true that a college professor will attempt to better himself by engaging in what may be termed horizontal, rather than vertical, attempts at advancement. Vertical advancement infers that the individual is somehow pushing his way up, while remaining within a single academic institution. Vertical advancement is sometimes more difficult undertaking than attempting to advance via horizontal promotion by changing institutions every few years, particularly when it is desired to advance from assistant to associate professor, and to the rank of full professor.

Jumping too rapidly from institution to institution brands one as an opportunist. Three or four changes during a career from one university to another will frequently broaden the professor's outlook, while at the same time insure him of fairer and more rapid advancement.

The final level, full professor, may be reached after another wait of four or more years, and a similar review by a faculty committee. During the early years of residence on a university faculty (the assistant professor stage), the faculty member's work undergoes almost yearly review. He is informed rather regularly whether the quality of his performance suggests that he will "make it," or that he will not receive advancement to the next higher faculty rank. The college instructor, while under some pressure to perform well in the classroom and often in the laboratory, at the same time is given frequent notice of whether his work is found wanting. Thus, the apparent shock that some students feel upon finding that their favorite professor's contract is not going to be renewed is usually not a surprise to the faculty member himself. He invariably has been told for the past several years that he is not going to be retained if his work continues to show a lack of promise.

Hopefully, college teachers responsible for educating teachers of either professorial or instructor's rank have had experience teaching at either the secondary or the elementary levels themselves, in addition to the academic background required of them when receiving their higher degrees. Many doctoral programs, particularly those leading toward the Doctorate of Education, require three years of public school teaching prior to receiving the degree. If the younger instructor has not had this experience himself, he may enter the college teacher-training classroom filled with facts and with a clear picture of the theoretical problems involved in human activity, while lacking an appreciation for the types of situations his students will meet when entering public school teaching. A lecture concerned only with theoretical facts can be as meaningless as one in which a former teacher simply recounts his adventures in sports or in the physical education class. College instructors need both experience and academic training to train teachers effectively.

Many professors, particularly those with positions at universities, are responsible for carrying out their own research as well as supervising the research of graduate students. Although there are varying opinions, on a whole, this is an important and healthy situation, particularly in the physical education field. For his work to be accepted by his colleagues and published, the researcher is forced to be a scholar; he must be up-to-date on the material in his field. His lectures, if he can communicate well, may be highly interesting. Much of the time he can recount firsthand experiences he has had by seeing people do things in his laboratory and perhaps in schools in which he has been researching. Research is the way to expand knowledge about human motor activity; and if carried out in a competent manner, it can lead toward helpful ways to improve service to children in the schools.

Most university professors in physical education who are doing any research at all devote only a portion of their time to this type of undertaking. Fifty to 60 percent of their time is usually spent in teaching and in other departmental functions. It is often difficult, however, to determine exactly how much time a given professor spends on each specific activity; for when he researches and writes about his findings, he is also by these same operations preparing and organizing material which he may later present to his classes.

It is a common criticism, and sometimes a well-founded one, that researching leads a college professor away from an interest in his students. A professor may become a less-than-adequate teacher because of an unusual absorption in work, plus perhaps an inability or disinclination to communicate to others what he knows. However, a researcher is *not* necessarily, *because of his interest in research*, a poor instructor. He may be a poor instructor because of an inability to communicate well; or perhaps he has chosen to submerge himself in his research because he does not relate well to students in classes.

There are a number of personal and professional qualifications needed to be an effective college or university instructor, in addition to the academic degrees previously discussed. Most professors and instructors do not possess all these to the same degree. At the same time, a severe deficiency in any one of them is likely to render an individual less than adequate as a college or university faculty member. Among these qualifications are:

1. *A good deal of physical vigor and stamina.* Writing, researching, teaching physical activities, obtaining advanced degrees, or writing dissertations requires a great deal of effort. Unless an individual has physical reserves to call upon, particularly during the early years of preparation, he or she is not likely to succeed.
2. *Organizational ability.* Securing advanced degrees, preparing for teaching, obtaining and organizing information, and similar functions require certain administrative abilities. An individual who is somehow disorganized much of the time is not likely to succeed well in college or university teaching and/or research.
3. *A scholarly approach to human performance, societal phenomena, and similar components of the world.* A university or college instructor should be continually questioning, and not satisfied with a pat answer to complex questions. Furthermore, he should be able to transmit these qualities to his students. And even more important, the instructor should be able to search, and to aid others to search, for some of the "whys" of human nature, even though these "whys" are usually only transitory in nature.
4. *Good communication skills.* Together with having something worthwhile to transmit, a highly important quality in a college or university professor is the ability to communicate well, both verbally and in written communication. These skills may often be acquired; but unless they are developed to a high degree it will be difficult for a professor to succeed. An inability to speak well will make years of lec-

tures painful for both the receivers and the sender; inability to write well, clearly, and concisely will render knowledge found in the laboratory laborious or impossible for others to peruse.

5. *The ability to work effectively with people.* The college years are among the most critical ones for the maturing youth. He is trying to find out who he is, where he is going, and the nature of his basic worth to himself and to society. The instructor who nourishes rather than simply tells, and who perceives that all people are not necessarily like he is, can be an asset on a university staff. Teaching and engaging in various physical activities involve interactions between people. The college instructor or professor who either dislikes people, or through some inadequacies of his own is unable to relate well to students, will perform inadequately.

Some undergraduates may have the mistaken notion that university teaching and researching is a kind of "glamour" occupation; a high-status, carefree "game" which only the privileged may play. It is often heard from undergraduates who may be performing less than effectively that they wish to become "researchers." This word has taken on some kind of status with many. Yet, this "rosy" picture of college and university teaching is not an altogether accurate one. While work at a university may be an extremely satisfying way to spend one's life, at the same time there are drawbacks which the enterprising student should consider prior to making his goal that of becoming a member of a college or university faculty. First of all, let us consider some of the *advantages* of university or college teaching and research:

1. The position on a university faculty, coupled with hard work, may earn the faculty member a satisfying change to make significant contributions to the community at large. This is particularly true if the faculty member writes, and attempts to work well with various community groups that may benefit from his expertise and background.

   Most important in this context, the college or university instructor, if he presents sound ideas and is persuasive in their presentation, is able to influence a rather large segment of the youth of the community. With the aid of scholarly writing, he or she may also be able to communicate ideas which at times will have a significant influence upon programs at the national level.

2. A university position affords the faculty member time, which others may not have, to peruse the library to gain background material which in turn may be transmitted to others, the chance to offer these types of services and to see the effects of one's contribution, constitute the more satisfying outcomes of university work.

3. A university position coupled with hard work may result in status

within the community. At the same time, the faculty member should remember that his position on a university faculty may leave him open to criticism if his work and contribution is inadequate or not helpful to others.

4. Another positive aspect of working at a college or university is that it keeps you in touch with the new ideas emerging from other fields, as well as those espoused by at least a portion of the nation's youth to which you are exposed. Hence, one may grow intellectually within a college community. The opportunity to work with select youth from a given area, during the time of life when they begin to show the greatest amount of intellectual and physical energy, can be a truly gratifying experience.

5. Continued growth and promotion on a college or university faculty can lead toward financial security. Writings, coupled with teaching salary, combined with consultant fees, will often enable a professor to maintain a comfortable standard of living.

6. Freedom from a strict accountability for one's time is an advantage of college teaching. You do not have to punch a time clock while on a university faculty. Your time may be budgeted to activities which you prize. Your actual teaching hours are usually less than those of teachers at other levels. This freedom from regulation must invariably be earned by the faculty member by first demonstrating to his superiors that he can engage in prolonged and extensive self-motivated work of a high quality. College teaching requires a great deal of time and energy outside of that usually devoted to lecturing. It has been estimated that approximately four to six hours must be devoted to the preparation of a one-hour lecture, if there is to be good content presented.

There are, however, a number of problems connected with college and university teaching, as is true in any occupation. Some of these drawbacks are unique to physical education faculties, and others are experienced by professors in other departments. For example:

1. Physical education faculty members may feel themselves members of a low status group, as viewed by their colleagues in other departments at the university. While at times this type of feeling may have been earned, I have observed that there are also usually a number of weak faculty members in other so-called "high-status" departments on the university campus; and that many faculty members in physical education departments make a contribution to knowledge and to their students.[1]

[1] I often make a quick and interesting test of the productivity of a colleague from another department by simply asking him what he is doing. Recently an individual of a "high-status" faculty committee of the academic senate informed me that he and three other colleagues were "busy" writing up research which they had carried out seven years

2. Many physical education major students may not be as academically capable as others on the college and university campus. This may be particularly true on campuses where the physical education department is still used as a "safe harbor" in which to protect athletes who may not be able students.

3. The demands on the physical energy of faculty members on physical education staffs may be enormous at times. Faculty members are often placed in the position of competing for promotion with other members of the college community on the basis of writing and research efforts; while at the same time their departments demand their energies in the teaching of an inordinate number of activity classes, or even require them to coach athletic teams. I have known several colleagues who have managed to initiate and to conduct research programs while coaching teams, but the energy cost in these dual endeavors is incredible.

4. The early years of preparation may be personally costly financially, physically, and in terms of human relations. You and your spouse usually will undergo several years of relative financial deprivation while obtaining your degree; and it may be several more years before your university salary will raise your pay scale to a reasonable level, comparable to other professional salaries in your community. The demands on your energy during these early years, and on the patience and energies of your family, may be formidable.

5. Research and writing, which is often a welcome part of your job at the university and college, may demand a considerable amount of time even during the latter years of your career; time which may be taken away from recreational activities and from time spent with your family.

6. Teaching activity classes at the university may require you to work with large numbers of students who have varying abilities, unlike the relatively homogeneous groupings found in other university classes. Students take your class because they have a time period available, not necessarily because they are physically qualified.

Despite these drawbacks, and others which might be mentioned, I personally have found university teaching and research a satisfying life. The advantages, in my opinion, more than outweigh the disadvantages and inconveniences. Some undergraduate programs at universities in our country have as one of their primary objectives the preparation of future college teachers. If you find yourself in a program whose primary

---

before! I was able to check up on the type of "research" this individual had been carrying out by questioning one of his students. I found that it consisted of compiling the results of a questionnaire sent home with his students which inquired how their parents were getting along!

objective is the preparation of elementary and secondary school teachers, you might select another university in which to pursue graduate work.

Summary

College or university teaching and research is a satisfying, but at the same time a taxing, career channel for you to consider upon graduation from college. The demands include a great deal of physical stamina, intellectual ability and curiosity, ability to communicate verbally and in writing, as well as personal qualities which enable you to work effectively with capable youth.

The rewards for college and university teaching include the opportunity for status, security, and the chance to enlarge your intellectual horizons. The opportunity to get across some of your philosophies and favorite practices and theories, which in turn may influence a rather broad segment of the nation's youth, is another advantage enjoyed by most college and university professors and instructors.

Student Activities and Discussion Questions

1. What qualities suit you or leave you unsuited for college and university teaching? How might you rectify or improve the negative qualities?
2. Interview faculty members of your college or university with several types of titles: professor, assistant professor, instructor, teaching assistant. Attempt to learn what they perceive as advantages versus disadvantages of college teaching.
3. Investigate the Ph.D. or Ed.D. degree program at your university or at a nearby university. How does your undergraduate program integrate, or fail to integrate, with the requirements for this program?
4. Consider the ways in which engaging in research may enhance or detract from the teaching competencies of an individual.
5. What national associations are available for college and university professors? What are the basic tenets of these organizations?

References

Caplow, T., *The Academic Marketplace*. Garden City: Doubleday & Company, 1965.

Cobb, L. S., *A Study of the Functions of Physical Education in Higher Education*. New York: Columbia University Teachers College Press, 1943.

CHAPTER TEN

Coaching Athletics

There are few people more important than the athletic coach in influencing the outlook of many male youths in the United States today. The coach is usually a central figure within an environment which is often highly charged emotionally. The boys and men who find themselves identified as athletes within this situation are likely to undergo a number of changes in both their emotional as well as their physical makeups—changes which the coach usually has some role in producing.

It has been traditional in our culture in educational circles (and recently in governmental circles) to state rather emphatically that only positive changes are produced in athletes by exposure to various sports. However, recent scientific evaluations of the psychological and physical effects of exposure to athletics upon youth suggest that a degree of caution should be exercised when evaluating the potential contributions to those participating in sports competition. Hopefully, coaches in the next decade will try in less evangelical ways than in the past to attempt to evaluate honestly the nature of their impact upon the youth with whom they come in contact, and whom they purportedly serve; and as a result of this assessment will try to instill or elicit positive changes in children and youth in their charge.

Coaches are essentially teachers of the more athletically-gifted youth in our culture. They deal with a variety of people in their work and are often forced to deal with pressures from a variety of sources. They may attempt, for example, to keep scholastically-unfit athletes eligible for competition so that they can please a community with a successful team; a community which both likes a spectacle and reveres the academic standards of the institution, standards which the coach may be attempting to "bend" so as to keep the team "show on the road!" The coach must often consider the personal problems of his athletes, problems which, if left unattended, are likely to detract from optimum performance. The coach is also beset with various organizational problems which require time and energy that may be better expended upon the team practices. Schedules often have to be made up, officials contacted, equipment ordered, and locker rooms supervised.

But, most of all, the athletic coach is concerned with producing individual and group athletic performances which are respectable, and which appear successful within the "goldfish bowl" of community judgment. If a specific sport is not followed closely by members of a school or village community, the conscientious coach applies pressure to himself as he seeks to optimize the potential of those youth who place themselves in his hands.

Coaching positions within high schools are invariably filled by individuals who obtain regular teaching certificates similar to those held by teachers in the various academic subjects. Coaching positions in community-supported junior colleges are similarly held by credentialed teachers. Coaches at the college level do not usually need state certification, but gain their positions by virtue of their potential excellence in teaching a specific sport, and hold their positions by the success they subsequently enjoy. However, the vast majority of college and university coaches hold at least the B.S. degree, and many have engaged in graduate work.

A high school coach may find himself fulfilling a variety of roles within the school, some related to and some independent of his coaching responsibilities. He may—and this is often the case—also be a teacher of physical education classes, dividing his time and energy between four to six classes during the school day and his athletic team practices in the afternoon. This division of time has several obvious drawbacks, including the fact that an inordinate amount of energy is needed to do both facets of the job well. Often the coach yields to the demands of the team practice, rather than expending his energy with the classes. While it is easy to criticize the coach for this manner of dividing his behavior—and indeed many writers have often made mention of this apparent character deficiency in coaches—at the same time there are obvious reasons why the coach will concentrate more on his team than on his classes.

For example, his job, and thus his salary with which he may be supporting a family, is more likely to depend upon his team's success than upon his performance as a physical education teacher. A man's energy simply stretches so far, and the team and the attendant pressures do not permit him to let up; while his conduct in classes is less likely to be so closely monitored. Superior athletes, because of their motivation and their ability to perform, are too often more satisfying to the coach than the sometimes disinterested, inept performances he observes in his physical education classes.

There are several administrative modifications which have been used with reasonable success to circumvent some of the problems discussed above. For example, in some schools the coaches are given reduced teaching loads; they may arrive at school about noon, teach a class or two, and then spend the rest of the afternoon with their teams.[1] At other times, to conserve their physical energy coaches teach inside classrooms during the majority of the school day, and only don their sweat clothes during the final portions of the afternoon.[2] In some schools coaches are permitted extra time to engage in team planning, diagramming plays, ordering equipment, mentally juggling personnel, and the like.

The vast majority of male physical education majors perceive themselves as future coaches of superior athletic teams. As the ambitions of those of you who feel this way are not likely to be realized, you should attempt to look ahead and to prepare yourselves for the possibility that (a) you may not obtain what you consider a satisfactory coaching position, and (b) that you may find yourself serving youth in physical education classes or in the classroom.

To prepare yourself for the most effective job of coaching possible, you should bring with you to your first coaching position technical competencies in the sport or sports you will conduct and the ability to work with a variety of types of people, both individually and in groups. Without either of these two general competencies you are likely to be inadequate as a leader of youth in the sometimes-stressful environment created by competitive athletics.

On the following pages are briefly sketched some of the ways you

---

[1]A coach in this situation would not receive extra pay, as is usually the practice when his coaching is added on to a full teaching load. The receipt of extra pay often provides an abrasive layer between the coach and other members of the school staff who, for example, may not get extra money for coaching drama clubs, drill teams, and similar extracurricular activities.

[2]This is not to infer that coaches should be assigned to classes in which they are not competent, and in which they should be allowed to rest for their later strenuous coaching duties.

may become competent in the techniques of coaching, and also in handling people with whom you are likely to come in contact in your chosen job. However, during your first year of coaching you are likely to find out rather quickly that experience is the best teacher; and that technical preparation, participation in psychology courses, and the like are effective only if you are susceptible to attempts to coach *you* in the various competencies you will require during your undergraduate years at college.

Technical Know-how

Inspirational pep-talks, a "warm" personality, "savvy" about people, or a hard-driving manner—none is a substitute for a thorough grounding in the essentials of the sport you hope to coach. You must be competent in several aspects of the game or games you administer, including knowledge in detail of the rules and their interpretations and game strategy. You should be aware also of the subskills that make up total performance competency in the sport in which you are expecting to participate as a coach. You should be able to teach these skills effectively, and should be aware of just how to elicit the expected level of physical conditioning needed for participation in the particular sport.

Thorough attention while an undergraduate to courses containing basic information about the mechanics of movement, data about motor skill learning, and work physiology, should give you basic information from which you should be able to evaluate the competencies and physical conditions of your athletes, to improve these abilities and qualities to the levels needed, and to evaluate various new practices to which you will constantly be exposed during the years after your graduation from the university.

As a coach you cannot expect to elicit the respect of your athletes if you are not fully aware of the technical questions they may ask. At the same time, you should be able to match the technical knowledge you require of them, such as the number of offensive formations used in football, to their level of maturity and understanding. When teaching individual skills and when attempting to elicit maximum physical condition, you should become able to impart to the athlete as much information about skill learning and the physiological bases of conditioning as he can be expected to understand and to profit from.[3]

[3]Superior, Eastern European athletes without formal university educations are given formal seminars in the scientific bases of human motor activity, containing psychological, physiological, as well as sociological principles, in addition to information specific to their sport. It is felt by many experts observing this program that the basic information,

You should, however, not engage in prolonged kinesiology lectures to individuals or to teams about some of the scientific underpinnings of motor activity which have relatively little value for the athletes.

Finally, you should be able to synthesize information and formulate meaningful practice sessions for groups of athletes, while concurrently accommodating to their individual differences in structure, personality, level of skill, and to the degree of physical conditioning they evidence and may require. In connection with the conducting of team practices, you should be able to assess accurately group mood, skill level, and condition as the season progresses, and become able to modify the intensity and content of your practices when appropriate.

Understanding People

You will be associated with a variety of people while coaching various sports, including the press, school administrators, community supporters (and detractors),[4] team "hangers-on," your fellow teachers, as well as the personnel and coaches of other teams. You must relate to and somehow "handle" all these individuals, in addition to forming effective relationships with members of your team.

It is not the intent here to present a "cookbook" for dealing with athletes, the press, etc. Such an undertaking is too complex to be written about here; but a few guidelines are suggested. The application of these guidelines depends to a great extent on how secure you are as a professional person, your own family background, the type of individuals with whom you must deal, as well as the personal needs you bring with you to the athletic field or to the gymnasium.

1. As a coach you should attempt to create an emotional environment on the team which permits the members to feel a certain amount of security that the "operation" is being well run, and that people are being exposed to experiences which will result in skill learning and proper conditioning; and yet an environment in which individual personality differences may be manifested, and to which they may be accommodated.

2. As a coach you must act, and at times act decisively, in the somewhat stressful situations found in athletics. You should also carefully consider your actions in the light of how they will be interpreted by your team members and by the community observing you. You should be prepared to modify your behavior when it is obvious that it is not achieving your goals.

---

when imparted to these athletes, aids them to understand themselves better, and, in turn, leads to more superior performance.

[4]These are often the same people at various times during the year.

3. You should become acutely and thoroughly aware of the many facets of the social unrest in the United States. Instigated to some degree by various minorities, these problems may impinge upon you in the athletic situation in which you find yourself.

There are several general procedures you might give some consideration to when the members of your team come from various ethnic backgrounds.

1. You should attempt to learn as much as possible about the facets of the community in which various members of your team reside. This information may come because you are invited to join, or speak to, various groups. Or it might come through personal, "man-to-man" discussions with various team members, instigated by you or by them. During these discussions you should attempt to listen well, try to ascertain how the athlete feels, and not be "turned off" or "turned on" (unduly influenced) by just what *words* he is saying.

2. When minority group members come to you for advice or help, extend your aid to them as honestly and completely as you can. The fact that they come to *you* means a great deal, and you should attempt to work with them in confidence and in a professional, honest, and warm manner.

3. Members of minorities should be led to feel that the coach's office door is open at *all* times; more than that, the coach should provide regular meeting times and office hours, so that scheduled "gripe sessions" may take place to air, and perhaps dissipate and rectify, dissatisfactions which may be real or imagined.

The black athlete during the early 1970s may be under considerable emotional strain. On one hand, athletics provides one of the few doors open to him which in some way may promise success. On the other hand, members of his race have demonstrated to him that athletic prominence may provide an effective means through which to protest what they feel are injustices perpetrated upon the race. The black athletes on your teams may thus be torn between acting in a manner which will insure team membership and optimum development as an athlete, and remaining true and faithful to their protesting soul brothers.

Many racial tensions on a team can be reduced if the coach indicates an awareness of the fact that a problem exists, and expresses a respect for the feelings of his black athletes. For example, the coach of a large west coast university, upon finding that the black athletes on his upcoming opponent's team were on strike against injustices they perceived in their situation, called his own athletes into his office one at a time and said that he was aware of the tensions they were under relative to supporting the strike of their opponents, and that he would not punish them if they as a group or as individuals decided to support the strike by refusing to play. This expression of his concern and understanding, coupled with the fact that he did not take the "hard-handed" approach, resulted in his own players supporting his team in their forthcoming effort. In addition, there apparently had been a solid background and team spirit formed during the previous months between team members and the coaching staff; so when this situation arose there were less tensions produced. Toughness begets toughness. It is sometimes remarkable what conversations, evidence of sensitivity, and the resultant understanding can achieve between players and coaches.

Competitive athletes are usually coached by white men, administered by white athletic directors, and paid for by white spectators. Many black athletes are wary and indignant, and perceive themselves as exploited through athletics by the "white power structure." Mere participation on a high school or college team may bring about personal feelings of guilt on the part of the black athlete, feelings which he may vent in the form of hostile verbiage or actions in or around the athletic environment.

For the coach of the 1970s to remain oblivious of these problems may be catastrophic to his career, and is morally inexcusable. A coach during the coming decade should be sensitive to the general social conflicts and problems which surround all of us, and make special provisions to permit athletes enmeshed within socially stressful situations, such as those described, to have some way to ventilate their feelings. At the same time the coach should take constructive action to remedy real injustices which may confront the athletes of minority races he may have in his charge.

This does not mean that the coach should be intimidated, either by his own ego needs to win at all costs (which may in turn lead him toward making unreasonable concessions to pressures applied) or by direct or subtle physical threats which may be directed toward him. Nor should the coach enter potentially troublesome situations without the necessary personal and professional tools with which to function. He should be armed with ways to make athletes better performers, and with a personal philosophy which permits flexible behavior toward others. He should also possess a broad social philosophy which permits not only unbiased understanding of the cultural unrest in which he may find himself, but also allows direct participation in constructive activities to rectify some of the social ills.

Your future ability to deal with athletes as individuals should be improved by participation in courses in the behavioral sciences, with emphasis upon material in the field of psychology. Additionally, constructive help in improving your interpersonal relationships as a student, through group interactions (sensitivity training, etc.) professionally conducted, should also be of immeasurable aid to you after graduation.

Your ability to work with groups in the community and within your teams should be enhanced by courses dealing with social psychology and sociology. The teams facing you not only interact with you in rather an obvious manner; their members also interact with each other in ways not always apparent. Sociology can improve understanding of the nature of team cliques, and of group pressures and aspirations. Knowledge about the manner in which group behavior may be changed through various role-playing techniques, the psychodrama and the like, similarly should make you a more effective leader of youth.

The athletes of the 1970s are likely to be more critical of the measures used to improve them physically, methods which were often applied in rather authoritarian ways by coaches in the 1960s and before. The constructive coach of the 1970s should come to terms with his own needs for authority, and with the needs the youth in his charge have for personal self-realization. Some educational philosophers have suggested that no true learning takes place unless the learners have some hand in deciding the nature of the tutorial activities directed their way. The gradual extension of decisions to your athletes, as is outlined in Chapter Twenty-three, may prove effective with the youth with whom you will later become associated.

The *younger* athletes in your charge may need to gain, through your direction, an awareness of just what discipline means; the discipline necessary for engaging in hard physical workouts, and regulating personal habits of health, sleep, and the like. However, when working with more mature athletes in their last years of high school and in college, you should hopefully find that *imposing your discipline* is not as effective an educational strategy as is permitting them to *develop a sense of personal self-discipline.*

Athletics in an educational context should provide the participating youth with a realization of various objectives associated with education, including an awareness of individual potentials in vigorous competitive sports, the ability to engage in self-discipline, and a heightened personal awareness. If entertainment of spectators, supporting the sagging ego of an ex-athlete coach, or financial gain seem paramount within a school program, the program's existence within an educational institution should seriously be questioned.

Most important, the fledgling coach seeking his first position should attempt to assess accurately the philosophy and objectives of the situation to which he may be seeking access. If these are incompatible with his own values, he should attempt to gain employment elsewhere.

Personal Evaluation

It is also important for the potential coach to engage in some degree of personal "sizing up." While the development of a philosophy, a degree of social sensitivity, and similar traits have been mentioned, there are other personal aspects which should be inspected. For example, the physical appearance you present to your teams is important. Obesity among coaches, who are usually attempting to enhance the fitness of youth, is inexcusable.[5]

The level of physical skills you possess as a younger coach may also prove an asset to you. It is generally found that male physical education majors tend to coach sports in which they participated while in college. Athletes may learn from your demonstration, if carried out with reasonable expertise, as well as from your verbal and visual presentations of various materials.

It is often found that athletes are unable to coach a sport well. This is due to a number of factors, including poor communication skills, and disinclination or inability to relate well and work effectively with youth. If you speak poorly, take a speech course and seek opportunities to present yourself verbally before groups. If you are not a participating college athlete in a sport which you may later prefer to coach, seek ways of improving your skills outside an organized team situation while you are an undergraduate.

It is important to seek situations during your undergraduate days in which you may obtain coaching experience. Often the local high school coaches welcome the regular assistance of college students in the conducting of team practices. Athletic clubs, YMCAs, and private schools may also provide a place in which you may "test your wings" as a leader of youth in vigorous physical activity.

During this period of initial experiences you may discover several things. You may find that coaching is not for you, or that you lack the ability to present materials clearly, or maybe that you need further grounding in tactics and in personal physical skills to make you capable as a demonstrator. If any of these problems arise, attempt to rectify them as an undergraduate, perhaps by changing your major. Entering a school as a coach, and finding out that you are not suited to the career you have selected, is an extremely painful experience for all concerned.

[5]A prominent coach in a western university recently received national publicity for chastising a black athlete for wearing a beard. This same coach appeared to be from 75 to 100 pounds overweight.

Women and Girls in Sports

The American culture is increasingly accepting girls in competitive and vigorous sports. Moreover, girls are finding out that vigorous participation in athletics does not result in any social censure, but indeed may lead to desirable recognition. It is obvious that more effective feminine coaches of these activities should be provided by teacher-training institutions.

In reading this text, and particularly this chapter, the female readers should not block out statements related to coaching as "something only for the boys." Female physical education majors often assume leadership roles and attempt to insert helpful practices into athletics for girls, practices which will lead toward wholesome and desirable educational objectives. The standards published by the Division for Girls' and Women's Sports should be consulted by female physical education majors. Girls who excel in sports should be given educationally sound environments in which to exhibit and expand their competencies. The quality of these experiences for women is to a large extent governed by the quality of the leadership to which they are exposed. The nature of this leadership is in turn dependent upon the type of preparation of, and attitude possessed by, the young women emerging from college and university physical education major programs throughout the country.

School and Community Relationships

The physical education major should come to terms with the truism that when he begins coaching he is likely to have constant community attention focused upon his efforts. Most sports, by their very nature, are exhibitions. Exhibitions are observed by spectators. The critical eye of many others will be cast in your direction, and your performance will be evaluated by virtue of whether or not your teams appear well coached.

If the community is reasonably small, your personal life will similarly be inspected at far-too-regular intervals. You should be prepared to react to this attention by presenting a picture to the community which, within reasonable degrees, adheres to the social and moral conduct generally accepted in your town. If not so prepared, you should seek another occupation.

Your relationships with your colleagues in the school are also likely to be interesting. Although some will feel that you are not academically acceptable because of your involvement in physical activity, if your sport is a prominent one its progress and your performance will also be regularly scrutinized. You will likely be the subject of some envy, as you may, for example, gain more attention from the community than do classroom teachers. The extra pay you may receive will also encourage some to direct displeasure in your direction. You should be aware that these feelings within the school community do exist. You can only rectify by your own conduct the feelings you find undesirable. You should attempt to present critics with a professional image by your conduct and attendance at faculty meetings, and by interests you direct toward *their* work. You may, by your personal impact, gradually persuade many of your colleagues that you consider the emotional needs of your athletes to be paramount. By the same token, if your conduct evidences an arrogant self-interest when coaching, this will also become clearly apparent to all who observe you in action with your teams. The choice of behavior will be yours.

Most athletic teams attract various kinds of "hangers-on," individuals who wish to associate themselves with your team for various reasons. They may be ex-athletes who wish to help you coach; or "never-were athletes" who hope to support somewhat sagging egos. While it might be your first tendency to dismiss these individuals summarily from your practice field or gym, many whose motives are wholesome may be helpful to you and to the youth you serve. They may, for example, possess real coaching skills, and if properly supervised can make a tangible contribution to your total effort. They may aid you in publicizing a game or in raising needed money. If by helping you they are in some way helping themselves feel important, perhaps this is not an undesirable outcome.

To attempt to present a complete spectrum of the problems which may confront you as a coach, and of the competencies you may need, is probably presumptuous, particularly within a limited number of pages. If helpful signposts have been erected for your consideration, the purposes of the writer will have been served.

Writing such a chapter without inserting one's personal philosophy concerning athletics and coaching is impossible; and indeed I have not held back expressing mine. To be completely clear, however, I should perhaps enumerate several points which I believe provide the bases for my feelings about athletics, and which I feel guided my behavior when coaching six sports over a period of fifteen years. The student reader should remember that these are *my* own; it is the student's task to compile his personal list of guiding principles during his formative years as an undergraduate in physical education.

1. An experience in athletics is seldom a neutral one for a youth. He comes away from it with either positive or negative effects on his physique, personality, and general outlook toward life, competition, and people.

2. The athletic coach has a profound responsibility, if he finds himself within an educational setting, to provide experiences on athletic teams which will result in positive changes to the various facets of the personalities of those he is purporting to serve.
3. The athletic coach should be a thoroughly-equipped professional person, possessing the knowledge and attitudes which will enable him to direct the efforts of athletes in specific sports, as well as the ability to work with the unique personality of each youth with whom he comes in contact.

Student Activities and Discussion Questions

1. Discuss with a local high school coach his coaching philosophy. Is he able to verbalize his general outlook toward sports and athletics? What does his philosophy contain which you might consider as positive and potentially adoptable by you? Which of his basic feelings do you reject? Why?
2. Discuss different approaches to motivating, and to personally interacting with, athletes in individual sports, and in team sports. What special methods might be used for making athletes in individual sports more cohesive?
3. Is the promotion of high levels of team cohesion, the "we" feeling, always important? What if a good performer makes a caustic remark about the poorer performance of a less adept teammate? Is this attitude likely to impede or enhance team performance?
4. List the multitude of coaching duties which may possibly be incurred, in addition to working directly with athletes. How may these various duties best be handled?
5. Talk to a top female competitive athlete. Discuss with her the feminine image of, and vigorous participation in, athletics. Does she feel that her participation poses any special social problems? What are these, if any?

References

Books

Beisser, A. R., *The Madness in Sports*. New York: Appleton-Century-Crofts, 1967.
Bonder, Jim, *How to Be a Successful Coach*. Englewood Cliffs, New Jersey: Prentice-Hall, Inc., 1958.
The Coaches Handbook. Washington, D.C.: American Association for Health, Physical Education and Recreation.
Cook, N. L., *Lifetime Sports: A Guide for Instruction and Administration*. Washington, D.C.: National Recreation and Parks Association, 1967.

Craine, H. C., *Teaching Athletic Skills in Physical Education.* New York: Inor Publishing Company, 1942.

Cratty, Bryant J., *Psychology and Physical Activity.* Englewood Cliffs, New Jersey: Prentice-Hall, Inc., 1968.

————, *Movement Behavior and Motor Learning.* Philadelphia: Lea & Febiger, 1st ed. 1964, 2nd ed. 1967.

DeWitt, R. T., *Teaching Individual and Team Sports.* Englewood Cliffs, New Jersey: Prentice-Hall, Inc., 1953.

Griffin, J. H., *Teamwork Between the Coach and the School Administration.* Danville, Illinois: School Aid Company, 1965.

Jokl, Ernst, and Jokl, Peter, *Physiological Basis of Athletic Records.* Springfield, Illinois: Charles C. Thomas, Publisher, 1968.

Means, L. E., *Physical Activities, Sports and Games.* Dubuque, Iowa: W. C. Brown Company, 1965.

Pearson, G. B., *Methods of Teaching the Fundamental Skills of Team Sports.* Dubuque, Iowa: W. C. Brown Company, 1960.

Scott, Jack, *Athletics for Athletes.* Oakland, California: Other Way Books, 1969.

Vanek, Miroslav, and Cratty, Bryant J., *Psychology and the Superior Athlete.* New York: The Macmillan Company, 1970.

Weiss, Paul, *Sport.* London and Amsterdam: Illinois University Press, 1969.

Periodicals

Athletic Journal, 1719 Howard Street, Evanston, Illinois 60602.

Coach and Athletics, 1421 Mayson Street, N. E., Atlanta, Georgia 30324.

Journal of Health, Physical Education and Recreation, 1201 16th St., N. W., Washington, D. C. 20036.

Scholastic Coach, 902 Sylvan Avenue, Englewood Cliffs, New Jersey.

CHAPTER ELEVEN

Special Education

The field of special education encompasses programs for children who are in some way "different" from the normal child in the elementary or secondary school. This difference may lie in the manner in which they function socially, emotionally, intellectually, and/or physically. Special education includes programs for children who are physically handicapped to various degrees; for those who are mentally retarded, or intellectually gifted; for those who are visually impaired, or blind or deaf, as well as for children who are emotionally disturbed in some ways which prevent them from functioning well within the usual classroom environment.

These classes and programs may take place within several types of school situations. At times, children who are different live in full-time residential schools. The staffs, usually supported by state and/or federal funds, are concerned both with the total welfare of the children throughout their waking and sleeping hours as well as with their education.

At other times these programs are found within school districts, in special day schools which are separate from the regular elementary and secondary schools. School districts may combine funds to provide special services to handicapped children, so that classroom units are formed which are large enough to be economically efficient. Classes for children who are "different" may also be found within schools for normal children. Additionally, various private schools of special education have been established in some parts of the country to deal with children with special learning problems. These schools are supported financially by the parents, and may offer special programs which are not found in available publicly-supported schools for special education. It is felt by some educators that if the handicapped child can spend part of the time with the normal child, and also acquire special help suited to his unique educational needs, he will grow to be a better-functioning member of adult society.

During the 1960s a great amount of attention was focused upon the potential role of movement within several types of programs of special education. Studies in England in the late 1950s spurred the adoption of an increased number of, and improvement in the quality of, physical education programs for the mentally retarded. This trend was supported and enlarged upon by the Joseph P. Kennedy, Jr. Foundation in Washington, D. C. Texts published during the latter part of the 1960s began to compile information relative to programs for the mentally retarded. Other research dealing with the blind indicated that early school preparation for later mobility in the city and neighborhood should include a sound physical education program.

The findings of the 1950s, which flowered in the 1960s with rather expansive publicity, suggested that motor activities which were formerly in the purview of physical educators could be used in a positive manner among children with learning deficiencies, to help them function better perceptually, motorically, and academically. While many of the more extravagant claims have been laid to rest following tests of their veracity by reputable researchers, this "movement" movement served to make all educators more aware of the potential for motor activities of various kinds within programs for the normal and for the atypical youngster.

A physical education teacher in special education may function at several levels. An instructor may work directly with students in a school for special education or in a resident home. He may serve as a special consultant working with teachers, aiding them to gain new skills and insights into the manner in which motor activity may be used to advantage in special education. Accompanying this work is often the task of "checking out" new claims and programs by conducting scientific research in which pre- and post-program test results are compared.

To an increased degree, teacher preparation schools around the country are incorporating courses, and at times designing entire curriculums at both the graduate and undergraduate levels, for individuals wishing to work with "special" children through movement activities. The pages which follow contain brief surveys of the unique training, activities, problems, and job opportunities relating to working with various subgroups within special education. For a more thorough discussion of how physical education, recreation, and athletics may serve these types of children, you might wish to survey some of the texts listed at the end of the chapter.

Physical Education and the Gifted Child

Special programs within public school districts and private schools which deal with the unique needs of the gifted child are appearing to an increased degree. Seldom, however, are these programs found to have made modifications in their physical activity programs to make them congruent with the higher intellectual abilities these children bring to school. Rarely do courses within physical education curriculums at the college level offer content dealing with the gifted child in athletics and at play. There are many who feel that special modifications should be made in programs for such children.

A trend which is emerging in the play characteristics of the normal child in the United States is an increased tendency to insert intellectual components into games, and to substitute more passive games of skill and strategy for the vigorous ones they formerly preferred. It might be hypothesized that the intellectually gifted child, exercising his capacities for thought, is even more likely to seek games which involve cognitive operations.

Effective work with the gifted through *vigorous* physical activity is possible, particularly if these children are given a number of decisions to make relative to the makeup and administration of the program in which they engage.

Within many groups of so-called "gifted" children, it is not unusual to find children whose parents have pressured them into some kind of pseudo-gifted performance which is not undergirded by truly exceptional intellectual capacities. In the case of this type of child, it may be necessary for the physical educator to provide methods which may be helpful in reducing the child's tensions by using, for example, various kinds of relaxation training. The truly gifted child may similarly need the tension-releasing activities which are found in most physical education programs, as at times his intellectual curiosity may lead him to "wind up tight" in his compulsive search for great amounts of information and new ideas.

Chances to learn about the principles behind muscular exercise, the physiological and mechanical principles of skeletal muscle actions, and similar concepts should, for example, provide a base from which the child may devise his own exercise programs. Providing the gifted child with opportunities to invent new games by giving him simple equipment, and then allowing ample time for him to think about modifications of activities he has previously been exposed to, and to create entirely unique games, is of vital importance.

As with any specialization within the broad field of physical education, potential instructors of the gifted should acquire information concerning the characteristics of gifted children; as well as a thorough knowledge of all related phases of physical activities, including a broad and deep grasp of a variety of teaching methodologies. Armed with this information, the outcome should be more meaningful programs for the more capable.

Retarded Children and Youth

A vast amount of literature reflecting an interest in the physical welfare of retarded children appeared during the 1960s. Even a cursory review of the important ideas contained in this material is impossible with the limited summary on these pages.

In essence the research indicates that retarded children are indeed less fit than normal children and, as would be expected, have greater difficulty in acquiring reasonably-complex skills than do their more intellectually-able companions. Their lack of muscular fitness and endurance may stem from poor programs to which they are exposed, or from the fact that some lack the opportunity to participate in any program at all. Skill deficiencies and the inability to engage in accurate movement are often, particularly in the more severely retarded, due to structural problems within the nervous system which are related to the intellectual deficiencies evidenced.

Programs for retarded children incorporating motor activities can have several purposes, depending upon the subpopulations of retardates to which they may be applied.[1]

The lower the group is on the intellectual scale, the more motor activities will play a part in their education. The trainable, for example, usually require help in speech (to some degree a motor act), in self-care skills including teeth brushing, dressing, and the like, as well as in appropriate recreational skills.

The educable, on the other hand, in many respects are functioning intellectually about two years below what would normally be expected. The label "educable" infers that a child is capable of being educated, and is, for example, usually reading about two or three years below the

---

[1]Depending upon the individual state, retarded children may be classified as severely retarded (30 I.Q.), trainably retarded (30-50 I.Q.), and educably retarded (50-79 I.Q.).

level expected for his chronological age. This latter type of child will generally need special help in understanding the rules of the more complex games, and may feel more comfortable participating in more simple games than are played by normal children of his age. It is the educable retardate who is often found within classes of physical education designed for normal children. The physical educator, in this case, should take special pains to educate the "normals" in how they might deal with their less gifted classmate. The teacher also should attempt to keep social pressure to perform well from descending upon the retarded child. During late childhood, the educable child may be able to gain accurate awareness of just how he is different; and special care should be taken that these possible negative self-feelings are not magnified by disadvantageous participation in physical education and recreational activities.

Increasingly, the severely retarded child is being given various kinds of movement therapies and other sensory experiences, usually in resident homes and hospitals for the retarded. If this kind of "intervention" is initiated early in the life of the child, and at times with the aid of various biochemical agents, more improvement is forthcoming than if he is left alone, as has been the case too frequently in the past. Research is making it quite clear that movement activities offer no magic panacea for the remediation of the many possible causes of mental retardation; but they do help some retarded children to perform some necessary activities more efficiently, and in general to lead more productive lives.

Movement activities correctly applied may help the retarded child to function better in several ways. Practice in necessary motor skills, if patiently applied, generally leads toward improvement of the skills practiced. Secondly, this improvement may lead to an increased inclination on the part of the child to try to do other things, including attempting to carry out more complex mental and academic operations.

Thirdly, motor activities and relaxation training can, if used properly, help to activate the habitually lethargic child; or conversely, aid to calm or slow down the retardate who may be habitually too active, and may be moving too rapidly to attend to any type of task for an amount of time sufficient to produce learning.

A fourth way in which motor activities have been demonstrated through research to aid retarded children is by combining movement and academic exercises so that they provide the child simultaneous intellectual and motor experiences. Research findings from the Perceptual-Motor Learning Laboratory at UCLA, and findings from other institutions such as the University of Wisconsin and the University of Maryland, have begun to confirm the axiom that movement activities will aid a child to think and perform various academic tasks to the extent that he thinks about the movements he uses.

A series of learning games have been published, and the surveyed results of the application of these to educable retardates are highly encouraging. For example, it was found that children with learning difficulties could be taught to identify the letters of the alphabet, and to write their letters and form geometric figures more accurately and quickly with learning games than through traditional methods of classroom tutoring. Remembering a series of pictures, numbers, and movements was enhanced and spelling also improved through various movement games. Thus, the physical educator may contribute in a number of ways to the education of retarded children: in direct ways through combining academic operations in learning games; and in more subtle ways by heightening the self-concept of retarded children by improving their social acceptance through increased capacity to engage in various recreational skills. The vocational success of a large number of retardates is predicated upon their ability to perform various simple manual skills. This is another type of attribute to which a physical educator who is well grounded in his subject (i.e., understanding movement and motor learning) may make a contribution to the development of many retarded children.

Exercising retardates will generally result in stronger and larger muscles, just as having them run may produce increased cardiovascular efficiency.[2] With a more scholarly application of various movement tasks, even more important contributions can be made to the welfare of retarded children than just creating better muscular and physiological efficiency.

Sensory Deprivation

The Blind and Deaf

Although there usually are not a large number of blind children within a given group of normal children, a large percentage evidence varying degrees of visual impairment. The deaf child is similarly difficult to

[2]Care must be taken with certain populations of retardates before indiscriminately exposing them to large amounts of physical exercise without proper medical supervision. Some may be more susceptible to epileptic seizures under the stress of exercise, while others may have structural abnormalities of the heart and associated systems which restrict the amount and intensity of activities in which they engage.

educate; and the problems he poses in physical education are unique and interesting.[3]

Research during recent years, particularly that carried out during the late 1950s and 1960s, has substantiated the importance of movement activities in the education of the blind youth. Not only, as would be expected, will his fitness and game skills improve, but his general spatial orientation may be enhanced by various kinds of body-image training applied in correct ways; training which involves a considerable amount of movement combined with cognitive and perceptual training. See *Movement and Spatial Awareness in Blind Children and Youth*, a text which examines in detail the contribution of movement to the spatial awareness of blind infants, children, and youth.

As with the profoundly retarded, there are usually found among populations of deaf and blind children an unusual number who evidence other neurological deficiencies, some of which are reflected in motor coordination problems of a moderate or severe nature. A good program of physical education for blind and deaf children should contain special activities designed to remediate motor difficulties, as well as others designed to meet their particular needs.

Working with these types of children offers physical education specialists a considerable number of challenges; but at the same time, observing their reactions and improvement will provide a teacher with deep satisfactions. As with all fields in special education, the physical educator should work quite closely with the classroom teacher and with available psychologists and physicians. He should also attempt to acquire basic information, both formally and informally, concerning the unique nature of the sensory-motor problems of the children with whom he attempts to deal.

Neurologically Impaired Children

Throughout the country during the last ten years, great emphasis has been placed upon dealing with the special needs of a large percentage of children found within the normal classroom. These children often evidence distinct coordination problems, and/or may be emotionally disturbed to a moderate degree. They have been grouped under several labels, depending upon the philosophical and legal conditions present within a given school district and state.

At times they are called educationally handicapped, or minimally

---

[3]He may, for example, decide to "turn off" his teacher's directions by simply closing his eyes, or turning his back to her while some distance away on the playground!

brain damaged (MBD), or minimally neurologically impaired, or dyslexic. In any case, they are not children who are severely emotionally disturbed, nor are they obviously physically handicapped. They fall in a category difficult to define, and at times to diagnose; which renders them, in turn, difficult to educate. These children have trouble learning, and are usually two or more years behind their classmates, although they may achieve average scores on I.Q. tests. They frequently, although not always, evidence coordination problems, resulting in social censure at play and an inability to keep up with their more able classmates when attempting to transcribe their thought to paper. They are frustrated in school, as their verbal comprehension, reading ability, and other cognitive processes are much better than their ability to express the quality of their intellectual efforts through handwriting.

They can usually be diagnosed during the early years of life, although identification is not always carried out. These children are confused in the manner in which they see things. Reading may be difficult for them, and they do not organize verbal directions to which they are exposed. These children, it has been estimated, comprise from 15 to 25 percent of the so-called normal population of children. They are the clumsy children who have throughout history frustrated the physical education teacher and coach, and who in turn have often been frustrated and punished by them.

The more progressive school districts are increasingly beginning to identify these children during the first years at school, and to offer them special help. Some of this aid is in the form of remedial classes, in which at least part of the program deals with motor training of some type. Special educators throughout the country appear to be engaged in a search for sensitive and well-prepared physical educators to work in constructive ways with these children; and employment opportunities are expanding.

Generally, the physical educator, when working with these children, should be capable of instituting and implementing a sound initial screening involving motor competencies. Furthermore, he should be capable of recommending remedial techniques to teachers, in addition to being able to carry on classes in which he has direct contact with the children.

Perhaps more than in other handicapped groups, with the exception of the severely retarded, one finds a large number of children within the group under consideration who may be classified as too active. They are constantly on the move, are hyperactive, and need to be slowed down in helpful ways. A real disservice can be done by the physical educator to the child, the parent, and the teacher, if he attempts to apply a "drainage theory" of physical activity to children or groups of children of this type. Attempting somehow to relax them by tiring them out in physical activity is likely to have reverse results. Vigorous, emotionally-charged physical activity, when applied to this group without subsequent provisions made to calm them down, is likely to raise their "movement barometers" so high that they are unable to settle down for the rest of the day in a classroom situation, or for that matter to sleep later that evening.

This group of children offers the physical educator interested in making a contribution to education a real challenge; while if work with these children is undertaken, real personal rewards should be forthcoming to the involved teacher.

Movement activities will not cure the educational ills of these children in the all-encompassing manner that has been suggested by some overzealous "educationalists" during the past years. At the same time, a lack of good self-control (of movements) and an inability to move accurately are qualities which detract in direct ways from the manner in which they function in school.

Other Types of Handicapped Children

There are other classifications of exceptional children which have not yet been discussed. The orthopedically-handicapped child, the child with obvious damage to those parts of the brain which control his movements (evidencing cerebral palsy and similar conditions), as well as the severely emotionally disturbed child, offer additional challenges to those attempting to work with children through movement.

By his very nature the child with cerebral palsy will have movement problems, and thus a great deal of his educational program may be devoted to attempting to improve his ability to control his actions. The orthopedically-handicapped child also needs special equipment and creative approaches, to help him to feel better about his obvious deficiencies in the usual childhood games.

The severely emotionally-disturbed child may also benefit from special programs of physical education. Generally, such children evidence either hyperactive behavior or extreme social withdrawal, either of which can make game participation a social trauma rather than a happy experience. Often, such children can be aided by making special provisions for calming them down, and by providing activities which are simple enough for them to master within social contexts which place little emphasis upon the winning or losing.

Summary

There are increasingly numerous types of opportunities through which physical educators may make a contribution to the education of children who are in some way different. These differences may evidence themselves in unusual emotional problems, in obvious or subtle movement problems, or in rather profound or mild sensory disturbances of some kind.

The feeling of success, together with the real help given such children in manipulative activities, handwriting, as well as recreational game skills, can make an important contribution to their total functioning in home, school, and community. Some of these children are presently trying to function within normal and above-normal populations, and are suffering because they lose most of the time. Others are obviously handicapped and are found in special classes, homes, and schools with children who evidence similar problems.

The physical educator hoping to work with such children should gain a good background in special education, directed toward the kind of "problem child" with whom he hopes to work, together with a kind of broad, practical, and theoretical knowledge about motor activity itself. The physical educator should, by gaining this background, become prepared to work on professional teams with physicians, psychologists, and educators who are also laboring within their specializations to aid such youngsters.

Student Activities and Discussion Questions

1. Visit a school for the mentally retarded and/or physically handicapped, paying particular attention to the type of physical education program they have available to them (if any). Evaluate the program upon your return, and design an ideal program for the children you observed.
2. As the result of reading and visits, design an ideal playground for the retarded, the physically handicapped, and/or the blind.
3. Compare the balance, agility, skipping ability, drawing ability, ability to name body parts, and ball-handling skills (throwing and catching) of two elementary school children similar in age and sex: one who is described by his teacher as "clumsy" and the other who is described as possessing normal or above-normal playground skills. Write up your observations and test scores. How would you accommodate program planning to the individual's differences you may have discovered?
4. Visit a mother who has raised a blind child. What unique problems has she faced relative to spatial orientation, cognitive and emotional development, as well as physical development? To what type, if any, of

physical activity program has the child been exposed? Report your findings to the class.

5. Visit a local agency or school which deals with the problems of the blind or the deaf. What provisions, if any, do they have for programs of physical education for the children and youth they serve? After such a visit design an ideal program, and facilities which will match your program.

6. Select a child whom an elementary school teacher has identified as "unable to sit still in class," "hyperactive," having a "poor attention span," etc. Assign him several tasks of "moving as slowly as you can" (e.g., drawing a line, getting up from a back lying position, or perhaps walking a line). How do his scores in these tasks compare to those of another child who is attentive and who exhibits good self-control in his school classroom? How might you work best as a physical educator with the more active child to improve his classroom attention?

7. Visit a program for the physically handicapped. Evaluate their program of recreation and physical education, if any. Design activities for the children, youth, or adults you observe. What special equipment might you need to develop to encourage their participation in various recreational motor skills?

References

Books

Arnheim, D. D., Auxter, D., and Crowe, W. C., *Principles and Methods of Adapted Physical Education.* St. Louis: The C. V. Mosby Company, 1969.

Clausen, John S., *Ability Structure and Subgroups in Mental Retardation.* London: Macmillan and Co., Ltd., 1966.

Cratty, Bryant J., *Developmental Games for Physically Handicapped Children.* Palo Alto: Peek Publications, 1969.

————, *Development Sequences of Perceptual-Motor Tasks for Neurologically Handicapped and Retarded Children.* Freeport, Long Island: Educational Activities, Inc., 1967.

————, *Motor Activities and the Education of Retardates.* Philadelphia: Lea & Febiger, 1969.

————, *Moving and Learning: Fifty Games for Children with Learning Difficulties.* Freeport, Long Island: Educational Activities, Inc., 1968.

————, *Movement, Perception and Thought.* Palo Alto: Peek Publications, 1969.

————, *Movement and Spatial Awareness in Blind Children and Youth.* Springfield, Illinois: Charles C. Thomas, Publisher, 1971.

————, *Trampoline Activities for Atypical Children.* Palo Alto: Peek Publications, 1969.

Fait, H. F., *Special Physical Education: Adopted, Corrective, Developmental*. Philadelphia: W. B. Saunders Company, 1966.

Joint Committee of the Council for Exceptional Children, *Recreation and Physical Activity for the Mentally Retarded*. Washington, D. C.: American Association of Health, Physical Education and Recreation, 1966.

Leland, Henry, and Smith, D. E., *Play Therapy with Mentally Subnormal Children*. New York: Grune and Stratton, Publishers, 1965.

Malpass, L. F., "Motor Skills in Mental Deficiency," in *Handbook of Mental Deficiency*, Norman R. Ellis, Editor. New York: McGraw-Hill Book Company, 1963.

Pomeroy, Janet, *Recreation for the Physically Handicapped*. New York: The Macmillan Company, 1964.

Robins, Ferris, *Educational Rhythmics for Mentally and Physically Handicapped Children*. New York: Association Press, 1968.

Walker, Leroy T., *Physical Education for the Exceptional Student: Principles and Practices of Physical Education for Atypical Students*. Dubuque, Iowa: W. C. Brown Company, 1963.

Wheeler, R. H., and Hooley, A. M., *Physical Education for the Handicapped*. Philadelphia: Lea & Febiger, 1969.

Periodicals

American Journal of Mental Deficiency. American Association on Mental Deficiency, P. O. Box 96, Wilimonti, Conn.

Child Development. 5750 Ellis Ave., Chicago, Illinois.

Exceptional Child. The Council for the Exceptional Child, N. E. A., 1201 16th St., N. W., Washington, D. C.

Perceptual and Motor Skills. Southern University Press, Box 1441, Missoula, Montana.

Psychology Monographs. The American Psychology Association, Inc., 1200 17th, N.W., Washington, D. C.

CHAPTER TWELVE

Recreation

A community planner in the mayor's office, a ship's captain, the principal of a high school, a psychologist interested in juvenile delinquency, as well as a factory owner, all may view a professional recreational worker as a valuable member of his staff. A career in recreation can take many forms, involve services to diverse types of people, and provide numerous interesting challenges to those participating and conducting recreational activities.

Throughout recorded history, those concerned about the harmonious development of man have written about the need to engage in recreational (literally, to create again) acts; and at times these writers have proposed programs designed to achieve this noble end. It has only been within recent years in our country, however, that a reasonable number of college-educated recreational workers have been graduated. As the needs and uses for recreation have continued to expand, there are seldom enough professional people available.

During the early years in this country, while the nation's leaders often expressed concern for the "vile" and "low level" ways in which youth occupied their leisure hours, little was done to provide facilities or programs which might engage the young people in pursuits more uplifting than the grog shop or the billiard room. However, the village greens of the colonial period did provide a place in which the children could play, and were the forerunners of today's large and complex recreation centers, parks, and playgrounds.

During the middle of the 1800s, following the Civil War, several cities of the United States, particularly around Boston, started to set aside areas in which children and others might play, although no formal supervision was at first provided. According to most authorities, the beginnings of the playground movement in the United States occurred in Boston in 1885, when the Boston Emergency and Hygiene Association placed two heaps of sand at the Parmenter Street Chapel and West End Nursery. The instigator of this action was Dr. Marie Zakrzewsky, who had recently observed the same thing in Germany. By 1893 so many "sand gardens" had appeared that a superintendent was hired to oversee the volunteer mothers who aided in these projects. Just before the turn of the century other cities, including Philadelphia, Detroit, Baltimore, Cleveland, and Chicago, also started small playgrounds, although the sums allotted to their building and maintenance were small indeed.

Paralleling these early playgrounds was the appearance of the first summer camps for children. Just prior to, and shortly after, the Civil War, the first camps for boys appeared, in general emulating the living conditions of the soldiers.

During these early years, however, it was found that while the playgrounds did indeed keep children off the streets, and were in other ways potentially useful to the community, they required professional supervision in a form other than just the local policeman. After the turn of the century various agencies were at work providing this type of leadership.

For example, in 1906 the Playground Association of America was founded, due to the leadership provided by Dr. Luther Gulick in New York and Dr. Henry Curtis in Washington, D. C. President Theodore Roosevelt was elected as its first Honorary President. This organization began at once to publish monthly pamphlets and magazines, including *The Playground*. In 1910 a comprehensive training monograph for recreational workers was published by this same organization, titled *The Normal Course in Play*.

The History of Recreation in the U.S.

Recreation and physical education were closely associated from the beginning, since many of the leaders of the Playground Association were teacher-educators and writers in physical education. By the end of 1912, large appropriations of money were advanced in Chicago, Los Angeles, Louisville, Philadelphia, Minneapolis, and other American cities for the building of more elaborate playgrounds, many of which included rather complex field houses for various kinds of indoor sports. The National Education Association, during this same period, supported the use of school buildings for recreational purposes. The intra-mural movement in colleges, which emerged slightly after this time, also tended to weld even more closely the objectives and practices of physical education and recreation.

During the 1920s the recreation movement waned, as the press of financial depression confined its expansion. However, federal projects during the 1930s tended to give it renewed vigor. With the help of the WPA and other federal projects during Franklin Roosevelt's adminis-tration, numerous facilities were constructed, play areas cleared, and programs initiated. Thousands of swimming and wading pools, 32,000 playgrounds, and many athletic fields and golf courses were built with federal support as a means of providing employment for those affected most severely by the depression. During this period these federal pro-jects provided an expansion of the activities consigned to recreational programs. Art projects, music, dramatics, and other similar diversions found their way into programs by the end of the 1930s.

Following World War II, further expansion of recreation organiza-tions and programs took place. By 1949, 40 colleges and universities offered major courses in recreation. Recreation programs flourished in governmental (national parks, wildlife services, etc.) as well as in non-governmental services (YMCA, Boy Scouts, WMHA, 4-H Clubs, CYO, and Girl Scouts).

Expansion of recreation was also apparent when one viewed the number of activities that various programs seemed to embrace. Expan-sion of types of activities was reflected by the annual report of the National Recreation Association published in 1948, in which compo-nents of recreation programs involving 75 activities were classified into nine categories, including arts and crafts, athletics and games, drama, music, outing activities, water sports, winter sports; and a miscella-neous division which included hobby clubs, motion pictures, commu-nity celebrations, and the like.

During the 1950s and 1960s, further enlargement of the scope of recreation was evidenced in the increased number of recreation pro-grams for the aged, as well as in the impetus given to industrial recrea-tion programs of various kinds. Many leaders of industry seemed to realize that not only was the mental health of workers enhanced by participation in meaningful recreation programs, but that such pro-grams more than returned their costs to the company in increased productivity.

Most recreational workers in the 1960s were well-trained profes-sional people, possessing at least a bachelor's degree, and were able to supervise and initiate a wide range of community programs. They have been sensitive to community needs when working in public programs, and occupy important roles in various private industries and agencies.

Background Needed

Generally, a recreation worker may begin a full-time career without the need for a degree past the bachelor's. However, many are working for advanced degrees or possess them at the present time. Usually, the undergraduate major in recreation contains relatively few courses dealing with the scientific bases of movement—anatomy, work physiology, and the like—and more classes emphasizing the social sciences, sociology, psychology, as well as those dealing with community planning and program planning. Additionally, most recreation curriculums contain courses dealing with the specific skills needed in recreation: various arts and crafts, music, as well as athletics and other recreational sports. In general, the more well-rounded the recreational worker is, and the more broadly he perceives his job to be, the more effective he will be in a variety of community environments.

Recreation majors usually take courses in administration and supervision. Much of their work involves the supervision of other volunteer workers, or of children, youth, and adults on their playgrounds and recreation centers. A professional recreation worker, particularly if he takes graduate work, should be exposed to techniques necessary for making community surveys.

Many times recreation directors are active in the planning of facilities. They must work together with architects and other community leaders in the initiation and design of facilities and equipment pertinent to the needs of a community.

Thus, the training of a recreation worker is relatively broad. He must work with people but must usually help people *do* something. He is an educator, and may be an informal guidance counselor to many more children and youth each week than the number visiting the office of the local child psychologist. He must be sensitive to the community needs, and at the same time lead the members of a community to expand their interests. The recreation worker must work in the planning of facilities and programs, and initiate through his personal behavior better ways to serve people.

Fields of Recreation

As has been pointed out, the types of recreational positions available vary widely. Only some of the facets of recreation will be considered on these pages. Your own community's recreational workers may have additional activities that are not covered on the pages which follow. A recreation worker may work for a township, a county, a state, or a federal agency. In private recreation, the possibilities for service are limitless.

Industrial Recreation

Industrial recreation programs have proliferated during the 1950s and 1960s. It had been discovered during World War II that when workers played together they tended to be better adjusted to their jobs; which, in turn, resulted in more tanks and airplanes being produced. Today's programs of industrial recreation in some of the larger companies are truly exceptional.

An industrial recreational worker may serve the employees of a company in several ways. Usually these programs contain facilities in which a harassed executive or an over-strained assembly-line worker may receive some kind of physical services immediately after work one or more times a week. There are often gymnasiums available for games and/or for formal conditioning activities (resistive exercises). Steam rooms, massages, saunas, and similar facilities also are found in the more progressive companies. Professional recreation people with strong backgrounds in physical education are needed within such programs, to suggest exercise loads, to design special programs of conditions, and often to work in conjunction with plant doctors to meet the special physical needs for workers who may have various physical disabilities which are the result of stress (physical or emotional incurred on the job).

Personnel working in industrial recreation are often organizers of leagues, tournaments, and the like for plant personnel. They form bowling, softball, and similar leagues, arrange for facilities or officials, and buy equipment. They also organize post-season banquets with all the trimmings, including food and drink, awards, and, of course, an appropriate speaker. The recreation worker must usually be responsible for publicity of various kinds. The plant newspaper usually has a large section devoted to recreational activities and the recreation worker must know how to write publicity and to otherwise familiarize people with his program. In this role he must be able to work in a helpful manner with a large number of people of various ages and recreational needs. Card tournaments for the more elderly, bowling tournaments and shuffleboard for the not-as-old, and basketball and softball for the younger employees, all must be the responsibility of the recreation worker at the plant.

Recreation for the Aged

More and more people are living to older ages in the United States. During the late 1950s and the 1960s, an increasing number of centers for the recreation of the elderly was found in both private and public agencies. Homes for the aged, supported by private and public capital, began to institute increasingly more programs in which professional recreation personnel were involved. Many city parks began to evidence facilities for bowling on the green and other more vigorous or less strenuous activities.

The elderly have special needs, not only because of their changing physical capacities, but also because of their changing outlook on life. They may be more easily depressed as they grow older, as their children move out of their homes, or perhaps when their spouse dies; and they need the companionship of others. They may be more reluctant to try new crafts, games, and intellectual and/or physical activities. They do not like to be reminded of the physical or intellectual limitations which may be pressing upon them, and which may result in the realization that they can apparently do fewer things as well as they once did. They may need special encouragement and help from sensitive leadership, often the leadership of a person trained to meet their needs.

At the same time, it has been found that when the aged are exposed to meaningful recreation programs, the aging process may be delayed to a remarkable degree. Old age is paired with inactivity and retirement; renewed interest in life can come with the assumption of new challenges, some of which can be found in the programs of recreation especially designed for the elderly.

Private Recreation

To an increasing degree, particularly in affluent communities, the 1950s and 1960s saw the establishment of numerous kinds of private recreational facilities. Bowling alleys proliferated. Camping facilities designed to take care of the recreational needs of various types of children, for an afternoon or for an entire summer, also appeared with more frequency. Many of these programs provided a good livelihood, for their owners free of the restrictions on time and income sometimes imposed in public recreation programs.

Private recreation may be a type of part-time business in which a physical education teacher may engage. A boys' club after school, a summer program emphasizing the coaching of skills in the various sports, or perhaps a camp for the physically or mentally handicapped also offers rewarding second occupations for hundreds of individuals who spend the major part of the year coaching or teaching physical education.

If you hope to become involved as manager and/or owner of some of these types of recreational programs, it is usually helpful to obtain a background in various phases of business administration. These enterprises provide needed services to thousands of children, youth, and adults in the United States.

Public Recreation

The vast majority of the positions available to students graduating with a major interest in recreation are to be found in the various public recreational agencies. Most of the time, experience within these programs can be gained while still a student. Upon graduation an individual should have a reasonably clear picture of the general types of situations in which he will later find himself.

Positions in programs supported by tax funds emanating from the city, state, and/or county are extremely challenging; however, they may be exhausting. Unlike the teacher in a school, the recreation worker generally is not working with a "trapped" audience; daily attendance at the high school is required by law, but participation at a local playground is not as closely monitored. Perhaps unlike anyone else in occupations associated with physical education, the recreation worker knows immediately whether he is conducting a meaningful program—if he is not, no one comes!

Much of the success of an individual in public recreation is dependent, therefore, upon the extent to which his program matches community interests and needs. He should be adroit at assessing the general tone of undercurrents of the sociocultural environment in which his facilities lie. This community evaluation usually consists of formal as well as informal assessments. Conversations with community leaders and with children on the playground should be coupled with the inspection of more scientifically conducted surveys of community opinion, interests, and feelings. Often the recreation worker will conduct these surveys himself. Generally a program should stem from the participants, and not rest totally upon preconceived interests and attitudes of the recreational worker himself. The recreational worker should be sensitive and also possess various professional tools; the children, youth, and adults he services should give him guidance in how to use his professional tools for their benefit.

The worker on a public playground is usually required to supervise, provide facilities, and provide leadership (either himself, or in the form of recruited instructors) for a wide variety of recreational enterprises.

The day may start with a child-care center, in which volunteer mothers take care of their children and those of other working mothers. Thus the activities involved require a knowledge of child development, as well as of just what two-, three-, and four-year-olds are interested in doing. A program of this nature may require a pre-program of training for the women volunteers.

Shortly thereafter, the older generation may arrive for their daily games of bridge, bowling on the green, and perhaps cribbage. Their tournaments must often be organized, the proper prizes awarded, and culminating ceremonies conducted. Within such a program the primary objective is usually to present a comfortable and yet a dignified environment, in which the participants may compete in reasonably nonviolent terms with one another.

By the early afternoon, the younger children will be coming from school. Prior to their arrival diamonds must be dragged and lined (sometimes with the help of a grounds keeper, and sometimes without this kind of help). During the middle or the latter part of the afternoon, high school students will arrive; and they will stay until the evening hours to close up the facility.

Often during the weekdays, both a male and female recreation supervisor are often present on the larger playgrounds. The woman may be in charge of instituting programs of dance, music, arts, and crafts among the girls; while the man's primary responsibilities may lie in the area of athletics. Both, however, usually cooperate when the relatively frequent special pageants occur.

Almost monthly, on some playgrounds, various special events will be scheduled. Halloween, Christmas programs, and others surrounding recognized national observances, along with various other events which may be dictated by the unique ethnic makeup of the community in which the playground is situated. Often these kinds of festivals can provide a helpful way for various factions within a community to learn to work better together, and to begin to appreciate each other's cultural heritages. The black children celebrating a holiday important to them may be aided by the brown youngsters; while later, when the Cinco de Mayo celebration occurs, both white and black children may take part.

Athletic contests, tournaments, and the like provide a large part of recreational programs. These events and regularly scheduled games are usually initially organized by the recreation director, who may or may not then turn over the actual coaching to various community volunteers. As the quality and outcome of most athletic programs are dictated by the nature of the leadership involved, it is an obligation of the recreational worker to attempt to select coaches who are not only qualified in the various sports, but who also possess other qualities which will make their associations with youth a positive experience for all concerned. Often older high school boys make excellent coaches for the sports of the younger children, an experience in leadership and athletics valuable to both. The playground competitions often provide a less competitive and stressful athletic environment, in which the inferior child may learn to experience the benefits of sports participation without the pressures that are sometimes seen in those more regimented and ballyhooed programs conducted in other facilities.

In addition to organizing programs, the recreational director must make his facilities available for the meetings and competitions of various groups. His general manner, his appearance, and the way in which he deals with adults, youth, and the aged from a number of organizations, will to a large extent determine how the overall community feels about him, and how much they will support his own programs in the future. There are both pleasant and unpleasant ways to unlock a door for these people.

The long hours during which many public recreational facilities must be kept open usually require part-time assistance for the professional workers. The overall image of the recreational facility may be either enhanced or detracted by the nature of the college-age youth who function during the evening hours and often on the weekends. Organized programs may be less apparent on Saturday and Sunday, but the number of people on the playground and park usually increases. Thus, the quality of part-time assistance is an important consideration in the effective administration and supervision of playground activities.

It is frequently assumed that the presence of recreational facilities will reduce various problems connected with juvenile delinquency. However, there have been several studies which indicate that these facilities may, in fact, spawn delinquency. Club meeting rooms become facilities in which a number of activities can be planned, from camping trips and cookouts to pot parties and stickups. Recreation facilities are places where one can collect all kinds of people. You should be prepared as a recreation worker to work with police and juvenile authorities, in the event that problems arise.

Your own background should prepare you for understanding signs of delinquent, immoral, and illegal behavior; and instead of registering shock when viewing and experiencing these kinds of "happenings" at your playground, you may deal in positive ways with social problems you see. The adolescents sitting on the grass and smoking pot near a clump of trees may also be telling the recreation director that he is not planning meaningful programs which would result in their behavior taking more positive directions.

The playground and recreation center are enlargements of a picture of the community. The activities at the center both reflect community problems and customs, and serve to modify the way in which members of the community grow, think, and feel about things. The challenges to the recreation worker during the next decades are likely to be even greater than they were during the past 50 years. The recreation worker is truly working at the grass roots level. He should be acquainted with community facilities, and professionals to whom he may turn for advice or for services for his playground flock other than those he can directly provide. The worker in public recreation is part of a community team composed of the social worker, the local clergy, the school teachers and administrators, as well as the directors of other private recreational agencies (YMCA, Boy Scouts, etc.). All of these at one time or another deal with the same people in a slightly different, but often related, part of their lives. The recreation worker has the obligation to provide his best services and leadership to those he is to serve; and the place to begin to undergird the quality of these services is during the undergraduate years at college.

Summary

Recreation is an enlarging and comprehensive field of service. Positions cover a variety of public and private institutions and agencies; and involve, in addition to athletics, programs in art, dance, music, and virtually any other part-time avocation that can be conceived.

A recreational worker often functions as a social worker, counselor, athletic coach, policeman, gardener, and door-unlocker during a given working day. His effectiveness in his job will come from his ability to work with a number of types of people who may be engaged in a number of recreational pursuits important to them. At the present time, about 20,000 to 25,000 full-time recreational workers are employed in the United States in various community agencies, with over 50,000 more employed on a seasonal basis; while an additional 100,000 work as volunteers in various public agencies. The numbers in private recreation are perhaps nearly as great.

During the 1970s and 1980s, recreational workers will work with community planners in the erection of even more facilities. It is important to see that the expenditures are well used; and their productive utilization is primarily dependent upon the quality of personnel arranging programs. Perhaps you will have a role in the planning and carrying out of these types of programs during the decades ahead.

Student Activities and Discussion Questions

1. Visit your local recreation center, and spend an afternoon there. Count the number of individuals on a given facility or facilities (such as tennis courts, and perhaps the diamond). Plot the number of participant-hours (people multiplied by hours) these facilities attract during this period. How might the number of participant-hours be expanded on this playground?
2. Visit a local playground at night from 7:00 to 10:00 p.m. Who is in

charge? What is his apparent background? What problems do you see within and outside organized programs? How would you handle these problems if you were the recreational worker in charge?

3. Outline the requirements in your state, if any, for certification of recreational personnel.

4. What are the qualifications for a recreational worker in the largest city nearest you? Do they consist of an interview, a performance test, a written test, or no test at all?

5. Interview a female and male recreational worker with B.S. degrees. Try to determine the nature of the problems and the rewards of their work. How do their philosophies toward their positions differ from yours; and in what ways are they similar? How might the differences result in different practices, if your behavior on the playground were later compared with theirs?

6. Whom might you interview, and how might the interviews be done, when conducting a community survey to determine recreational interests and needs? What questions would you place on a questionnaire?

7. In your community, whom would you contact to publicize the events occurring in a recreational program?

References

Books

Brightbill, Charles K., *Man and Leisure*. Englewood Cliffs, New Jersey: Prentice-Hall, Inc., 1961.

Danford, Howard G., *Creative Leadership in Recreation*. Boston: Allyn and Bacon, Inc., 1964.

Dulles, Foster R., *America Learns to Play*. New York: Appleton-Century-Crofts, 1959.

Dulles, Foster R., *A History of Recreation*. New York: Appleton-Century-Crofts, 1965.

Ginzberg, Eli, ed., *The Nation's Youth*. New York: Columbia University Press, 1960.

Green, Arnold W., *Recreation, Leisure, and Politics*. New York: McGraw-Hill Book Co., 1964.

Groos, Karl, *Play of Man*. New York: Appleton-Century-Crofts, 1913.

Hjelte, George, and Shivers, J. S. *Public Administration and Recreation Services*. New York: The Macmillan Company, 1963.

Kaplan, Max, *Leisure in America: A Social Inquiry*. New York: John Wiley & Sons, Inc., 1961.

Kerr, Walter, *The Decline of Pleasure*. New York: Simon and Schuster, Inc., 1962.

Menninger, Karl, *The Vital Balance*. New York: The Viking Press, 1963.

Nash, Jay B., *Philosophy of Recreation and Leisure.* Dubuque, Iowa: William C. Brown Co., 1960.

Outdoor Recreation Resources Review Commission, *Outdoor Recreation for America.* Washington, D.C.: Superintendent of Documents, 1962-63.

Riedman, S. R., *The Physiology of Work and Play.* New York: Holt, Rinehart and Winston, Inc., 1950.

Shivers, Jay S., *Leadership in Recreational Service.* New York: The Macmillan Company, 1963.

Smith, Julian W., Carlson, P. E., Donaldson, G. W., and Masters, H. B. *Outdoor Education.* Englewood Cliffs, New Jersey: Prentice-Hall, Inc., 1963.

Tunley, Roul, *Kids, Crime and Chaos.* New York: Harper & Row, Publishers, 1963.

Ykic, T. S., *Fundamentals of Recreation.* New York: Harper & Row, Publishers, 1963.

Periodicals

American Recreation Journal. Fenner Hamilton Co., 3200 So. Zuni St., Englewood, Colorado.

Parks and Recreation. National Parks and Recreation Association, 1700 Pennsylvania Ave. N. W., Washington, D. C.

Recreation. 315 Fourth Ave., New York, New York.

CHAPTER THIRTEEN

Health Education

Beginning with the 1800s, physical education and what was then termed "hygiene" were closely associated. In the 1830s, five texts were written by American authors, dealing with physiological processes, exercise, and hygiene. The early program of college physical education, instituted in the middle of the 1800s, often combined lectures in health with exercise classes; and attempted to give the students a theoretical perspective which would enable them to perceive the values of education to the human physique.

By the 1860s and 1870s, classes in hygiene were commonly taught in the secondary schools. Their content generally emphasized the control and prevention of communicable disease, with particular reference to material on the then-new germ theory. The dangers of narcotics and alcohol were also covered in these courses given over 100 years ago.

Around the turn of the century, there was an explosion in the field of health knowledge, as well as in private and public agencies concerned with the health of the nation and of her youth. By 1920 a "Modern Health Crusade" was promoted by the National Tuberculosis Association. In 1923 the American Child Health Association was formed. In 1913 the National Safety Council had been created, the forerunner of over 20,000 volunteer health agencies which finally emerged by the middle of the twentieth century.

The widest growth of school health education occurred after World

War I, arising partly from the concern registered when the public became aware of the medical rejections of men examined for possible military service. The National Education Association in the 1920s selected "health" as the first of the Seven Cardinal Principles of Education that they proposed.

The national concern for health during this period was not reflected in the number of college courses dealing with the subject. Those which did exist were usually taught by physicians, because there existed few teacher-training courses specifically designed to train health educators. At the same time, the health courses in secondary school did tend to proliferate. Special attention in these classes was devoted to cleanliness, proper exercise, fresh air, brushing the teeth, food nutrition, and normal growth and development.

In the 1930s, 1940s, and 1950s, changes in the school environment were incorporated into many new buildings. The concept of healthful school living was adopted by many, replacing the narrower idea of personal hygiene. In 1930, the White House held a Conference on Child Health and Protection; and in 1940, 45 national agencies formed the National Conference for Cooperation in School Health Education, with a full-time coordinator appointed to head their efforts.

The initiation of better health teaching in the school was aided in 1936 by the pronouncement of the National Conference on College Hygiene that college instruction in hygiene received the poorest teaching in colleges. But by 1947, it was found that basic courses were required in most colleges; they were taught in small classes and offered sound content. By the end of the 1950s, some courses in the secondary schools and many more at the university and college levels began to expand their offerings to include material on personal adjustment, mental health, as well as various topics relating to sex education (family adjustment, social hygiene, etc.).

During the latter part of the 1960s, increased community concern directed toward the drug problems among the nation's youth has caused health education curriculums, both in high school and college, to be modified and expanded. Instruction of this sensitive and important subject has been extended into the upper grades of some elementary schools.

Increased concern has been directed toward the changing sexual mores purportedly taking place. With this concern have come two trends: an increase in the number of courses in health education, with content related to sex practices; and secondly, a community reaction in some areas on the part of conservative elements, which decry the assumed weakening of the traditional role of the home in providing family life education. By the late 1960s, in the majority of communities in which some form of sex education was carried out, instructors usually had taken great pains to present information devoid of religious or moral overtones. It is to be expected that the issue of whether, and precisely how, to inform children and youth about the biological, sociological, and psychological information in this sensitive area, should be a continuing one in the decade ahead.

Health education as a major curriculum may be found within a physical education major course, usually modified in ways to be described; or within departments or other administrative subdivisions separate from physical education. At the university in which I teach, for example, health education is presently found in the department of public health. Certification to become a health education instructor is gained through the state in which the college or university resides, and is similar to certification issued to other types of elementary and secondary school specialists. Student teaching and graduate work, in addition to obtaining a B.S. degree, is often required prior to issuing a teaching certificate.

The health education major usually includes courses during the first two years which emphasize the biological sciences, human physiology, and nutrition; and content courses in health education. During the final year or two, courses in instructional methodology, related to health teaching and the like, are often found in the curriculum. In addition, the health education major often takes part in some of the applied science courses found in the physical education program.

The expanding health needs of children and youth in the 1960s, and presumably in the 1970s, has prompted, and should encourage, future health educators to obtain broad backgrounds consisting of courses dealing with family relations, mental health, drug addiction, social psychology, sociology, and similar topics. It is apparent that there will be a further expansion of the content of these curriculums in the 1970s, which should continue into the 1980s.

Health educators often work with a wide range of professional people in planning a total health program for an entire community. Public health officials, physicians, educators, psychologists, police officials, social workers, and others often pool their ideas, resources, facilities, and backgrounds into formulating comprehensive approaches either to solve community health problems or, more positively, to prevent potential problems from arising.

Often the health educator will be an important part of a health committee within the school. Such a committee, which might consist of administrators, students, the school physician and nurse, physical education teachers, etc., is generally concerned not only with the health problems and needs of the students, but also with creating and maintaining a healthful school community. Attention on these committees is paid to specific students with health problems, general problems evidenced by the entire school population, the scheduling of health screening examinations (in which the health educator may take part, together with the school nurse or physician); as well as the nature of the colors and general condition of the campus classrooms and buildings, the noise conditions prevalent on the campus, and similar facets of the total school environment. In this context, the health educator aids in the provision of health services, as well as serving in the usual role of providing health instruction.

If the health educator's background is adequate, he is often able to conduct student surveys effectively, covering the entire student body or only the students in his classes, to determine what attitudes, needs, and questions they may have relative to their physical and emotional health. The construction of more fruitful curriculums should hopefully terminate this assessment effort. This is a method of curriculum construction which is increasingly seen in the schools.

Ideally, the background of a health educator in a school should encompass information obtained in medical school specialization in psychiatry, child development, and pediatrics; as well as the content obtained when earning Ph.D.s in sociology, psychology, and perhaps police science—a background which no one individual can possibly obtain. The effective health educator, however, while remaining aware of his or her lack of background in all these areas, should be able to supply the students with sufficient information on the vital subjects related to their personal well-being, which they will eagerly seek or will at least need. Additional help can come in the form of speakers from the community visiting the class. The psychiatrist, psychologist, social worker, and the like provide added in-depth background to all health education courses. At the same time, the teacher should be able to direct her students, if they are mature enough, to specific readings which will expand their backgrounds relative to questions they may hope to have answered.

The health educator should be able to work effectively within a community, and devise a meaningful curriculum which both reflects community mores and meets the needs and questions of students. Although the differences between the students' questions, mores, and needs, and those mores prevalent in the community, may be great indeed, often the health educator can, together with others, help the two generations somehow bridge the gap of understanding.

Summary

Health instruction in schools encompasses a comprehensive content area, including information related to physical health, personal grooming, mental health, family problems, sex education, drug use, and the like. The preparation that the health educator obtains should be very broad. While many times the health education major in the colleges and universities is found, modified to some extent, within physical education departments, there is an increasing trend in this country to separate the preparation for the two disciplines.

However, historically and administratively, health instruction and physical education are closely associated. The physical educator often is qualified to teach courses in health. The basic science courses in human physiology and biology are often similar in both health education and physical education majors during the first two years of college. At the service level, both the health educator and physical educator serve the health needs of youth, although through different methods.

The health educator must often work in various committees within the school and within the community. These groups are often concerned with total community health planning, creating a healthful school environment, providing adequate health services to students in the form of physical screenings and remedial services, as well as with the content of the health education courses themselves.

It is likely that in the 1970s and 1980s there will be an increased need for effective and pertinent health instruction, extending down into the elementary years. If the pressures of the 1960s continue to impinge upon the nation's youth, to some degree they will look to health educators for background information from which they may, hopefully, form answers which are compatible with living the "good life." The health educators of the future should be able to meet these kinds of challenges if their background preparations are adequate; and if their personal philosophies are flexible enough to enable them to work both within communities of adults who to a large degree control the schools, and at the same time to function well within communities of youngsters, who to a large degree may be unable to deal with the pressures surrounding them without mature guidance.

Student Activities and Discussion Questions

1. What community health services and facilities are available in your community? In what way should a school health educator use these, be able to explain them to students, or in other ways take advantage of them?
2. What volunteer health agencies in the community are potential sources of teaching materials? Contact one and determine what films, pamphlets, etc. they have to offer.
3. What needs do you feel that junior high school students have which

may be dealt with in a health education course? High school students? College students?

4. In what ways might health instruction be taught which may differ from the methods used in other secondary school and college courses?

5. In what ways do the health needs and attitudes of various ethnic groups differ?

6. What do you see as definitions of health attitudes, practices, and knowledge? Do you believe that all of the above are necessarily congruent in students; e.g., do students act in accordance with their knowledge? What are the influences of attitudes about health upon health practices?

References

Books

Beyrer, M. K., and Nolte, A. E., *A Directory of Selected References and Resources for Health Instruction*. Minneapolis: Burgess Press Co., 1966.

Daugherty, G., *Methods in Physical Education and Health for Secondary Schools*. Philadelphia: W. B. Saunders Company, 1967.

Foder, J. T., and Dalis, G. T., *Health Instruction: Theory and Application*. Philadelphia: Lea & Febiger, 1966.

Johns, E. B., and Sutton, W., *Health for Effective Living*. New York: McGraw-Hill Book Co., 1966.

Knutson, A. L., *The Individual, Society, and Health Behavior*. New York: Russell Sage Foundation, 1965.

Means, R., *History of Health Education*. Philadelphia; Lea & Febiger, 1962.

Obertuffer, D., and Beyrer, M. K., *School Health Education*. New York: Harper & Row, Publishers, 1966.

Paul, B. D., ed., *Health, Culture and Community*. New York: Russell Sage Foundation, 1955.

————, *Report of the National Advisory Commission on Health Manpower*. Vols. I and II. Washington, D. C.: United States Government Printing Office, 1967.

Walker, Herbert, *Health in the Elementary School: The Role of the Classroom Teacher*. New York: The Ronald Press Company, 1955.

Willgoose, C. E., *Health Education in Elementary School*. Philadelphia: W. B. Saunders Co., 1969.

Periodicals

American Journal of Public Health and the Nation's Health. American Public Health Association, Inc., 1740 Broadway, New York, New York 10019.

Health Education and Welfare Indicators. United States Government Printing Office, Washington, D.C.

Journal of School Health. American School Health Association, 515 E. Main St., Kent, Ohio 44240.

CHAPTER FOURTEEN

Physical, Occupational, Dance, and Recreational Therapy

There are a number of career channels involving service to physically handicapped individuals which are open to physical education majors emerging from many curriculums throughout the country. These are, to some degree, auxiliary occupations to the medical profession. Training in the specialties of physical therapy, occupational therapy, and recreational therapy usually involves at least one year of graduate work after completing the bachelor's degree; accompanied by supervised clinical work of some kind, usually at a hospital or similar facility. Each of these careers deals in some way with atypical children, youth, or adults. At the same time there are certain differences among these careers, which will become apparent as you read the chapter.

The qualifications for entering these interesting and worthwhile jobs are usually set by the state in which you reside, in cooperation with various colleges, universities, and hospitals. Two of these jobs, occupational and physical therapy, usually require an extensive background in anatomy, physiology, and at times neuroanatomy (the makeup of the nervous system); while recreational therapy usually requires some basic background in recreation theory and practices and abnormal psychology, plus graduate work involving work with the physically, emotionally, and/or mentally handicapped.

Occupational therapists and physical therapists usually work with individuals whose primary problem is an inability to move well. These individuals are often beset with other personality problems, and may evidence varying degrees of mental retardation. Frequently, however, even the more severely physically handicapped will possess intellectual capabilities which are normal or above average in nature.

If you are interested in any of these types of positions, you should, during your first year at the university, obtain the requirements for the entrance to the graduate programs in which you may be interested. If there is no formal program for physical therapy (or pre-physical therapy) on your campus, you may wish to transfer during your junior and senior years to a college which has one.

Individuals in all three professions may work with people evidencing a variety of problems. There are also a number of types of jobs within each profession which may be carried out by individuals entering each career field. On the pages which follow, only a most general description of the characteristics of each professional subdivision may be carried out. For further details, you might obtain counseling in your department, and/or from a graduate school, in any of the therapies in which you may be interested.

Physical Therapy

Physical therapy is remedial work with individuals evidencing motor problems gained either through some kind of accident or disease, or evidenced from birth (as is seen in those afflicted with cerebral palsy). Physical therapists also work to rehabilitate people following operations, or after they have received injuries of various kinds. A physical therapist's background usually consists of undergraduate preparation in physical education, a pre-physical therapy program, a pre-med preparation, or perhaps a pre-nursing major. This undergraduate background should contain courses in the mechanics of movement, human anatomy, and physiology; together with chemistry, psychology, and similar courses. The graduate preparation trains the individual to work under the supervision of a physician (usually an orthopedist, or doctor of physical medicine) in the remediation of a number of motor problems and structural problems evidenced by children, youth, adults, and the aged.

There are a number of possible sites in which a physical therapist might work, including a hospital, a school of special education, a doctor's office, an athletic team training room, or in a special facility dealing only with physical therapy and staffed only by therapists to whom patients are referred by doctors. During training, and shortly thereafter, you will be rather closely supervised by physicians whose patients you will be serving. After you gain experience, this supervision may become less marked, as the physicians with whom you work may begin to rely more and more upon your judgment concerning the specific applications of various remedial techniques at your command.

In general, physical therapists are concerned with improving or restoring normal function of all the movement patterns which human musculature is capable of making. Focus is usually placed upon the actions of the larger muscle groups, the trunk and limbs. Occupational therapists, on the other hand, concentrate their efforts on improving or restoring motor functions which are integral parts of basic vocational and life skills. Thus, the occupational therapist will often attempt to aid in the improvement or restoration of various manual activities needed by the factory worker; as well as improving various manipulative self-care skills, including dressing, shaving, combing the hair, eating, and the like.

Following undergraduate preparation, the physical therapist is exposed to more detailed accounts of human anatomy. Particular emphasis is placed upon the manner in which the nervous system controls various movements, and the way in which various structural and neural abnormalities detract from normal functioning. When engaged in actual work with patients, during the latter part of his training, the physical therapist is usually exposed to one or a combination of the various theories of muscular rehabilitation. Even a cursory analysis of these theories requires a book several times the size of this (e.g., Reference 6). However, the theories may be compared and contrasted according to whether they emphasize the use of some kind of mechanical aid, or rely upon the natural movements and manipulations of the body; whether or not they rely upon a rather total approach involving psychological as well as physical rehabilitation; and whether or not they involve assisting the individual by triggering various reflex patterns. In general, in most modern schools of physical therapy the student is exposed to a practical assessment of all of these various methods, and is aided to select from among them those principles and practices which are most appropriate to the treatment of specific movement abnormalities.

The student in physical therapy is taught to assist the movements of an afflicted individual if necessary, to know when the individual should be permitted to perform various movements under his own control, and also how and when to add resistance to various movements it is deemed necessary to improve.

Furthermore, the physical therapist learns to employ various therapeutic tools other than his own hands: these include whirlpools, diathermy, ultrasonics (high frequency sound waves), and the like. Some physical therapy programs help the student to employ his own hands as "tools" in an effective manner, as he becomes able to assess muscular proficiencies by various tests. He may, for example, hold a limb and ascertain the resistance or lack of resistance a patient is able to muster; or perhaps become able to administer a soothing and scientifically correct massage.

Among the problems handled by the physical therapists are the post-operative cases; the infant, child, youth, or adult afflicted with severe damage to the areas of the brain controlling movement (cerebral palsy and similar conditions); muscular dystrophy; arthritic conditions of various kinds; damaged peripheral nerves resulting in localized movement problems; or other more exotic conditions such as Parkinson's disease. Often the therapist may not be able to correct a problem because a method to insure its true remediation has not been discovered; this is the case in some conditions occasioned by malfunctions of the central nervous system (the brain and brain stem). For this type of problem however, the therapist can often afford the individual much needed relief or may bring about a moderate degree of change.

In other cases, such as postoperatives, the therapist's ministrations under the direction of the physician can often totally restore muscular capacity.

More courses dealing with the psychology of illness, abnormal psychology, and the sociology of physical disability, are appearing in catalogs outlining curriculums for physical therapists. More often physical therapists, in common with physical educators, are beginning to consult the helpful data available from the fields of psychology and social psychology.

Educators of physical therapists, to an increasing degree, are training the newer members of their profession to make a careful survey of the total individual when attempting to rehabilitate a movement problem. This trend seems to suggest that some of the more sagacious in this field are beginning to consider the individual more than merely a complex set of levers and pulleys moved by muscles. Instead of asking a child simply to "pull on my arm" when attempting to obtain increases in muscular strength, they are attempting to devise ways to make the child try harder when pulling on an exerciser.

Occupational Therapy

Occupational therapy also requires at least a year in addition to a bachelor's degree in a specialized program which is usually licensed by the state in which the training facility resides. The training, while in some ways similar to that of the physical therapists, is likely to contain more courses in the social and behavioral sciences, with particular emphasis on all aspects of vocational rehabilitation.

The occupational therapist is more "task oriented" than the physical therapist, who is primarily "movement oriented." The occupational therapist sees movement as a means toward an end, with the final objective consisting of making his patient a more productive member of society, able to function better when executing the necessary activities of life.

The occupational therapist does not usually employ the various machines familiar to the physical therapist. The tools of the occupational therapist may consist of a large panel containing doorknobs, switches, hinges, and other household devices for manipulation practice by his patients. The occupational therapist may survey the needed motor skills in a factory assembly line, then design tasks for their patients to match those which may be required on the job. Frames containing zippers, buttons, snaps, and the like are likely to be used by the younger children whose movement capacities the therapist is attempting to improve.

Recreational Therapy

Recreational therapy is a newer member of the "family." In general, the recreational therapist is likely to work with a wide range of individuals in various situations. He may be found, for example, in a state mental hospital attempting to "bring out" some of the more severely depressed patients from their chronic depression. He may work with a dance therapist in a school for the mentally retarded, attempting to improve the students' self-concepts by teaching them socially desirable recreational activities. A home for the aged may also use his services; in such a situation he may be asked to develop games and other recreational activities which may tend to slow the onset of senility.

Essentially, the recreational therapist works through movement to improve other personal and social attributes of the individuals in his charge; although it is usual to find that movement capacities also will improve. Recreational therapists are not officially licensed in all states. Those states which do issue licenses usually require a year of graduate work coupled with intern experiences with individuals possessing various problems, as well as proven ability to work well with people.

As in all fields of therapy, the personal rapport that the recreational therapist can gain and maintain with those he serves is an important consideration. The recreational therapist must like people, be sensitive, and be able to tolerate various kinds of rather severe personality disorders in others. He should also possess the technical background to enable him to discern the "whys" of such atypical behavior.

The academic training of recreational therapists during their college years may consist of several courses in the social sciences, abnormal psychology, social psychology, the psychology of the handicapped, mental retardation; as well as work in the philosophy, theory, and practices of childhood and adult recreation.

Dance Therapy

Dance therapists may not be officially licensed in some states; however, their numbers are growing throughout the country. Their role is to work through rhythm, dance, and total body movement, in an effort to improve the same personal qualities upon which the recreational therapist may be focusing. The recreational therapist may employ a wider range of tasks, including art work, games, dances, and the like; the dance therapist, while employing a smaller number of movement "tools," usually has them honed to a sharp edge.

The research on the effects of dance upon personal, emotional, intellectual, and movement attributes has become increasingly scientific. The findings of these investigations do indeed point out that many useful ends can be served if children and adults with various personality disorders are exposed to the sensitive, dynamic, and expert guidance often offered by the dance therapist. The results are often dramatic in the case of individuals who may formerly have been out of contact with reality in the atmosphere of the mental hospitals. With increasing efforts to learn just why and how dance and rhythm work with certain kinds of people, even further progress should be forthcoming.

The dance therapist should possess a wide and deep technical and performance understanding of several phases of dance. He should possess the ability to teach and to demonstrate various modifications of modern dance, various types of rhythmics, as well as social and folk dances. He should also be aided in his work by the ability to play a piano and various percussion instruments. Like the recreational therapist, his background should be rounded out by the inclusion of courses in the psychologies needed to deal effectively with the wide range of personal disorders to which he may later be exposed.

Overview

The practitioners of the various therapies previously described invariably function professionally in a team of individuals interested in, and

capable of, eliciting improvement in the behaviors of various classifications of atypical individuals. Not only are they likely to work with each
other, but they also may work at various times under or with a physician, psychiatrist, psychologist, speech therapist, coach, educator, or
reading specialist. Their backgrounds often begin with an undergraduate major in physical education or recreation, while their graduate
work is more highly specialized. The opportunities to serve humanity in
these professions are limitless. The energy required to carry out their
duties is great. The number of individuals potentially requiring their
assistance is limitless, while the skills needed for their effective functioning are considerable.

Most of these therapists require a great deal of research to undergird
their practices; while at the same time many practicing these professions are unaware, or have had no opportunity to become aware, of the
newer work which has been produced. Of particular need is the deter-
mination of just what kind of results will accrue from the application of
just what specific types of activities, with a special effort to extract the
influence of the therapist's personality from the post-testing results
obtained. A second basic question which should be more thoroughly
researched, and considered by therapists, concerns just how many types
of activities are needed within a program of remediation to affect just
what range of abilities.

It seems to me, after observing therapists in action, that they often
engage in either too wide or too narrow a range of activities which they
hope will transfer to various other tasks in life. Efficiency in educational
programs of all kinds involves making the best use of the time (and thus
of the money) available. At the present time this principle appears
sometimes to be ignored by too many individuals working in these
paramedical professions.

Student Activities and Discussion Questions

1. Visit a physical therapist, occupational therapist, dance therapist, or
   recreational therapist at work. Following your observations, attempt to
   interview them concerning their feelings about their chosen profession:
   the drawbacks and advantages, the satisfactions and frustrations.
2. Collect information from your college counseling office concerning just
   where graduate schools for these various therapies are located near
   you. What are the entrance requirements? Will the physical education
   major program in which you find yourself fulfill these requirements? If
   not, what additional courses are needed? Are these available in the
   university or college which you are now attending?
3. Review a research article in a journal dealing with one of the

professions discussed in this chapter (*Physical Therapy Review, Exceptional Children, Research Quarterly of AAHPER, Dance Therapy, Music Therapy,* etc.). Is the research well carried out? Are the results confirmed by objective testing and sound evidence? How might the research have been improved? What other groups of subjects might have been used in the experiment? Was the experiment theoretical or applied in nature?

4. Invite a registered physical therapist, or a member of the other professions described, to speak to your class.

References

Books

Cratty, Bryant J., *Developmental Games for Physically Handicapped Children.* Palo Alto: Peek Publications, 1969.

————, *Developmental Sequences of Perceptual-Motor Tasks for Neurologically Handicapped and Retarded Children.* Freeport, Long Island: Educational Activities, 1967.

————, and Martin, S. M. M., *Perceptual-Motor Efficiency in Children.* Philadelphia: Lea & Febiger, 1969.

Daniels, A. S., *Adapted Physical Education.* New York: Harper & Row, Publishers, 1954.

Dayton, W. O., *Athletic Training and Conditioning,* New York: Ronald Press Company, 1960.

Licht, Sidney, ed., *Therapeutic Exercise,* 2nd edition, revised. Baltimore, Maryland: Waverly Press, Inc., 1965.

Logan, G. A., *Student Handbook for Adapted Physical Education.* Los Angeles: Adadon Press, 1956.

MacDonald, E. M., *Occupational Therapy in Rehabilitation.* Baltimore: The Williams & Wilkins Company, 1964.

Morehouse, L. E., *Scientific Basis of Athletic Training,* Philadelphia: W. B. Saunders Company, 1958.

Rathbone, J. L., *Corrective Physical Education.* Philadelphia: W. B. Saunders Company, 1965.

Stafford, G. T., *Sports for the Handicapped.* Englewood Cliffs, New Jersey: Prentice-Hall, Inc., 1947.

Wheeler, R. H., *Physical Education for the Handicapped.* Philadelphia: Lea & Febiger, 1969.

Periodicals

American Journal of Physical Medicine. The Williams & Wilkins Company, 428 Preston St., Baltimore, Maryland 21202.

PART THREE

Reaching
Your Goals

CHAPTER FIFTEEN

Course Content: A Survey

Outlined in the following chapters are some of the traditional, as well as some of the more modern, types of content you are likely
to find in the courses you will take in your physical education major.
Emphasis is placed upon courses and subject matter which are the exclusive concern of physical education, health, and recreation teachers
in training; excluding to some degree the basic courses usually taken
during the first years of college, which are broader in their scope.

The student should perceive some of the interrelationships involved
between the first course taken and those later encountered in the major.
For example, the freshman and sophomore courses in anatomy and
physiology, in which the muscles, bones, nerves, and physiological
processes are examined from a basic standpoint, lead naturally into
courses in the physiology of exercise and the physical principles of
movement. This basic knowledge is applied and related to humans
engaging in sports skills, and in other vigorous physical activities
involving the larger muscles in concert with each other.

Lower-division courses in history, psychology, and sociology are
also necessary underpinnings for upper-division courses in the history
of physical education, the sociology and psychology of sport and motor
activity, and the cultural bases for physical education.

Activity courses in which physical education major and minor students are encouraged to attempt to improve *their own* physical skills

are usually the forerunners of other courses encountered during the upper division years, in which these same students try to find out how to improve the skills of others who will later be in their classes and on their teams.

It is probable that some of the content outlined in Chapters Sixteen through Twenty-three will not presently be found in the curriculum in which you find yourself. You may find that some of these content areas are potentially so important, and currently interesting enough to you, that you will either (a) attempt to get content of this type inserted into the curriculum through the work of a student-faculty curriculum committee, or (b) you will try to enlarge your own background by consulting the recommended literature on the subjects. Some of the content areas reflect a look ahead. The outlines proposed may give direction to the planners of future curriculums.

Other course content areas dealt with in the following chapters are currently and traditionally found in physical education majors, and represent a look ahead for the student who may wish to prepare himself academically for what is to come.

While reviewing the pages which follow, the reader may feel that somehow all knowledge which physical educators must acquire has come from sources outside physical education. However, upon consulting the literature in depth, the student should uncover the fact that while indeed physical educators have borrowed from the basic knowledges of the behavioral, life, and physical sciences, this information impinges upon several courses central to physical education, athletics, and associated careers. Physical educators are interested in explaining, describing, and otherwise categorizing information about vigorous muscular activity, the primary role of which is to somehow develop people, to change them in desirable ways. Much of the research on the part of physical educators during the past several years has sought to discover just what changes may be termed desirable, and exactly what methods are most productive for these hoped-for changes.

Our society has developed, prescribed, and otherwise dictated a number of recreational and athletic activities to which it has given status; participation in which elicits social acceptability and at times an inordinate amount of prestige. Many physical educators, as well as researchers and teachers in training, have focused their efforts on learning more about the underpinnings of these socially-prescribed activities; and on the ways improvement in motor activity can change emotional, perceptual, intellectual, as well as other personal traits. Some of the subject matter areas described in the following chapters deal with these parts of the field of physical education.

From the late 1920s through the 1950s, many physical educators produced writings which were not so much professional as they were evangelical. Instead of taking a truly professional approach to the problems of physical activity by examining just what types of activity should be carried out and to what degrees these activities could elicit positive or negative changes in children, they sometimes inferred, and at other times directly stated, that unequivocally physical activity is good—in all measures, for all people—and indeed often went further in their simplistic statements to say that the more physical activity you have the better off you are!

In a way this was like the medical profession stating that all medicine is good for all ailments, and the more pills you take the better your health will be. Indeed, some physical educators are just now beginning to admit that great amounts of strenuous exercise (i.e., movement "pills") will not necessarily make one less susceptible to infectious diseases.

On the other hand, a number of physical educators with a more scientific and hopefully more objective slant to their efforts have attempted within a number of subdisciplines to take a less value-oriented approach to the role of physical activity in education, leisure time, and the total life space of the infant, child, youth, and adult. They seem to be seeking precisely how much and what kind of motor activity, if applied in what particular ways, help what aspect of life.

Many of these "newer" (they are not always the youngest) physical educators have been struck with the need for evidence to substantiate claims which formerly graced the pages of "principles" books in physical education which were not based upon research data. They have, for example, seen evidence of the fact that not all people of all ages need or can partake of similar amounts of physical exercise. They have questioned the frequently voiced and written assumption that somehow playing games will make people more sociable; and have begun to look at just how game participation reflects cultural patterns, what games are played by children left to their own devices, and have collected a good deal of evidence which suggests just how curriculums can best be planned while keeping in mind the propensities of children as well as the potentials of group interactions.

Some of these physical educators have been struck by the emergence of exercise parlors in the 1950s and 1960s, which reflects a need on the part of people to exercise; but have noticed that customers who signed up for one to five years often gave up after six or seven workouts. These same physical educators, who are not overly emotional about movement but are intellectually agreeable to the ideas behind movement, have been struck by the possibility that a great deal of psychological harm may be done to some children in little league situations, and on junior football teams, while other children seem to flourish within such environments. They seem to be seeking the reasons for the damage, and also the reasons for the uplifting results that seemingly can come to some children within the same situation. Some have traced these differences in program effects to the quality of the leadership available to children, both from organized programs in their schools as well as from the "nonprofessional" leadership emerging from the community (which may be better than the trained physical educator). Most individuals in our field should be impressed by the presence of the various age-group programs in swimming, football, baseball, ice hockey, and other sports, which by their very existence signal the fact that perhaps the needs of children (or of their parents) are not being met by the presently-constituted school programs.

These are some of the principles underlying the information which is to follow. It has been attempted, although somewhat superficially, to awaken the beginning student to some of the *whys* of physical activity; rather than attempting to indoctrinate him with "all is good," "exercise is fun," "athletics are wonderful," or some of the other simplistic and at times simple-minded platitudes to which students in our field have been traditionally exposed. The content attempts to respect the student readers, most of whom are hopefully looking deeply for meanings, and who are better prepared academically upon entering school than were the students of the 1940s and 1950s who are now their teachers.

CHAPTER SIXTEEN

Physiological Basis

Most programs of teacher training in physical education and associated disciplines contain one or more courses dealing in some way with the physiological principles underlying exercise, athletic participation, and similar strenuous types of motor activities. At times this type of information is found in courses dealing rather broadly with kinesiological principles, in which content dealing with mechanical analysis of movement, motor learning, and similar topics are found. At other times, however, separate courses are contained in the undergraduate curriculums dealing with the manner in which physiological functioning reflects, and in turn is modified by, varying degrees of vigorous action.

There are a number of topics important to the physical educator and coach to which knowledge about the physiological underpinnings of human movement may contribute. For example, to train an athlete or group of athletes to achieve maximum performance in some kind of endurance or strength effort, one should know something about the type of strain placed upon various of the bodily systems when maximum effort is required; as well as about the manner in which the various components of the physiological apparatus can be expected to change due to the imposition of strenuous exercise.

Knowledge about physiological principles associated with exercise is also helpful when dealing with the normal child, youth, and adult.

Information of this nature should enable one to determine within reasonable limits just how much exercise should be engaged in by people of various ages, who may vary in their apparent capabilities for strenuous endeavor. The ill-informed exercise zealot usually suggests that all-out exercise is good for everyone. The professional physical educator upon graduation from college should be able to be more precise in the amount of exercise that should be prescribed for an individual; and most important, should know *why*.

Another important professional service that physical educators can, if properly prepared, provide is the evaluation of the various fitness fads which enjoy frequent exposure in the press. The true values of belts which belt people, the wiggly tables that wiggle, the bumpers that bump, and the shakers that shake are often questionable. Only with a sound scientific background can the possible worth of these be accurately surveyed.

Interest in man's physiological functions is as old as recorded history. Knowledge gained by eighteenth- and nineteenth-century scientists undergirds our present ability to analyze physiological processes during strenuous exercise. During the middle of the 1800s the first physiology text in English appeared, as even the early American physical educators began to attempt to base their programs of activities upon sound physiological principles. During the 1920s and 1930s, physical educators began to write texts dealing with the physiology of exercise. Some of these are listed in the bibliography at the completion of the chapter.

At the present time, some physical educators at several colleges and universities have begun to take a closer look at various aspects of human physiology associated with motor activity. This branching of interest has been evidenced in the institution of new courses. For example, in some graduate programs one may take a course in the cellular and biochemical changes which occur within the exercising muscle. Other classes deal primarily with work physiology, and examine how the various components of the physiological apparatus function. Still others have become interested in the neuroanatomical and neurophysiological mechanisms which function as man moves in various manners. Research concerning how the motor nerves affect muscle tissue, and how biochemical changes at the synapse (the physiological space between nerve cells) influences motor activity and motor learning, have occupied the time of other scientists in physical education departments in various parts of the country. Still another approach is in the institution of new courses focused upon the physiological factors eliciting optimum performance.

Upper-division courses dealing with the physiology of exercises are invariably preceded by other more basic classes in biology, human anatomy, and human physiology, taken in departments other than physical education. These courses provide basic content, which later may be employed when attempting to understand the physiology of man in action.

A brief survey of the possible content of courses dealing with the physiological bases of vigorous activity may be found in the outline on the following pages. A more thorough grounding in this type of information awaits you when you actually participate in classes of this type, unless you are enterprising enough to "attack" some of the texts listed at the completion of the chapter.

The Immediate Effects of Exercise
upon Human Physiology

The manner in which activity affects bodily functions may be considered within several contexts. For example, one might examine the immediate as well as the long-term changes in physiological functions in organ efficiency and the like, which are apparent when some type of exercise stress is imposed. The following immediate changes are usually found to occur. These processes are of two types: those which support and supplement the increased amount of exercise engaged in; and those processes which do not directly contribute to the effort expended, and if continued at their higher rate could conceivably interfere with the activity engaged in.

1. The heart may enlarge during exercise, with the walls of the heart thus becoming thinner. If the individual is accustomed to vigorous exercises, his heart will sometimes (not always) squeeze out a greater amount of blood during each heart cycle as the amount of exercise increases.
2. Rate of breathing increases, as the body prepares itself to send increased amounts of oxygen to the blood.
3. The location of the blood in various parts of the body tends to shift in order to accommodate the increased need for blood, and thus nutrients, by the skeletal muscles. For example, decreased amounts of blood are likely to be found in the kidneys and in the organs of the stomach area. The peripheral blood supply to the skin decreases. The blood supply to the brain, however, remains relatively constant, unless an unusual amount of exercise is engaged in. Nature seems to be protecting this vital "signal organizer" even though the individual seems intent upon expending maximum energy.
4. Digestive processes tend to diminish, due to decreased supply of blood to these areas, as well as to the influence of automatic control mechanisms within the nervous system. The churning digestive movements of the stomach will usually become reduced, a phenomenon which some

have suggested can lead to an upset stomach if vigorous exercise is begun too soon after eating.

5. If exercise is continued for a period of time at levels near the individual's maximum, various other physiological phenomena can occur, depending upon how fit the individual happens to be. As the blood sugars (fuel) diminish in the blood and muscles and are used up in energy for the exercise, the effects of various biochemical fatigue products may be evidenced. Increased deposits of acids in the urine may be found, for example. Muscle cramps can occur due to the inability of an untrained set of muscles to dispel waste products effectively.

   Continued vigorous exercise can affect the blood supply to the brain; and contrary to an often-voiced opinion, it *has* been found that some young children can be driven to unconsciousness and nausea with an exercise program which is too vigorous and to which their physiological constitution has not had time to accommodate.

6. Blood cell changes also occur during exercise. While there is not always marked increase in the oxygen-carrying red cells except during the early stages of exercise, the white cell count does rise. The more stressful the exercise, the higher the white blood cell count becomes. The usual explanation for this is that the white blood cells, due to the activity, are washed into circulation from the sides of the blood vessels to which they had been adhering.

Long-Term Effects of Exercise

The long-term effects of exercise depend upon the age of the individual and the intensity and type of exercise imposed. Some of the changes which can be noted in the individual exposed frequently to exercise are rather obvious, while others take place in the various organs and systems which support continued physical effort.

For example, at the surface level there are several obvious changes occurring as the body accommodates to the demands of strenuous exercise over a period of time.

1. A muscular system develops which evidences what may be called hypertrophy (muscles get larger). If this happens, the nature of the exercise has been more toward the production of muscular strength than toward activities designed to promote endurance.

2. The ability to sustain strenuous work for prolonged periods of time increases, and there is an absence of an undue amount of breathlessness at the end of exercise periods. Hard breathing and a fast heart rate quickly subside in well-trained athletes, as their systems do not need to "pay back" the same large amount of oxygen "debt" which will be incurred by the less fit individual. The well-trained athlete or fit worker

is able to do physical work and sustain himself with the physiological processes taking place while performing the work, rather than having to "pay back" his system at the completion of his efforts.

3. The fit individual will evidence less effort when performing a given task. He will have learned how to pace himself, and to avoid undue strain; while his muscles, usually at the unconscious level, will have learned how to work together for greater efficiency.

4. Long-term and sustained regular exercise will result in gradual weight reduction, if the individual maintains a constant diet. Exercise in specific body areas will not result in what has been termed "spot reducing," but will reduce fatty deposits over the entire body; with the amount of fat disappearing in one area dependent upon the percentage of fat normally found there in a given individual.

More basic organ changes will usually occur as the result of prolonged exercise.

1. The heart muscle will grow larger and more efficient, just as will any other exercised muscle. While the heart is in many ways different from muscles you can see, it will become larger with increased work load placed upon it. The myth of the danger of an over-large "athletic heart" has largely been put to chase by most available evidence.

2. Muscle changes at the cellular level will occur, including the enlargement of the muscle cells and increase in the number of small capillaries pushing their way into the muscles.

3. The walls of the blood vessels will become more elastic and stronger. The increased general muscle tension maintained in various skeletal muscle groups, particularly those in the legs, will aid the heart muscle in the pumping action needed to send blood along the arteries and veins.

4. The nature of the chemistry of the blood and muscle cells may also change with the introduction of prolonged exercise. These changes reflect an increased efficiency, at the biochemical level, in utilizing blood sugars when working, and in dispelling waste products which collect in the muscles and blood as the result of hard physical effort.

Designing Programs

In addition to explaining organ changes and more obvious changes due to exercise, your course in the physiological bases of physical activity should help to explain a number of other basic phenomena connected with athletics and physical education. With a clearer understanding of these principles, you should be able to design more valid exercise programs for individuals with various kinds of physical attributes and for athletes in several sports. For example, one of the more basic principles

which should be brought out in such a course is the difference among
the ways in which various types of exercise programs may be applied to
improve muscular strength, strength-and-endurance, or primarily
endurance.

One scale upon which physical activity may be considered contains
"pure" strength acts at one end, while at the other end are activities
which are more dependent upon the efficiency of the heart and lungs.
This scale might be illustrated as follows:

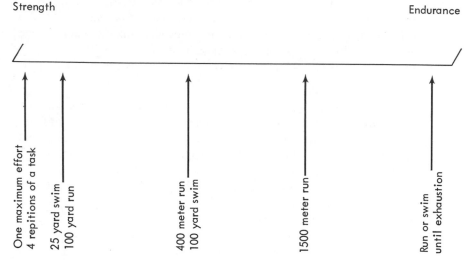

Figure 16-1. Scale showing pure strength items on one end, running or
swimming to exhaustion on the other, with intermediate activities placed in
between.

It is believed by most authorities on this subject that the type of
training to which an individual is subjected will rather specifically train
him for those levels of strength and endurance which are inherent in the
methods used. Thus if single-strength efforts are required, the training
should be of this nature. If a combination of strength and endurance
activities are desired as an outcome of a physical conditioning program, then the training tasks should parallel these.

The often-used method of interval training, to which athletes in track
and swimming are exposed, has been found to produce a great deal of
strain upon the physiological systems supporting sustained effort. In
this method, a group or an individual athlete will be exposed to repetitive "bouts" consisting of, for example, running ten 100-yard dashes
with given intervals of time between. The speed of the runs are kept

constant if the athlete is able; and the strenuousness of the training may be increased by shortening the rest intervals between runs, and/or by decreasing the time in which the athlete is required to run each dash. An interesting new modification of this method results in "sending" each athlete on each repetitive effort when his heart rate reaches a certain level. For example, it may be desired to maintain a constant stress upon the athlete by requiring him to evidence a minimum heart rate of 120 beats per minute during the interval between trials. Thus, the criterion used to "send" the athlete on his second and subsequent trials is not the length of time he rests, but when his heart rate comes down to 120 beats per minute after a higher rate is evidenced at the completion of the first and subsequent trials. The correct application of this method for athletes in various sports, of several ages, and of both sexes, who are training for various events, is dependent upon a sound knowledge of the physiological principles underlying exercise.

Incorrect application of training purporting to prepare an athlete for a given sport, due to a lack of awareness of correct training principles, is commonly encountered. For example, an interior lineman in football, if he plays most of the game, must possess both strength and endurance. Strength is needed for the reasonably frequent one-shot or two-shot efforts he makes against the man facing him across the line of scrimmage, and for the quick burst of effort he needs when tackling a runner. If he is to perform well during an entire game, he needs some measure of endurance. His ability to start quickly and to maintain effort during the last quarter depends upon the ability of various components of his physiology to deal with the biochemical wastes in his muscles due to prolonged exertion.

Despite these obvious needs for both strength and endurance, most football practices during the season seem to produce endurance rather than strength. It is common to see the teams run laps at the beginning and at the end of practice. A professional football team was reported to be proud of its record when running a cross country course during the season. The heavy weight-lifting, strength-producing workouts, in many cases, are engaged in *prior* to the season; rather than interspersed with practices *during* the season, when they are likely to do the most good.

Researchers in the midwest have discovered, as expected, that members of university football teams and swimming teams, if not exposed to strength-producing activities during the season, evidence significant strength losses when weekly strength scores are contrasted! In the case of the football team, however, this loss of strength did not seem to make any difference, as their opponents were found to be losing strength at the same time!

The football coach who finds his linemen not hitting as hard during the latter part of the season, and the swimming coach wondering why his sprinters do not post good times in the final meets of the year, are probably not following sound conditioning procedures, and should look to themselves rather than to their "lazy" athletes when discovering these types of performance changes.

In general, sound athletic training should attempt to duplicate the physiological and psychological stresses the athlete is to encounter in the competition which he will face. Several suggestions for this type of "model" training (model training after the stress of competition) are to be found in the first text reference listed at the end of the chapter. No teacher in your teacher-training curriculum, however, can possibly design for *you* the training programs which will correctly satisfy *all* the possible people, sports, and situations in which you may find yourself later as a coach and teacher. Your professors may only outline general principles based upon sound physiological evidence. The translation of these principles into effective practices will be up to you.

A number of other phenomena should be discussed in a course dealing with the physiological bases of physical activity. For example, such a class may contain information which will aid you to evaluate the manner in which various diet supplements may or may not aid in the production of better performance. The effects of various other substances upon the human system, including drugs and the like, should also be carefully considered in such a context. Many coaches in the 1970s and 1980s will find themselves attempting to deal with a drug problem on their teams. Help in working with youth who believe that the use of one of the milder drugs somehow contributes to their personality growth may come by referring to information you obtained while an undergraduate.[1]

Such common experiences as seeking or obtaining a "second wind" can often be explained by reference to material in textbooks dealing with the physiology of exercise. In a similar manner the nature of fatigue, late season staleness, and the like can also be explained and perhaps overcome, if the coach or physical education teacher comes to his classes and teams equipped with more than a ball, a whistle, and a roll book.

Among a number of new trends seen in the literature is an increased emphasis upon individual differences in physiological makeup. With a sound grounding in this interesting subtopic the prospective physical educator and coach may better understand the less-capable children

---

[1]Recently a gymnast had an article published concerning how the use of marihuana aided him to be more creative when developing and executing his routines!

and youth whom he confronts, by being able to attribute their lack of strength or endurance to factors at the cellular level rather than to a character deficiency.

Summary

Information concerning the physiological bases of physical activity can lead in many directions. Data concerning how exercise elicits immediate changes in organ systems can be found in such courses, in addition to research dealing with the long-term effects of exercise upon the muscular and cardiovascular systems (heart-lungs). Armed with information of this nature, the prospective physical educator should be better able to formulate adequate training programs, and to devise exercise regimes which suit the needs of a variety of participants of various ages, sexes and capacities for activity.

The subtopics often found in courses of this nature include:

1. The effects of various nutrients and drugs upon performance.
2. The matching of training intensities, and the makeup of training programs geared toward specific needs of athletes in various sports.
3. Analysis of long-term and short-term changes in physiological and muscular makeup due to exercise.
4. Evaluation of physical fitness, including cardiovascular efficiency of the heart-lung system, as well as the efficiency of muscular tissue.

Student Activities and Discussion Questions

1. Compare the speed with which two individuals' heart rates drop off, following the same amount of exercise. Have both subjects run a 100-yard dash and then take their heart rates, using the pulse at the wrist, at 30-second intervals for five minutes after exercise. Graph the two scores you obtain. What can you conclude about the physical condition of these two people?
2. Select five people and determine how strong they are in a single effort (i.e., pounds per square inch on a hand-grip device). Ask these same five people to jog 400 yards, and perform the same heart-rate monitoring as was outlined in activity 1. Is there any relationship between their strength scores and the level of cardiovascular condition they evidence after the running task?
3. Discuss with a distance runner the phenomenon of second wind. Has he ever gotten one? If so, when and under what conditions? How does it feel? To what has he attributed it?
4. Devise a preseason conditioning program for a football player (lineman

and back), a swimmer (a sprinter and a distance swimmer), a high-jumper, a shot-putter, or perhaps a basketball player. How have you attempted to match the later physical requirements the athletes will face with the components of the exercise program you have outlined?

5. Collect some research evidence concerning the possible positive and/or negative effects of various dietary supplements upon performance. Evaluate the evidence you have collected.

6. What if you found some of the "star" players on the basketball team you were coaching "turning on" with pot Friday and Saturday nights? What might your course of action be?

References

Books

De Vries, H. A., *Physiology of Exercise*. Dubuque, Iowa: W. C. Brown Company, 1966.

Guyton, A. C., *Function of the Human Body*. Philadelphia: W. B. Saunders Company, 1969.

Hetlinger, T., *Physiology of Strength*. Springfield, Illinois: Charles C. Thomas, Publisher, 1961.

Karpovich, P. U., *Physiology of Muscular Activity*. Philadelphia: W. B. Saunders Company, 1965.

Mathews, O. K., *Physiology of Muscular Activity and Exercise*. New York: The Ronald Press Company, 1964.

Ricci, B., *Physiological Basis of Human Performance*. Philadelphia: Lea & Febiger, 1967.

Vanek, M., and Cratty, B. J., Chapter 8, "Model Training," in *Psychology and the Superior Athlete*. New York: The Macmillan Co., 1970.

Periodicals

Physiology and Behavior. Brain Research Laboratory, Syracuse University, 601 University Ave., Syracuse, New York 13210.

CHAPTER SEVENTEEN

Psychology in Action

The beginnings of formal physical education programs in the United States during the middle part of the nineteenth century often received impetus from physicians. By the turn of the century literature dealing with the values of physical activity began to contain mention of the psychological values of sports participation and of engaging in programs designed to improve fitness.

Psychologists before the turn of the century began to study motor activity and the nature of sensory information from receptors in muscles, tendons, and joints. Indeed, the first experimental psychologists in German laboratories during the 1800s focused upon what was termed the "muscle sense."

By the 1920s statements which might have come from a clinical psychologist were being made by various writers interested in physical education. At the same time several research laboratories in departments of physical education, notably at the University of Illinois and Penn State University, were beginning to study motor learning and motor performance, using the tools of the experimental psychologist.

In 1924 Griffith, a physical educator, authored the first texts in this country dealing with psychology and athletics.[1] During the 1930s, more authors in physical education began to publish their experimental and

[1]These were preceded by several books by European psychologists and physical educators, written during the nineteenth and early twentieth centuries. A review of the history of literature in sport, psychology, and motor activity may be found in the text by Vanek and Cratty, in the references at the end of this chapter.

clinical observations. In the late 1940s and early 1950s two psychologists, Dr. Slater-Hammel at the University of Indiana and Dr. Franklin Henry at the University of California at Berkeley, began to research the psychological factors related to motor performance and motor learning within physical education departments at the two institutions.

American psychologists during the 1950s also began to explore motor performance and motor learning. Prominent among researchers during this period was Edwin Fleishman, who explored the basic abilities underlying the performance of manual skill and big-muscle activity, including physical fitness tests. He used hundreds of air force candidates as subjects in these studies.

In the 1960s there appeared several texts written by physical educators both in the United States and in England. These books provided the impetus for the establishment of courses dealing with the psychology of physical activity in teacher-training institutions during the last decade. Much of the research work upon which they were based was carried out by experimental psychologists who used motor performance measures as convenient ways to explore factors other than movement, including motivation, group interaction, and the like.

Another interesting trend began to appear on the scene in the middle of the 1960s. While American researchers had occasionally evidenced interest in the psychology of the superior athlete, in 1965 this interest began to coalesce, and 35 physical educators and psychologists from the United States journeyed to Rome to participate in the first International Congress of Sports Psychology. While attending this meeting, which had been organized by Professor Feruccio Antonelli, an Italian psychiatrist, the American delegation formed a North American Society for Psychology in Sport and Physical Activity, which is affiliated with the International Group. Its first president was Arthur Slater-Hammel from the University of Indiana. This organization continued to meet yearly just prior to the meeting of the American Association for Health, Physical Education and Recreation, and in October of 1968 sponsored the Second International Congress for Psychology in Sport in Washington, D. C. Over 200 scientists from 35 countries participated in this meeting.

At the present time, many institutions of higher education in the United States have courses at the graduate or undergraduate level in motor learning (or some similar title), which reflect the content obtained from the pages of psychology journals, and from those physical education researchers who have explored the manner in which various psychological variables interact with the movement of the larger skeletal muscles.

There are many facets of psychology which can contribute to the understanding of motor activity. Indeed most branches of psychology can make a contribution to the knowledge which may be important to physical educators or athletic coaches. Traditionally, experimental psychology has been divided into research dealing with motivation, perception, and learning; and indeed all of these subjects are potentially important to the understanding of human movement. Additionally, the investigation of personality has often produced findings of interest to those using physical activity to deal with children and youth in educational settings.

In a more global sense, information from the scientist studying human behavior can lead to the better understanding of how individuals function, as well as to illuminating just how skills may be taught. Some of the information with which you may later become more familiar has been outlined in the paragraphs which follow. For more detailed accounts of the subject matter, which is only hinted at in this chapter, you may want to read some of the texts listed at the end of the chapter.

The Nature of Movement Behavior

Some of the information with which the physical educator should become familiar deals with the identification of basic ability traits which apparently underlie the performance and learning of a number of motor skills. Studies in which a large number of subjects have been given an extensive battery of motor tasks have culminated in findings which suggest that with children and youth one must consider, and at times attempt to improve, a number of separate *motor abilities,* rather than simply practicing a few coordination tasks which are expected to aid that general quality sometimes referred to as "coordination."

In addition to the isolation of these basic ability traits found when subjects are urged to try as hard as they can, it has been found that there are personal inclinations to move in various ways which also probably influence the final effort exhibited in sports skills and in similar activities. People have different preferences for the amount of force they habitually like to expend, or for the rate of speed they prefer to exhibit when engaging in rhythmic tasks. Also, there are individual differences in the space people prefer to use in various motor tasks when moving their limbs or their total bodies.

A thorough understanding of the personal preferences to be expected of individuals of various ages, personality types, and sexes, as well as a clearer picture of the ability traits which have been identified by researchers, will hopefully lead a physical educator to deal more effectively with individual differences seen in the children and youth he is attempting to serve.

Motor Learning

A vast body of knowledge is present in the psychology, education, and physical education literature which elucidates the ways people learn motor skills, as well as the multitude of factors which influence the rates and final performance levels reached following a series of practice trials. Variables which influence the rapidity with which a skill is learned include the manner in which it is taught, the duration and spacing in time of the practice trials, how much of the total skill is practiced at one attempt, as well as the unique characteristics, abilities, and past experience of the learner himself.[2]

For example, it is usually found that there is some optimum amount of spacing of the practice trials, which is productive of the best skill learning. Practices placed too closely together in time often tend to somehow "blunt" performance; while giving the learner a rest between trials perhaps permits the motor patterns to "set-in" the nervous system in some way.

Important also is data which clarifies which conditions lead to the best retention of skill, the ability to re-perform a task after an interval of time. For example, it is usually found that best retention occurs when initially the task has been over-learned. Thus, if the ability to shoot ten free throws perfectly in basketball is desired, practicing until 15 perfect throws are mastered is more likely to produce better retention (of ten perfect throws) than is practicing until only ten successive efforts are perfect.

Retention is also enhanced if the learners are told in exact terms that they are expected to remember the tasks practiced. People seem to practice in more thorough ways if they are aware of the fact that they will need to re-perform at a later date.

Motor skills seem more easily retained than most verbal information, because the former are more likely to be rhythmical, which is usually not the case with verbal information (with the exception of poetry, which is likely to be as easily remembered as are rhythmic movements). Verbal information may also be harder to remember than

---

[2]The research dealing with teaching methods is covered briefly in Chapter Twenty-three, so it will not be dealt with extensively within these paragraphs.

are motor skills because of the manner in which other information dealt with during the retention interval may interfere with remembering, unlike what usually occurs between practices in various movement tasks.

There are numerous other factors which may affect remembering which are covered more extensively in the texts on the subject. The reader would do well to consult them prior to teaching motor skills.

Transfer of training is covered in most learning theories, and is an important consideration when studying motor learning and motor performance. Transfer refers to the fact that learning and performing one skill may either aid or interfere with the performance and/or learning of a second. The concept of transfer permeates most teaching endeavors. The coach attempts to construct practice sessions containing drills and exercises which transfer to the actual game, while the classroom teacher tries to construct a curriculum containing tasks which will transfer to facets of life which will later confront the maturing child.

Generally, the most positive transfer from one task to another will occur if all the elements of the two tasks are similar. Shooting baskets in practice is more likely to aid game shooting if the players during the preparatory period must shoot over and through waving hands, and in the presence of crowd noise. Kicking field goals on the football practice field is more likely to produce good game effort if similar distractions are present.

Improper applications of the principles of transfer by constructing drills in sports skills which do not resemble closely enough the game situations for which they are designed can actually result in more inferior game performance than if the preparatory drill is not engaged in at all! For example, the basketball tip-in drill, in which the centers tip the ball to each other against the backboard and over the basket, might lead to the same inappropriate response under the stress of game conditions (i.e., tipping the ball *over*, instead of *into*, the basket!). Other similar examples could be cited in a number of sports.

Another factor which elicits maximum positive transfer from skill to skill is the construction of cognitive bridges of understanding between the tasks, by specifying to the learners exactly how practice in one may contribute to performance of the other, and noting the elements common and dissimilar within each of the skills involved. Principles of cognitive bridge transfer are not relevant to the athletic coach, but are important when devising programs purportedly helpful to the later achievement of elementary school children.

Motivation

Research in human motivation generally deals with the apparent reasons individuals *select* certain tasks as being important to them, the things that seem to impel them to engage in these tasks for various periods of time, as well as the factors that influence them to exhibit varying degrees of intensity when performing a task. The concept of motivation is usually an integral part of motor learning theories, and is often discussed by lay people, coaches, physical educators, and others. At the same time the measurement of degrees of motivation, and of the influence and nature of motives, is often a rather inexact and difficult undertaking.

In general, motives may be evaluated by the direct means of asking people, via a questionnaire or some similar tool, why they enjoy or dislike something; or in more indirect ways, for example, by measuring performance changes under various purportedly "motivating" conditions. A favorite study of physical educators seems to be to measure the levels of performance achieved by children or youth when subjected to various kinds of verbal encouragement.

The exact motive or motives influencing performance in athletics or in a specific motor task are often difficult to ascertain, because most of us are potentially swayed by a variety of reasons which constantly surround us, any one of which (or combination of which) may, at a given moment, influence our tendencies to perform. The nature of motives which may modify physical performance changes as people grow from infancy into childhood, and adolescence, and finally adulthood. The infant, for example, may be active to satisfy somewhat generalized activity needs, while the adult may participate in certain recreational skills for more complex and specific reasons.

The motivational state of an individual performing motor skills has been demonstrated by experimenters to be not only modifiable but also to influence his performance to a marked degree. Particularly susceptible, for example, are the fitness test scores of boys in late childhood. If members of this group are told, for example, that they are being compared to another similar group, they can usually be counted upon to perform significantly better than if they are not given this type of information.

Motives for action arise from a number of sources. Basic physiological needs for activity impel some to move strenuously, and indeed a reasonably good case can be made for the existence of inherent activity needs at birth.[3] On the other hand, various reasons for the quality and

[3]Marked differences are seen in the activity levels of babies at birth, differences which seem to persist into late infancy, early childhood, and even into adulthood.

quantity of activity evidenced in people can be derived from various kinds of social stimulation; such as the presence of an audience, or the individual's psychological needs for the mastery of his environment.

Although somewhat difficult to come to terms with in objective ways, the study of motivation, and the thorough understanding of unique motive systems in the various children and youth with whom they come in contact, should enable physical educators and coaches to work more effectively within their chosen portion of the educational environment. Perhaps even more important, as educators in activity become more sensitive to the motives of others, they may become better able to assess their own needs. And having acquired this understanding, they may become more sensitive to the ways in which their personal reasons for dealing in physical activity interact with the things that spur their students to action.

Motor Performance and the Development of Other Capacities and Attributes

Even the primitive caveman was aware that practice in skill elicited skill; and the Greeks, 3,000 years ago, were cognizant of the fact that exercise produced strength. However, within recent years findings from the psychological laboratories have begun to suggest that perhaps motor activity in some way favorably changes other components of the human personality. Observations of the maturing child suggested, for example, that the early manual explorations and trunkal movements of infants aided and enhanced their ability to deal visually with seen objects both stable and moving. Several writers and researchers in physical education and psychology have produced findings which indicate that some perceptual attributes are improved by engaging in certain types of movement tasks.[4]

While physical educators for years have insisted that participation in sports and physical education activities contributes positively to emotional health, findings from the psychologists' laboratories have begun to illuminate this complex relationship (i.e., between emotional health and motor fitness and ability). For example, it has been shown that men who in their thirties and forties would be evaluated as the most stable and productive were those who matured earlier and thus enjoyed earlier success in highly valued childhood sports. On the other hand,

---

[4] "Perceptual attributes" refers to abilities based primarily upon the ability to synthesize, select, or interpret information received through various sense organs (eyes, ears, touch, etc.).

their late maturing, and thus not as adept, classmates evidenced less productive adult behavior and less appropriate social and emotional adjustment.

On this subject, as in many within this general area of study, research will sometimes, and helpfully so, contradict assumptions which have been generally accepted for long periods of time. For example, recent data has shown that engaging in vigorous physical activity or observing contact sports as a spectator will not necessarily reduce aggressions contained within the emotional makeups of the participants and spectators. Indeed, some findings suggest that unhealthy aggressive behavior may be magnified as a result of sports participation or observing vigorous athletic contests!

The interactions which might occur between intellectual and academic endeavors and physical activity have been the subjects of researchers in the United States, Japan, and Europe during the past 40 years. And while their findings are too extensive for a thorough review by any publication shorter than a full-length book, there are some interesting indications of which physical educators should at least gain a superficial understanding. For example, it has been found that the intellectual achievement of the more fit children with high activity needs in late childhood may suffer if they are confined to classrooms for prolonged periods of time; while the intellectual performance of less fit children may not be similarly affected by immobility. Treadmill running at about 45 percent maximum produces higher scores in mathematical tasks performed simultaneously than does standing immobile on the treadmill, or running on it at about 80 percent maximum. In studies we have carried out in our laboratory, it has been shown that for some children playing various learning games elicits more improvement in basic academic operations, including spelling and letter recognition, than will extra classroom tutoring carried out in the usual manner, while sitting at a desk.

These and other findings suggest that motor activities can be inserted into educational programs at all levels in more helpful ways than they have been employed in the past. Justification of the use of games and other vigorous movement tasks within the school's total program can only come about if physical educators become aware of the research supporting some of the claims which relate movement and academic performance, and justify the new practices they may attempt by carefully measuring the outcomes of the movement interventions they initiate.

One of the primary movements within the 1960s has been prompted by several educators, psychologists, and others around the country who have suggested that movement activities are somehow the key to unlocking the intellect. By the end of the 1970s most of these pronouncements will have been placed in perspective by the emergence of research which either supports or refutes these claims. The publicity these movement fads have obtained, and the resultant research which they have instigated, are providing for many educators, psychologists, physicians, and others interested in the welfare of children an impetus to examine in greater detail the more obvious aspects of a child's behavior, and bodily efficiency in various movement tasks. This close inspection by others of our "thing" (movement) has been in some ways a boon to physical education; a boon which, if exploited properly (scientifically and educationally) could result in greater service to children on the part of physical educators working through movement. More of this trend was outlined in Chapter Seven, dealing with elementary physical education.

Psychology and Superior Athletes

One of the more recent trends relating psychology to physical activity has been referred to previously in this chapter. The child's, youth's, and young adult's participation in a sporting event is usually a highly important experience to him. The more attention his performance elicits from others—as when trying out or competing at a national or international contest—the more pressure is placed upon the athlete, and thus his emotional (psychological) state has a greater influence on his performance.

Although in Eastern Europe, perhaps for political reasons, the superior athlete has come under the scrutiny of competent psychologists for the past 30 or 40 years, within the United States high-level athletes have received relatively little attention by qualified members of the psychological community. The available research until the latter part of the 1960s usually consisted of isolated studies, rather than coherent and sustained efforts with a large group of athletes or within an important problem area.

At the same time, researchers both here and abroad have begun to form helpful guidelines for the coach dealing with the competitive athlete.[5]

There are reasonably sound techniques emerging which may aid the coach to either calm the too-excited athlete, or to activate the athlete

[5]The more "scholarly" physical educators sometimes scoff at the necessity for dealing with information concerning athletes, and high-level athletics, as such attention will purportedly take attention away from the "average" child, etc. I believe, however, that physical educators should not ignore the more gifted performers in their midst, just as the mathematicians should not ignore the more able within their classes. Indeed the boys or girls who are placed in the stressful position of competing in highly competitive athletic programs probably deserve extra attention to their emotional needs, and to their potential emotional problems.

who is too passive prior to a contest. Reasonably manageable evaluation instruments are becoming available, which will enable coaches to engage in cursory personality trait assessments of boys and girls on their teams. This type of evaluation should help the coach to deal more effectively with each individual according to his individual needs, motives, and characteristics.

To an increasing degree throughout the world, qualified psychologists are becoming attached to high-level teams and engaging in assessment functions, as well as counseling the competing athletes. For example, in the 1968 Olympics two psychologists were officially attached to teams: Dr. Miroslav Vanek worked with the Czechoslovakian team, while Dr. Frederick Blanz evaluated and counseled the Finnish team. Other psychologists accompanied teams as unofficial observers, including Professor DeSilva who functioned in this manner with the Brazilian Olympic team.

There is enough data stemming from research with superior athletes at the present time to construct an entire course dealing with the psychology of the superior athlete. An increasing number of behavioral scientists and psychiatrists have begun to focus their attention upon this interesting group of high achieving and highly motivated men and women.

Overview

There are several other types of problems which might be considered in courses dealing with psychology and physical education, including information regarding the interaction of visual perception of moving objects with various sports skills, and the examination of the movement sense (kinesthesis) which gives an awareness of the nature of our movements without the necessity of constantly watching our limbs and bodies in action.

Findings from the physiological psychologist can extend our knowledge of the mechanisms underlying emotions connected with sports participation. Research of this type, some of which is being carried out by physical educators in our larger universities, may contribute in positive ways to practices in physical therapy and occupational therapy.

An increasing number of physical educators whose doctoral programs have contained a large number of courses in psychology and related subjects are carrying out psychological research, and imparting their findings to undergraduate students. Additionally, physical educators who have been in the field relatively long have retreated from the more applied courses, and have begun to devote their efforts to gaining an understanding of the manner in which various psychological parameters can enhance our understanding of man in action. At a recent national convention of AAHPER, 43 research papers were delivered which had something to do with the psychological bases of physical activity, while only 30 papers concentrated upon the physiological underpinnings of human action. It seems that more and more physical educators, coaches, and physical therapists are beginning to realize that it is *behavior* rather than nerve impulses, and observable movement rather than blood enzyme changes, with which they are primarily concerned. Psychology, the "study of behavior," seems to be providing a great deal of helpful information to these members of your chosen profession.

Summary

To an increasing degree, principles derived from research in psychology have come to influence the thinking and practices of physical educators. Psychology, the study of behavior, has been found to be useful in the understanding of a number of facets of physical education, athletic coaching, and associated subjects. The study of motives has prompted physical educators to become more sensitive as to why people select certain sports in which to participate, why they participate with various intensities once they choose their sport, and also why they practice the activity for certain durations of their lifetimes.

Findings from research in perception, personality, and intelligence have often given physical educators cues concerning how they may make a contribution to broader aspects of the personality than are usually thought of as associated with motor activity. Learning games seems to help some youngsters to acquire certain academic operations; and observation of the first movement behaviors of infants and children has aided students of child development to understand the early beginnings of perceptual development.

Future progress in work relating psychology to physical education and athletics will probably be given impetus by the increasing number of teacher-educators who are obtaining backgrounds at the doctoral level in the behavioral sciences. More understanding of the manner in which psychology enlarges our understanding of people should lead toward more sensitive and effective physical education instructors and coaches who are working directly with children, youth, and adults through physical activity.

Student Activities and Discussion Questions

1. Take one or two tennis balls, and devise a motor performance task which is reasonably difficult (an example would be to juggle two balls

with one hand). Plot a learning curve as the result of ten trials of practice. Study the shape of the curve you produce, and attempt to explain fluctuations in progress you might observe.

2. Discuss the nature of various motives that might influence the performance of an infant of one year, a school boy of ten years, and/or a college girl of 20 years, in various motor tasks.

3. Ask your classmates to "tap rhythmically" with a hand or foot. Observe or measure any differences in speed preferences between individuals. Discuss the reasons for these differences, and how they might influence initial progress in dance. Can you devise other rather unstructured movement tasks which might bring out personal preferences for moving in various ways?

4. If there are athletes in your class, discuss with them why they feel they participate in athletics. Have their reasons changed over the years? Do their motives fluctuate from day to day, from week to week?

5. Devise an ideal elementary school day, placing physical periods at optimum times during the day and making them what you think to be an ideal duration of time. Keep in mind some of the information contained in this chapter, and also the fact that it has been found that reasonably intense physical activity immediately following learning can sometimes obliterate the memory of that learning.

6. Rank your classmates in some measure of strength, then rank them according to their scores in another measure of running speed. How do the two sets of rankings compare? What do the similarities or differences tell you about how you might have to train individuals for athletics?

7. Review one of the books on motor learning listed in the references. Present your opinions of the content to your classmates.

References

Cratty, Bryant J., and Hutton, R., *Experiments in Motor Performance and Motor Learning.* Philadelphia: Lea & Febiger, 1969.

———, Martin, S. M. M., Jennett, C., Ikeda, N., and Morris, M., *Movement Activities, Motor Ability, and the Education of Children.* Springfield: Charles C. Thomas, 1970.

———, *Movement Behavior and Motor Learning.* Philadelphia: Lea & Febiger, 2nd ed., 1967.

———, *Movement, Perception and Thought.* Palo Alto: Peek Publications, 1969.

———, *Psychology and Physical Activity.* Englewood Cliffs, New Jersey: Prentice-Hall, Inc., 1968.

———, and Vanek, Miroslav, *Psychology and the Superior Athlete.* New York: The Macmillan Company, 1969.

————, *Some Educational Implications of Movement Experiences.* Seattle: Special Child Publications, 1970.

Knapp, B., *Skill in Sport.* London: Routledge & Kegan Paul, 1964.

Oxendine, J. B., *Psychology of Motor Learning.* New York: Appleton-Century-Crofts, 1968.

Singer, R. N., *Motor Learning and Human Performance.* New York: The Macmillan Company, 1968.

Whiting, H. T. A., *Acquiring Ball Skill.* London: G. Bell & Sons, Ltd., 1969.

CHAPTER EIGHTEEN

Sociology in Sport
and Physical Activity

The study of sociology in essence involves the study of society. There are many ways in which society can be studied and many facets of society which can be explored. The interaction of the individual with his society is also the legitimate concern of the sociologist.

Physical educators interested in the sociological implications of sport and physical activity have begun with increasing energy to study several possible societal-activity relationships. Some, for example, have focused their attention upon the nature of sport in the American society, and within other nations of the world. Others have taken a broader outlook, and have become interested in the manner in which game participation by children and adults both reflects and in turn molds various types of cultures and subcultures.

A fruitful field for exploration, and one which has been little tapped, involves an examination of the various types of games prevalent within various subcultures on the American scene in the 1970s. Many ethnic, racial, and national groups remain relatively intact within the larger American cities; while various nationals from some of the European countries have indicated a propensity to move to small towns in America, towns whose climatic and cultural characteristics generally resemble those of the homeland. A more thorough understanding of the manner in which the various racial groups (e.g., the Negro children of the ghetto) play, and the factors which govern their play will lead toward more effective and meaningful physical education programs in the schools within these same segments of society.

Another important source of information for the physical educator is the literature in social psychology. In addition some physical educators, employing variables first identified by the social psychologist, have begun to study the influence of various aspects of society upon the individual performing, and also have begun to illuminate principles of small-group interaction which may be applied to situations in recreation, sport, and physical education.

Among the subjects found in this part of the literature are studies and information dealing with the social organizations of children at play, the effect of the audience upon team and individual performance, the nature of competitive and cooperative behavior in sports and in less formally organized physical activities, the nature of leadership on teams and in children's games, as well as the influence of the family and peer group upon an individual's performance and feelings about physical performance.

An increased interest in and emphasis of the sociological context in physical education is reflected in the formation of various national and international organizations during the 1960s. For example, in April 1966, a committee on sport sociology, part of the International Council for Sport, met in Cologne, Germany, with the theme "Small Group Research in Sport." The "Big Ten" schools sponsored a seminar on sport sociology at Madison, Wisconsin, in 1968. Papers were read by outstanding sociologists interested in sport and by physical educators studying the manner in which sport interacts within the total cultural context.

More important, reasonably objective information is beginning to be synthesized for physical educators, and additional data is being obtained in this country and abroad, some of which should be immediately helpful to the physical educator and coach. The more sensitive worker in a physical activity environment has long realized the importance of the nature of the broad culture, and of the subculture in which he is working. With the increased understanding provided by this new scientific emphasis, physical educators and coaches should become more effective in their dealings with groups, and with individuals who are in turn influenced by group pressures, goals, and expectations. Some of this information is summarized in the pages which follow.

Individual-Group Expectations and Pressures

As a single youth performs a motor task he is either directly or subtly influenced by two types of audiences. One kind of audience may consist of a crowd of his onlooking friends on the street corner, his peers in the physical education classes, or members of the community in the bleachers on the side of the athletic field.

The second type may be thought of as an unseen audience. These are the people always present in spirit, and in the mind of the performer; they are children against whom he may be comparing his performance, the family at home who may later learn about and either praise or ridicule his efforts, or other members of his subculture who have attached varying degrees of status to his efforts.

For the physical educator or coach to remain unaware of the marked influence of either of these two groups, who either obviously or subtly "look over the shoulder" of the children in his charge, seems worse than short-sighted. Certainly the performing child or youth is unable to ignore them, and is consciously or unconsciously reacting to them most of the time he plays and competes, and when he wins or loses.

In general, it has been found that the audience physically present when an individual performs a motor task can have various effects upon his efforts. If the performer is proficient, experienced, and exerting less than his best efforts, urging by a crowd is likely to improve his performance. On the other hand, if a child or youth less adroit and/or experienced is subjected to some type of audience reaction when performing, he is likely to manifest less than his best effort.

Complex skills with which the performer is not familiar may also be disrupted by the audience, while simple skills and reactions may improve with the added spur to action provided by onlookers.

Athletes in high school, college, or competing professionally are likely to be sensitive to the social status which a group of spectators can bestow upon them, and the financial rewards which may be forthcoming from this same group of people. It is interesting to note, however, that in-depth research with reasonably good athletes at several levels has revealed that these performers were found not to like their fans very much. Apparently it was felt by the athletes that even their more rabid supporters were likely to become severe critics when they were not too successful, a transformation which usually occurs at some time or another. Additionally, athletes were found to be somewhat resentful of those among the throngs of cheering fans who attempt to gain their status, manhood, and feelings of success from the sweat of the athlete's brow, rather than earning these qualities from their own efforts.

Audiences are rarely silent. They may encourage, support, or disparage and ridicule performing athletes or children in the playground. The effects of this audience behavior has also begun to be investigated by several scholars in our field. It has been found, for example, that if the supporters are highly valued friends their remarks can have a marked impact not only upon the performer's immediate efforts, but upon his long-term feelings about himself and his "friends." Children, particularly boys, whose physical ineptitude elicits ridicule from their playmates not only admit to receiving this type of social censure, but as a result may evidence a generally low concept of themselves.

There are many lessons to be learned from the type of findings outlined above, as well as from other information now emerging. To suggest that participation in games will be helpful socially and/or personally to a child or youth is imprecise. Rather, one must consider the quality of the social environment in which the participation takes place before attempting to evaluate whether physical activity has indeed been "good" or "bad" for the child.

Competition and Cooperation

Competition is another facet of the social context which has come under consideration recently, although one may read in literature dating back over 100 years about how important competition in athletics is to a maturing child.

In general, the data suggests that competition is an extremely basic facet of the human personality. Babies a few months old compete for objects placed between them, while animals rather low on the evolutionary scale evidence competitive behavior under certain conditions.

Competitive behavior will occur in children when two or more see themselves as being able to gain some advantage through their participation, and as having some chance of occasionally winning. Their competitor must be perceived as being not more than 25-35% better or worse than they are for striving competitive behavior to occur, according to some researchers.

A question which some of the information on competition should pose for budding physical educators and coaches is: With whom should a particular child be encouraged to compete in order to encourage the most vigorous participation? It has been found, for example, that by late childhood a child can predict with accuracy in just what place he will finish in a wide variety of physical tasks, when confronted with a number of competitors whom he may not even know. Thus, it might be assumed that for maximum effort a child might also be encouraged to compete against himself. Children may be encouraged to better their own efforts in succeeding exposures to activity, even within highly competitive situations, as well as trying to best their opponents in more obvious ways.

In most physical education and athletic situations, both cooperative behavior and competitive responses occur. A youth competes with others on his team for a place on the squad, then he cooperates with those who also made it in order to compete against those on other teams. The obvious and less obvious factors which mold both competitive and cooperative efforts seem well worth the serious consideration of all purporting to lead vigorous physical activity toward objectives helpful to the unfolding personalities of children and youth.

Children left to their own devices, within highly competitive cultures as exemplified by the United States in the 1970s and 1980s, are likely to insert a great deal of strategy and skill into the game patterns they evolve. Thus a study of the nature of a culture may be, and has been, made by reference to the types of games which are developed by its children.

Social Evolution in Children's Play

The characteristics of children at play have been studied as an important part of several noted scholars' efforts to measure the basic natures of both primitive and "modern" cultures around the world. Within the American culture this same type of examination has been carried out with increased attention.

Curriculum designers and others working directly with children at all ages should be aware of what children and youth of these various ages will do, with reference to the simple social organization they evolve if left to their own devices. Inappropriate activities which do not correspond to a child's "motor age" or "emotional age" or actual chronological age are not helpful. On the other hand, with some awareness of the social stages children normally pass through while at play a physical educator is more likely to match complexity of activity with the complexity of social organization a specific group of children can tolerate.

In general, a child at about the age of two or three years engages in what has been termed "parallel play"; that is, two or more children may tend to play at the same thing, but do not directly interact with each other. Each child may bounce a ball, and be socially stimulated by an adjacent child bouncing *his* ball, without throwing the ball to another child.

Later, children begin to play in small groups of two or three children, usually of the same sex. A further stage consists of larger groups, with the boys in late childhood evidencing a tendency to play games with reasonably complex rules.

Several trends may be noted in the social behavior of children at play in the American culture, trends which should be carefully considered by physical educators. In general, girls are seen to play vigorous games previously thought of as the exclusive property of the boys. More important is the tendency seen in American children to engage in games in which there is a large amount of intellectual content, strategy, or other type of thoughtful experience. American children, just as children have been seen to do in every other culture around the world, tend to insert into their game patterns qualities which they perceive will "get them by" as adults. Children in the United States are undoubtedly beginning to realize that large muscles are not as consistent a criterion to success as are intellectual capacity and cleverness, and thus they are inserting intellectual qualities into their games. At the same time, these children possess muscles which require action and bodies which demand action. It is believed that successful elementary school physical education programs will in the future contain vigorous activities, which the children will have had some part in planning, and the execution of which will require a good deal of intellectual involvement. This point was discussed previously in Chapter Seven, dealing with elementary physical education.

The Family and the Child's
Performance

Interesting data have emerged from studies carried out in my laboratory relating the performance of children and youth with their families. Information obtained in the early 1960s suggested that the performance of adolescent boys in various running and jumping tasks was correlated rather significantly with that of their fathers during these same years of life.

More recently, high positive correlations were obtained in young children between their physical performance and the attitudes of their parents about the worth of physical education and physical activity. Parents who have positive feelings about activity produced active and proficient children; while those who held less positive feelings apparently transmitted the disinclination to perform well to their children.

Taken together, these findings are probably what one would logically expect. It is apparent that how the child acts and reacts within a physical education setting is to some degree dependent upon the physical "equipment" he has inherited from his parents, as well as the attitudes about activity the parents may have instilled in him prior to his being confronted by a physical educator.

The physical educator may, therefore, have a relatively easy time instructing, motivating, and improving some children and youth with whom they work; while other children, due to negative parental feelings and/or poor inherited physical attributes, evidence less zest and ability.

The former type of child is usually lauded, and related to well by the physical educator; while the other child may suffer further social punishment by his peers and even by the athletic coach and physical educator with whom he is confronted, a situation harmful to the child's capacity for and inclination to engage in physical activity.

The Child and Youth in
Various Subcultures

Not only game characteristics but also the performance capacities of children are probably molded to a marked degree by the values and conditions within the part of the culture in which they find themselves from birth. We are finding in our studies, for example, that the black child in the ghetto seldom lacks development in and capacity for engaging in activities requiring effort of his larger muscles. He can run fast, jump high, and otherwise evidence physical vigor and toughness, as these are qualities which may contribute to his success in his unique subculture. This same child may evidence the ability to engage in imaginative verbal interchange, while sometimes lacking the ability to read well—at least to read the middle-class, white jargon usually presented to him in the available texts.

On the other hand, the child in the more privileged part of town less often evidences reading problems. He is highly verbal and may possess an extensive vocabulary. Having had the opportunities to color and to draw since infancy, he can often write well; but he may lack the expected development of the larger muscles.

At another level, it is obvious that various subcultures in America encourage, and at times facilitate, proficiency in various competitive sports. Players of the "rich man's sports," well-known and superior teams in tennis, golf, and swimming, are usually found in the high schools within the economically more privileged areas of the larger cities. Contact sports, football and the like, are more often found to consist of teams of youngsters from the less-advantaged portions of a city, perhaps partly because of the feeling on the part of boys in these areas that athletics is one of the few avenues of success. Also, there is evidence that boys of some racial groups found more frequently in the less-advantaged sections of town tend to mature earlier (e.g., the black and Chicano) than do boys with Anglo-Saxon ancestry. Early maturity leads to more strength and endurance, and to earlier and thus more prolonged success in athletics.

Specific national groups also have made, and continue to make, specific contributions to the development of sports in the United States. For example, the German and Czechoslovakian immigrants brought their *turnvereins* and *sokols* to American cities, breeding places for boys and girls interested in and proficient in gymnastics, many of whom became coaches of the sport when adults. Recent immigrants from Puerto Rico, Cuba, and Hungary similarly have spurred the emergence of soccer and water polo within certain parts of the country.

It is believed that an effective physical educator, finding himself within his first school or recreation center, should come equipped with the ability to perceive accurately the signs which will lead toward an accurate "reading" of the needs, inclinations, and physical skills of the members of the subculture in which he finds himself.

Acquisition of knowledge about the social dimensions of physical activity should enable the physical educator and coach to determine how he might better work with children at several levels. At one level, for example, he may acquire information which will enable him to engage in curriculum planning, and to meet the needs of children with a view to making his program congruent with the broad cultural and social environment in which he finds himself. At a second level, he may become more sensitive to various social pressures impinging upon individual children. For example, the physical educator may be able to deal with the demands and attitudes of their parents.

At a third level, increased awareness of the manner in which various factors within the social clime may influence the performance of groups and of individuals may enable the physical educator or coach to manipulate components of his program to produce better outcomes. He may, for example, become better able to help children choose up sides without the accompanying social stigma which comes from being chosen last, by using the roll book for this type of selection process without allowing a youth to be aware of whether he was chosen first (or last).[1] The physical educator may also become better able to arrange competitive situations by handicapping contestants in a desirable way; and become able to detect and develop leadership in some of the children and youth whose social development may be aided by leadership experiences.[2]

Summary

The coach and physical educator must invariably work within some cultural context. The team members confronting the coach not only

---

[1]Team captains might do this type of selection, by using the roll book, attempting to make up teams of equal competence, and *then* drawing to determine which captain will lead which team.

[2]One amazing example of being insensitive to the effects of social censure upon performance, which came to my attention recently, involved an elementary school physical education teacher who permitted team captains daily to "fire" and "trade off" their most inept players.

react to the leader selected by the board of education, but also select their own leaders and interact with each other in complex ways, which if understood enable the educator to work with them toward educational and performance goals in a more effective manner.

Children at play, both in the prevalent white, middle-class environment, as well as within various subcultures, may evidence inclinations for activity and motives directed toward specific activities which should be accurately evaluated by those attempting to work with them in physical education and/or athletics.

Information concerning the nature of group motives, competition, the influence of the peer group and family, as well as data dealing with broader social and cultural considerations, are all important for the "well-armed" and well-equipped physical educator and coach to possess.

Student Activities and Discussion Questions

1. Visit an elementary school for an entire day (or for a week, one hour a day). Survey the types of games the children seem to be engaging in spontaneously, and note the complexity of the social organization they bring to these games. Are there discernible sex and/or age differences? What other characteristics do you notice? Are these influenced by the unique cultural setting in which the school resides? In what way?
2. List the factors influencing competitive behavior. What are the specific influences of these factors?
3. Devise a game program for elementary school children containing a maximum number of opportunities for their intellectual involvement. At what stages, or in what games, might this type of involvement be greatest? In what types of activities or games is there likely to be the least amount of intellectual involvement on the part of the children?
4. What types of physical activities might be engaged in most by the ghetto youngster of Puerto Rican heritage, by the middle-class Jewish child, and by the white, male adolescent in a wealthy community? To what factors can you attribute the differences seen?
5. Go to a recreation center in a section of town unlike the type in which you were raised. What do you notice about the manner in which activities are chosen? How are the recreational choices and other behaviors in physical activity different from those which might be observed in recreation centers to which you were exposed while growing up? Can you account for any differences seen?
6. Obtain a sociogram of an athletic team by plotting the responses to a questionnaire in which team members indicate their first, second, and third choices of friends, as well as their least-liked teammate (be sure to

keep the information collected confidential). What do you notice about your diagram? Are there cliques, or team members whom no one seems to feel strongly about in either a positive or negative manner? What do you predict may happen to this team when confronting competition?

7. Using the team above, observe the manner in which they interact in a game. Who tends to cooperate with whom? If it is a basketball team, who tends to pass to whom? Do these direct interactions at play tend to be predicted by the sociogram you collected prior to observing them? What guidelines can you formulate for the most effective handling of this team and of the individual members making it up?

References

Cratty, Bryant J., *Social Dimensions of Physical Activity*. Englewood Cliffs, New Jersey: Prentice-Hall, Inc., 1967.

Kenyon, Gerald, ed., *Sociology of Sport*. Chicago: The Athletic Institute, 1969.

————, "A Sociology of Sport: On Becoming a Sub-Discipline." *New Perspectives of Man in Action*. Cratty and Brown, eds. Englewood Cliffs, New Jersey: Prentice-Hall, Inc., 1969.

Loy, John, and Kenyon, Gerald, *Sport, Culture and Society*. New York: The Macmillan Company, 1969.

————, "Game Forms, Social Structure, and Anomie." *New Perspectives of Man in Action*. Cratty and Brown, eds. Englewood Cliffs, New Jersey: Prentice-Hall, Inc., 1969.

Ulrich, Celeste, *The Social Matrix of Physical Education*. Englewood Cliffs, New Jersey: Prentice-Hall, Inc., 1968.

CHAPTER NINETEEN

Historical Perspectives

Introduction

Most college curriculums purporting to prepare physical education teachers contain one or more courses in which the historical backgrounds of physical activity and athletics are considered in some detail. This type of information should not only enrich your knowledge in general, but should also enable you to assess the sources from which various components of current programs have sprung. Furthermore, an in-depth awareness of the historical bases of physical education should better help you to perceive new directions which are presently apparent in physical education in the United States, or which might come about in the near future.

The history of physical education can be studied in a variety of ways. In addition to surveying the usual "what happened in what decade" approach, as is employed on these pages, the enterprising student may follow an historical trend, tracing physical education from the time of the ancient Greeks to contemporary happenings in the United States. Individuals who have had important influences upon physical education throughout the centuries may also be studied. A given practice or teaching method may also be researched, with the attempt made to discover its historical roots.

Prehistory, Cultural Anthropology

In general, information concerning the history of physical education cannot be divorced from the total study of history itself. Throughout the time written records have been kept, the type of physical activities and sports a people have engaged in both reflected and molded the type of civilization and culture in which they resided. Warlike civilizations have engaged in vigorous activities, which in some ways prepared their populations for the rigors of conflict. Competitive cultures similarly have evidenced competitive games. In all cases the young have been taught the physical skills which they would need as adults by their elders.

Much of the literature dealing with cultural anthropology is rich with information concerning how primitive tribes still existent today interact with each other in various games and sports. These same journals recount the manner in which their child-rearing practices reflect the problem of preparing the young for the physical prowess they may later have to display. Through a perusal of this type of information one is able to at least catch a glimpse of the manner in which prehistorical man became "physically educated."

A thorough review of this literature has led one author to state that "play, games, athletic sports and dances have been recognized as universal to cultures the world over." However, this same writer cautions that the manner in which these movement ingredients are woven into the entire cultural pattern may differ markedly from culture to culture. For example, research suggests that in countries with warmer climates, one is likely to find fewer games of physical skill. Among tribes and peoples who inhabit high altitudes, endurance is found in various sport and game forms, often including the apparent preference for long-distance runs.

Other investigators have found moderate relationships between child-rearing practices and game patterns. A moderate relationship was found when the incidence of games of skill, strategy, and chance were tabulated within 56 societies. Games of physical skill were found in tribes in which rewards for achievement permeated the parent-child relationship. Games of strategy were found in cultures in which obedience was emphasized in childhood. In cultures which emphasized responsibility, games of chance seemed to predominate.

Many interesting parallels can be perceived between activities in so-called modern societies and the various cultural patterns of the primitive tribes. For example, the extensive preparations for war, with the secret planning, war dances, conditioning, and the like, have their counterpart in the elaborate training, game plans, strategy meetings, and pep rallys which accompany American football. The substitution of games and warlike dances for actual physical conflict is seen in various existent primitive cultures, and also perhaps in various international competitions engaged in by societies higher on the technological and social scale.

Recorded History of Physical Education

Books dealing with the history of physical education seldom dwell overlong on the beginnings of physical activity before the dawn of recorded history.[1] Rather, they usually begin their narrative describing the manner in which sport permeated the life of the ancient Greeks and Romans.

The historical discussions available usually pay relatively little attention to the history of physical activity in the various countries of Asia, while the development of programs in Europe during a period of 2,000 years is given rather extensive treatment. Scanning of these documents reveals that components of programs which resembled physical education as we know it today were at various times closely aligned with classical medicine, religion, art, politics, and, of course, the total educational program as perceived at a given time in a given country.

Several major threads can be traced through the history of physical education. For example, through the centuries one can discern varying degrees of importance attached to physical activity in the total educational program. In the same way, today within various schools in our country there may be found different educational philosophies that dictate the amount of time to be devoted to physical education classes, to the content of these classes, and even whether they are permitted to exist at all within the program.

The early Greeks and Romans seemed to feel, particularly during their earlier periods, that the physical and the intellectual abilities of man were inseparable. The alert faces which were placed over the muscular bodies of their statues attest to the nature of the close association they perceived between the mind and body.

During the Dark Ages there was a deemphasis on physical activity in educational programs, and emphasis was placed upon the development of religious values. During that time only the nobles engaged in exhaustive training programs, designed to make them fit for combat. Among

---

[1]For information of this type one must consult the literature in archeology, cultural anthropology, ethnology, demography, and cultural geography.

other things, these armored warriors attempted to become agile on the saddles of their horses while swinging their large swords. The wooden horses they sometimes practiced on in the gymnasiums were the fore-runners of the side-horse seen today in gymnastic meets.

The deemphasis in sport and physical activity during medieval days was due to the strong negative feelings churchmen developed after observing and considering the pagan rites connected with the Roman spectacles which had occurred during the early part of that era; as well as to the Christian deemphasis upon consideration of the human body, as opposed to the propagation of spiritual and religious truths.

The creative, religious, and scientific awakening experienced in Europe during the fourteenth to the seventeenth centuries was triggered by a number of factors. The writings of Aristotle were rediscovered, and the crusaders made inroads into new lands and contacted new peoples. Universities were founded in Italy, France, and Germany. In general, people began to look at contemporary occurrences and phe-nomena rather than being only concerned with preparing themselves spiritually for their place in the afterlife.

Greek ideals were renovated, and to an increasing degree physical activity programs were instituted in the new schools emerging in both northern and southern Europe, again to educate the "whole man." School programs were expanded in other directions, and the prolonged hours devoted to the consideration of theology in the medieval schools were displaced by courses in drawing, painting, rhetoric, history, phi-losophy, as well as physical education.

During the Renaissance, outside of the schools an individual with means could practice in fencing schools, and in tournaments devoted to emerging sports such as tennis, bowling, and the like. Track and field events were rediscovered, and archery was practiced as a sport rather than solely as an activity of war.

The strict Martin Luther advocated the use of gymnastic exercises, fencing, and the like in educational programs, in order to, as he put it, "keep the limbs strong." However, other religious orders, notably the Puritans, still looked askance at any physical activity which did not resemble the hard work needed to "get on in the world."

The educational philosophers during this period, notably those in Italy and France, began to produce writings outlining their ideas con-cerning the ideal education of the child and youth. Invariably there was reference to the role of physical activity in their texts. At times they advocated activities as a kind of relaxant which would enable children to get on with intellectual endeavors, the "real" work of the school. At other times, however, programs of movement activities formed an inte-gral part of the educational programs; and children and their teachers were often seen running on the grass together as they chased butterflies, or perhaps just enjoyed the experience of movement.

By the early 1800s, marked feelings of nationalism were reflected in the establishment of extremely vigorous strength-developing physical education programs. The most pronounced of these programs were reflected in the heavy apparatus installed in the German gymnasiums, with which the youth could be developed for service in the armies of the republic.

By the late 1800s, however, many Germans, and others in Eastern and Central Europe, perceived broader goals for physical education; and the writings of this period reflect an interest in the manner in which physical activity and play might contribute to the emotional, social, as well as the physical beings of participants.

By the end of the 1800s compulsory programs of physical exercise and gymnastics were found in most of the German schools. The strains of German nationalism, reflected in mass exercise programs of various kinds, lingered on until the 1930s, during which time the Nazis imposed a vigorous, Spartan-like regime upon their youth as they prepared for World War II.

During the early and middle 1800s a program termed "medical gymnastics" arose under the inspiration of Per Henrik Ling, in Sweden. Pointed not only toward the remediation of physical defects and the training of a fit army, the Swedish gymnastics were designed to promote aesthetic as well as educational goals. Although the original system was modified toward the end of the 1800s and the movements became more stultified than were those originally proposed, the basics of this program are to be found today in the movements seen in free-exercise events in modern gymnastics and in the rhythmic gymnastics employed by women in Europe and the United States.

The physical education programs which evolved in the various European countries after the turn of the 1900s in general reflected the national ideal of what constituted a "well-rounded" and "well-educated" man. Finland and Denmark, for example, have developed their unique variations of the Swedish rhythmic and the German gymnastics, coupled with modification of various field sports, plus "athletics" (track and field). The French and British have emphasized games rather than formal exercise, while the Germans have to some degree made less militaristic and harsh the programs to which they previously exposed their children and youth. At the same time, following the Revolution the Soviet Union has made physical education compulsory not only for school children, but also for factory workers at periodic intervals during their working day. The aim of this latter society is to provide movement experiences which not only contribute to physical development, but also reflect upon the way both the adults and children perform intellectually as well as in manufacturing tasks.

Physical Education in the United States

Formal physical education programs were nonexistent in the United States in the early days of the nation. Heavily influenced by the puritanical approach to work and play, the early schools of the 1700s contained few or no facilities to encourage a child to develop physically, and confined the available educational tools to improving reading, writing, and ciphering. However, even during this period, in writings by Benjamin Franklin, one can detect the beginnings of a concern on the part of the nation's leaders about the lack of some kind of physical activity within educational programs for children and youth.

During the 1800s, the new democracy began to evidence a number of trends relative to physical education, recreation, and related movements. As waves of immigrants from European countries arrived, they brought with them components of their previous cultures, which usually included some favorite type of physical experience.

Displaced German physical educators in Boston, by the beginning of the 1800s, with previous exposure to the gymnastic programs indigenous to their native land, began to stress physical activity in programs at several schools in the area; and partly due to their encouragement the city of Boston, in 1853, instituted required physical education programs in the public schools. But prior to the Civil War the only facilities provided for college youth consisted of small exercise rooms in which undirected activities could be engaged in. And while two teacher-training institutes were started in the years just prior to the war, their doors closed after only a few months.

During the Civil War, military training replaced physical training; but following this conflict there were signs of a renewed effort on the part of many national leaders to construct a stronger government educational system, and as a by-product they organized programs of physical education. Leadership during this period, and during the next 20 years, usually came from various college physical educators, many of whom were physicians. They had begun to institute what they believed to be scientifically sound programs whose primary goals were symmetrical development of the physique and physical vigor. However, by the 1880s some of these pioneers in American physical education had begun to expand their goals. Dudley Sargent, for example, included hygienic (optimum physical development), educative (special powers of the mind and body, physical skill, etc.), recreative (release

from tensions of daily work), and remedial (restoration of bodily malfunctions) as the primary objectives of his program at Harvard.

A number of programs from other nations began during the late
1800s to take their places in various school districts and colleges,
depending upon the nationalities of their proponents. German-Ameri-
can gymnastics, Swedish gymnastics, as well as various more aesthetic
dance and rhythmic programs appeared and were often modified, then
either disappeared or were continued while evidencing unique American flavors.

One of the most important influences upon American physical education during the middle and latter parts of the 1800s were various
games which, with modifications, had been imported from England.
The start of intercollegiate sport began on the campuses initially under
the leadership of exuberant undergraduate students. Cricket was
rounded into the shape of a baseball bat, modern tennis evolved out of a
more stilted English version, and the fat rugby ball became the slender
football. In 1891 a unique American court game was invented at
Springfield College when James Naismith nailed a peach basket to the
wall of a gymnasium.

Physical education and recreational activities were not confined,
during this period, to organized school programs. The YMCA movement, the establishment of recreational programs and parks in some of
the larger cities, combined with the growth of clubs of amateur athletes,
together provided strongly nationalistic Americans with ways to work
off their abundant energies in constructive ways.

Organizations to regulate and administer various athletic and physical education programs began to appear just before and slightly after
the beginning of the nineteenth century. The AAU was established in
1888; The American Physical Education Association in 1903; and The
National College Athletic Association in 1910.

As is usual during wartime, the colleges and secondary schools in
1917 and 1918 emphasized physical preparedness for military service.
But following World War II, expansion of American physical education proceeded along many channels.

The movement to evaluate scientifically the outcomes of education,
instituted at Columbia during the early 1900s, began to "rub off" on
physical education. Reflecting this trend were measurement programs
in colleges and universities, designed to detect fitness and performance
problems of entering freshmen, and to evaluate the extent to which the
goals of physical education programs were realized. Achievement tests
were also beginning to be employed in high schools during this same
period of time.

Health instruction began to permeate the secondary schools and colleges, and was often coupled in the 1920s and 1930s with courses in physical education. The growth of recreation was aided by the scouting movement, which appeared in America about this time. Modern dance, due to the influence of Isadora Duncan and others around the turn of the century, began to appear in both college and secondary programs for women and girls.

In the 1930s the *Research Quarterly* appeared, in which scholarly research relating to health, physical education, and recreation could be published. During this decade there appeared an interesting controversy concerning the "true" goals of physical education. Some claimed that physiological objectives should be paramount (fitness, cardiovascular endurance); while others wrote that a broader list of goals should be adopted, and the scope of programs expanded to include the development of social and emotional attributes, as well as strong muscles and "unfagging wind."

The years from 1930 to 1950 saw many changes in physical education at the national level. Graduate programs began to appear in the nation's colleges and universities during this period. Research laboratories also began to appear in increasing numbers, and their participants began to look at a remarkably wide range of possible effects of activity upon children and youth. Scholars in physical education began at times to team up with researchers in other disciplines on the university campuses for helpful interdisciplinary investigations.

The national organizations changed, combined, split apart, and became associated with other ancillary groups. In 1937 the old American Association for Physical Education evolved into the presently-constituted American Association for Health, Recreation and Physical Education, which by 1950 boasted a membership of 18,000 people.

The NCAA enlarged upon the number of sports in which they sponsored national competition. In 1932 boxing was started by the NCAA; gymnastics, tennis, and cross-country appeared a year later. Basketball began in 1939; and golf, fencing, baseball, and ice hockey followed in the 1940s. In 1932 the organization of women's sports was overseen by the National Section of Women's Athletics, a move which resulted in the establishment of a nationally-recognized standards and policies group to which all women could appeal when instituting and conducting programs of this nature.

Health instruction in elementary and secondary schools at the beginning of the 1930s was given impetus by a White House Conference on Child Health and Protection. In 1947 a National Conference on Health in College similarly provided leadership and guiding principles for programs of this kind in institutions of higher education.

Although during World War I most college programs were administered by the military, the same was not true during World War II. On most campuses the responsibility for conditioning the military was assumed by civilian athletic directors and department chairmen, while many researchers in physical education and athletics worked within the military services to improve standards and to conduct scientifically sound programs.

Contemporary Trends in Physical Education

During the 1960s several trends seem to have emerged which may have implications for any future directions that physical education, health instruction, and recreation may take during the decades ahead. Some of the trends had their beginnings in the middle and late portions of the 1960s, many seem imminent in the 1970s, while still others may be merely figments of your writer's imagination! Among recent trends are the following:

1. There is an increased tendency for various educators to question the value of physical education in the schools as a regularly-conducted daily program; particularly in light of the cost of such programs in terms of staff and facilities. Physical educators are increasingly called upon to produce data justifying their very existences, particularly with regard to compulsory programs on the college campuses in the nation.
2. Standards of teacher accreditation have been getting higher, and in many states secondary school teaching requires an individual to spend five years in college, including a year of graduate training. This trend may have both negative and positive effects upon the services rendered to children in the schools. On one hand, more people with well-qualified backgrounds are likely to confront these services; on the other hand, many qualified people may be lured toward lucrative professions with more status for which training may not be as extensive nor as expensive.
3. Physical education has become international in scope. Increased international cooperation is seen at several levels, and among many organizations. The jet plane flies rapidly between countries, and ideas and personnel of various countries have contributed to, and in turn are aided by, American physical educators. National groups for the study of sports sociology and sports psychology are affiliated with international societies. The United Nations' UNESCO has provided a number of international meetings to promote the value of physical activity during the 1960s, and such meetings should increase in number during the decades ahead.
4. The value of intercollegiate sports is continuing to be questioned, with

regard to the educational outcomes they purportedly offer the competitors in light of financial costs to the institutions which support them. A new breed of campus militant is often not only unconcerned with athletic programs, but openly hostile to their goals and practices. The black athlete, a football and track star of the 1930s, 1940s, and 1950s, began to question the motives of the white "hand that fed" him during the latter part of the 1960s.

5. International sports competitions are increasing in frequency as well as in the number of sports they encompass. Annual world championships are held in gymnastics, while track and other sports hold similar frequent encounters in addition to the Olympic competitions.

6. Health educators, dance instructors, physical educators, and coaches are beginning to seek membership in, and the support of, organizations more suited to their individual needs than the sometimes-unwieldy national organizations. Local organizations of physical educators in the country are beginning to operate with more vigor; while at the national level special interest groups, including the College of Sports Medicine, The College Men's and Women's Physical Education Associations, The National Society for Psychology in Sport and Physical Activity, The National High School Athletic Association, and The National Society for Sociology in Sports, among others, are attracting memberships with special needs and interests.

7. There seemed to be an increased tendency for teacher-educators during the 1960s to consider information obtained from psychology and sociology as pertinent when formulating their curriculums. Courses in the psychology of sport sociology and of motor learning began to appear with frequency, and took their place beside classes in biomechanics, work physiology, and the mechanics of movement, that formerly provided the scientific core of the physical education major.

8. At several levels sports competition for girls and young women is increasingly provided for, and is being accorded social acceptance. Girls engage more in vigorous activities, formerly the sole purview of the boys; while in high schools and colleges, well-run programs of competitive athletics for females increased during the latter part of the 1960s.

9. Physical educators will begin to render more services to children and youth taking part in programs of special education. During the 1970s it is likely that special physical education programs for the gifted may emerge, together with an expansion of those currently available to the retarded, the blind, and others with various problems.

10. Physical education curriculums during the 1970s in our colleges and universities will begin to achieve a balance between theory and practical or applied courses. The out-of-contact, highly-theoretical university

course will be made more realistic in terms of the needs of students; while the "athletic harbor" still seen too often in colleges and universities will begin to grow some academic "muscle" in the form of more and improved theory courses.

11. Graduate training in the 1970s, particularly doctoral programs, will continue to improve. Graduate programs have existed in the United States almost since the beginning of formal college programs; however, even during the final years of the 1960s, their quality has been highly uneven. It is possible that a national accreditation board, similar to that seen in medicine, might be formed to attempt to establish minimum standards of staff competencies, libraries, course offerings, and laboratory facilities. Institutions of higher learning may be evaluated by comparing them to these standards, and in turn they may be employed so that institutions of higher learning may assess themselves with more validity.

These and other signs point to interesting decades ahead, decades of challenge requiring alert, perceptive, professional participants. It is hoped that upon graduation you can serve youth in the "game" called physical education. A deeper appreciation of the events, and your role in shaping them during the 1970s, should be gained by a thorough understanding of what has gone before.

References

De Grazia, S., *Of Time, Work and Leisure*. New York: Doubleday and Company, Inc., 1962.

Hackensmith, C. W., *History of Physical Education*. New York: Harper & Row, Publishers, 1966.

Huizinga, J., *Homo Ludens*. Boston: Beacon Press, 1950.

McCloy, C. H., *Philosophical Bases for Physical Education*. New York: F. S. Crofts and Company, 1940.

Menke, F. G., *The Encyclopedia of Sport*. New York: Barnes Publishers, 1963.

Miller, N. P., *The Leisure Age*. Belmont, California: Wadsworth Publishing Company, Inc., 1969.

Rice, E. A., et al., *A Brief History of Physical Education*. New York: The Ronald Press Company, 1968.

Sapora, A. U. H., *The Theory of Play and Recreation*. New York: The Ronald Press Company, 1961.

Van Dalen, D. B., *A World History of Physical Education*. Englewood Cliffs, New Jersey: Prentice-Hall, Inc., 1953.

Vanek, Miroslav, and Cratty, Bryant, *Psychology and the Superior Athlete*. New York: The Macmillan Company, 1969.

Weston, A., *The Making of American Physical Education.* New York: Appleton-Century-Crofts, 1962.

Zeigler, E. F., *Philosophical Foundations for Physical, Health, and Recreation Education.* Englewood Cliffs, New Jersey: Prentice-Hall, Inc., 1964.

CHAPTER TWENTY

Mechanics of Movement

Traditionally, a body of knowledge to which physical educators have been exposed while undergraduates deals with the physical and mechanical principles which govern, regulate, and otherwise determine the nature of human movement. At times this information is incorporated into a rather broad course, sometimes titled kinesiology, in which principles relative to the physiology of exercise are also covered. At other times this information is presented in a separate course.

In this type of course, man's action system is compared to a complex system of levers and pulleys. The physical forces which govern movement of the total body within various environments (water, under the influence of gravity, relative weightlessness, etc.) are dealt with in one portion of the course, while in another part the principles are described which explain the manner in which various bodily components interact and move (the limbs, trunk articulations, etc.).

Dealing with subject matter of this nature requires two basic types of knowledge on the part of the student. He must be well-grounded concerning the nature of human anatomy, including the manner in which the skeleton is constructed, the way in which the muscles are placed on the bony frame, as well as the manner in which they move the bony parts as they contract and stabilize in various ways. Secondly, the student should have at least an elementary grasp of the principles of mechanics. Newton's laws, the nature of levers, as well as some information concerning velocity and mass, are needed to understand the manner in which the human body exerts force and moves. Information of this kind is usually obtained during the first year or two as an undergraduate, while a course containing information dealing with human physics and mechanics is generally forthcoming during the final two years.

Knowledge of the mechanics of movement can provide the physical educator and coach a great deal of practical help while working with children and youth. Maximum effort in various sports skills requires forces to be directed properly through correct placement and movements of the body and of body parts. The feet and trunk of the shot-putter, and the velocities of the discus thrower, must be within reasonable limits before their implements will be well "sent."

New practices and performing styles which emerge in track and field, swimming, and other sports, may be more accurately evaluated if the coach possesses an adequate background concerning the mechanics of movement. The rather extreme high-jumping style which emerged in the latter part of the 1960s, the lunging fall employed by some when hurling the javelin, and the newer place-kicking styles borrowed from soccer and used in football, may be better assessed by those possessing a good background of the physical principles governing human motion.

Even more basic actions become amenable to analysis with a thorough grounding in the mechanical principles underlying movements. Correct running styles can be ascertained for individuals of various body builds and gait characteristics; while various running styles which may be inefficient can similarly be identified.

Throwing balls of various kinds for varying distances can also be scrutinized, by applying principles dealing with the summation of forces to the components of human behavior involved in this highly-prized skill.

Undergraduates interested in physical therapy should be especially attentive to lectures in courses dealing with the mechanics of movement. Correct identification of inappropriate gait characteristics and other movement disabilities of atypical children and youth is necessary before remedial efforts can be applied. The ability to analyze mechanically correct and incorrect walking patterns, and to determine exactly why the latter are inefficient, is vital to those dealing with the orthopedically handicapped or brain-damaged child.

There are many other facets of this interesting subject area which may be brought out in your course in the mechanics of movement. For example, students should be able to analyze and predict the mechanical advantages and disadvantages which are likely to be realized by individuals possessing various body-build characteristics when attempting to perform specific motor acts. Instructors in the mechanics of movement should bring out the nature of individual differences in both body build and in the manner in which muscles are attached to various bony surfaces and promontories. For example, the mechanical advantage when running and jumping of the manner in which the heel tendon is attached, and of the length of the heel bone (calcaneus), might be considered in this context.

In addition to learning about how the body may move totally and how its parts interact mechanically, a course in the mechanics of movement should deal with material which teaches how missiles and other implements may act when given impetus by humans in various ways. The manner in which a ball will travel when released at various angles, for example, should be thoroughly covered. The actions of the discus, shot put, javelin, and similar objects should also be analyzed closely.

Another reasonably complex subtopic within a course in mechanics concerns how the body moves when impelled in various ways. What is to be expected, for example, when the human rebounds in various ways from a trampoline, a diving board, or a take-off board within the gymnasium? A thorough grasp of the principles involved within this component of the course should not only be helpful to those interested in promoting better performance, but would also seem to be imperative for the prevention of accidents on some of the potentially dangerous apparatus in gymnasiums, on athletic fields (e.g., the resilient pole-vaulting pole), and equipment near swimming pools.

In the pages which follow, only some of the primary mechanical principles which may be applied to human motion are outlined. Additionally, some of the ways in which these principles may be applied to the better understanding of basic human actions, as well as to relatively complex sports skills, are covered. It is hoped that through this brief introduction the student will become more sensitive to the basic physical factors underlying human motion; and during the years which follow will attempt to gain even deeper insights into this important topic by more careful observations of the actions of others, by independent reading, as well as by participation in formal courses.

Principles of Total Body Movement and Stability

It is apparent to all that the lower the center of gravity, the more stable the object. A pyramid with a broad base is more stable than a tall, thin rectangle placed on its smallest side. The same is true of a human being, although rather than being composed of a single unchangeable mass as is a cement pyramid, the human can lower his center of gravity through changes he initiates in his arm positions, through bending his knees, and in other ways.

Various exercises may be performed by children, and by the reader, to demonstrate the manner in which stability is increased or reduced by various shifts in the center of gravity, as well as by changing the nature of the body's base of support. For example:

1. Run in a straight line for about 30 feet; then attempt to stop while remaining relatively upright, as opposed to dropping the arms to the sides and quickly bending the knees. Experiment with *either*, ending your run with a quick knee bend, or dropping the arms. Which seems more efficient?
2. Stand in the center of a trampoline and, without bending your knees, quickly move your arms up and down, at the same time keeping your elbows straight. Study the effect upon the body's center of gravity as reflected in up and down movements of the bed of the trampoline.
3. While standing with your eyes closed and head slightly back, experiment with various reductions of your base of support: by standing with feet together, in a heel-toe position, on one foot, and on one foot (your nonpreferred one) with arms folded across your chest.
4. Practice jumping upward with and without simultaneous arm extension. What does arm extension do to the body's center of gravity?

A Law of Motion: Action and Reaction

To every action there is an equal and opposite reaction. To run rapidly forward you must push backward hard with your feet upon the running surface; a jump upward with the body is accompanied by a vigorous downward push. A number of simple experiments can demonstrate the application of this principle to human actions of various kinds. The reader is encouraged to attempt some of the activities in the water, to delineate more clearly the principle involved.

1. Stand on a bathroom scale, or a more substantial scale if available. Jump upward, trying to jump to various heights on subsequent jumps. Have an observer record how many additional pounds of push you apply to the scale as you try the higher jumps.
2. Float in a swimming pool with your body extended in a face-down position. Pull directly backward with both hands and arms at the same time. Note the reaction of your body. Experiment with various arm pull angles; e.g., pulling back with one arm and permitting it to move away from the hip as the pull finishes. Start one and then both arms back by the hips, while still in this face-lying position, and move them directly forward toward your head. What does your body do in this case?

3. Illustrative of a law of the manner in which direction of moving objects is sustained is the movement forward of the body in the water with repeated applications of force applied backward. Experiment with your crawl stroke, and attempt to increase efficiency by varying the tempo with which you make repeated arm strokes. Try first pulling with alternate arms in rapid succession. Next place both arms to the front, pull hard backward with one arm, return that same arm to the front again, and *then* pull with the second arm, returning the second to the front before pulling with the first again. Continue this action, and also experiment with varying degrees of force applied on each arm stroke. How do you seem to be most efficient, getting the most speed out of a minimum of effort on your part?

Principles Governing the Throwing
of Balls

All other things being equal, it is obvious that the harder you throw, the farther the ball will travel. All other things, however, are seldom equal. For example, the angle at which the ball is released is critical, as are other factors such as the extent of the windup and the manner in which body parts, other than the arms, are incorporated into the throwing act. The spin placed on the ball, the air resistance, the altitude, and similar factors also influence what the ball does after you release it. In the exercises which follow, only two of the many mechanical and physical principles governing throwing will be explored.

1. Efficient throwing involves what has been termed a "summation of forces." The final force applied to the ball as the hand releases it is the result of .actions starting at the feet and continuing up through the thighs, aided by a shift forward by the total body at the moment of release; accompanied by a twist of the trunk, as well as by actions of the shoulder, arm, and finally the wrist. If any of these components of the total throwing action are reduced, the final effort is likely to result in a throw of reduced distance. The nature of this principle can be illustrated as you either observe children of varying ages and sexes throwing with varying degrees of arm-leg-body involvement, or as you attempt to vary the nature of the throwing action yourself. For example, sit in a chair, keeping your back against the back of the chair, and throw as hard as you can for distance using just your throwing arm. Using the same ball, stand on a line, feet parallel, without shifting your weight forward, and again throw the ball. Note the differences in distance achieved by throws 1 and 2.

Now stand with one foot (the one opposite the throwing arm) slightly ahead of the other, and concentrate upon a throw which starts on the rear foot, continues up the trunk, and finishes with a weight shift to the front foot accompanied by the fast arm action and release. What difference do you now note in your throwing distance when comparing the distances achieved in throws 1 and 2?

2. Throwing is an extremely complex act, and many other physical principles are involved in its execution. For example, it is a truism that the longer the distance through which an object (in this case a ball) is moved, the greater the speed which can be imparted to it. The principle is best illustrated by the extended windup used by some pitchers, in which the throwing hand is brought back initially almost to the ankle of the leg under the throwing arm, and then continued forward in a long arch up over the shoulder, terminating in front of the foot of the leg opposite to the throwing arm. The ball, of course, is usually released at about chest level during the forward trajectory of the arm. Another experiment which can be performed is to attempt to throw varying distances by changing the amount of windup applied prior to the release of the ball.

Levers, Joints, and Movement

The various ways in which muscles and tendons attach to and move bones can be likened to a large and complex system of levers. When in action, not all parts of the human muscle system move. Many muscles merely stabilize limbs and portions of the trunk, which in turn provide strong bases from which other parts may move. Movement itself, initiated by impulses and finally manifested in actions at the numerous joints of the body, in some ways resembles the action of mechanical contrivances usually associated with the levers and pulleys found in a factory.

A thorough analysis of the manner in which principles of levers interact with human anatomy is predicated, of course, upon a thorough knowledge of human anatomy. A superficial examination of the nature of the three classifications of levers, as they correspond to various levers within the human body, may give the student an initial look at mechanical principles of movement governing actions of various body parts.

1. A first-class lever may be likened to the seesaw found in elementary school playgrounds. The fulcrum, or pivot, is placed between the resistance and the place force is applied. The first-class lever can be illustrated as follows:

If the force arm is long, as illustrated below, more resistance can be moved with relatively less force.

Several muscular systems in the body act upon joints to move the weight of various limbs and body parts in this manner. For example, if the leg is crossed and the foot is unsupported, the weight of the foot provides the resistance, the long leg bone acts as a fulcrum, while the calf muscle attached to the heel provides the force. Perhaps with the help of your instructor you may identify additional first-class levers in the skeletal-muscular system, and can also decide what effects will occur if the relative lengths of the resistance and force arms are changed in various ways.

2. In a second-class lever the resistance is placed between the force and fulcrum as shown. An example of a simple machine incorporating a lever of this type is the wheelbarrow.

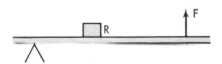

Relatively few joint-muscle systems within the body evidence this type of force-resistance-fulcrum arrangement. Perhaps with the help of an anatomy text you can identify various second-class levers, and can determine what effects changing the placement of the resistances along the lever arms might have upon the efficiency of the levers. Attempt to analyze jumping with this type of lever in mind.

3. A third-class lever involves placement of the resistance at the distal end of the lever arm, as shown, with the force between the fulcrum and the resistance.

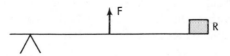

The flexing forearm is a good example of a lever of this type, with the resistance composed of the weight of the hand and forearm, the force being applied upward by the tendon coming from the biceps (the large muscle in the front of the arm); while the fulcrum, or pivot point, is the elbow joint itself. Perhaps you can locate others.

Many joints do not act as simple hinges, as exemplified by the simple lever systems outlined above. Some, for example, involve a kind of pulley arrangement; as exemplified by the long upper tendon of the biceps, which travels upward through a groove in the upper arm and attaches to the scapula at the rear of the upper back, thus providing additional mechanical advantage when the arm is lifted upward and forward at the shoulder.

The interaction of the various joints is an extremely complex process in most motor skills. For example, many joints that seem to act directly upon a given movement are actually passive and automatic in the degree of involvement they really manifest. This is particularly true in various throwing movements and rapid kicking movements, in which the elbow and knee joints may actually be "thrown" by other previously-involved joints, rather than moving in controlled and forceful ways in and of themselves.

Summary

A course in the mechanics of movement is likely to incorporate information from several areas. Principles of the various actions in which the total body participates constitute one section; a second portion involves the nature of the muscular-skeletal lever systems within the body; while a third portion of the course likely will cover the manner in which objects external to the body may be acted upon by human effort, and can add impetus to the body in various ways. Additionally, a thorough examination of the physics of movement should deal with the way in which working in various media, such as air, water, and weightless (or near-weightless) environments, would be analyzed.

The student gaining a good understanding of the various aspects of the mechanics of movement should become better prepared to:

1. Analyze a given athlete performing a specified skill; and offer constructive suggestions, if any are needed, for the improvement of performance.
2. Assess new ways of performing familiar skills, to determine whether valid physical principles are violated, or whether the athlete has discovered, perhaps by chance, a truly better way of utilizing the body by exploiting sound mechanical principles.

3. Survey individual differences in body build, and in more specific aspects of the skeletal-muscular system, in order to determine better ways in which a single athlete might perform, as well as to ascertain whether a given youth has a reasonable chance for success in various sports.
4. Design more efficient apparatus and facilities for propelling the body (e.g., trampoline, diving board), for throwing (balls, etc.), to run on, as well as to promote fitness and strength (exercise equipment of various kinds).

Student Activities and Discussion Questions

1. Select a sports skill, and analyze it mechanically. What modifications in the manner in which it is performed are likely to improve efficiency? Which modifications are likely to reduce efficiency?
2. Select a recent innovative technique espoused by a prominent athlete. Why does it seem to result in better performance than a more traditional manner of performing? Is this improvement caused by the unique body build of the performer using it, the amount of practice devoted to it, or to some real mechanical advantage?
3. List the joints of the body which seem to provide speed, and those which seem to result in the application of force. What kinds of levers are involved in each? Where are the forces, resistances, and fulcrums placed in each joint you have analyzed?
4. Study a trampolinist and attempt to answer several questions: When can he initiate rotation when doing front and back somersaults? Can he turn to the left or right in the air after leaving the bed (while in an upright position)? In what positions can he rotate fastest and slowest? Can you explain your findings by reference to information gained from a study of body movement mechanics and of the physical principles of motion?

References

Books

Broer, M. R., *Efficiency of Human Movement*. Philadelphia: W. B. Saunders Company, 1966.

Bunn, J. W., *Scientific Principles of Coaching*. Englewood Cliffs, New Jersey: Prentice-Hall, Inc., 1960.

Rasch, P. J., and Burke, R. K., *Kinesiology and Applied Anatomy*. Philadelphia: Lea & Febiger, 1967.

Scott, M. G., *Analysis of Human Motion: A Textbook in Kinesiology.* New York: Appleton-Century-Crofts, 1963.

Wells, K. F., *Kinesiology.* Philadelphia: W. B. Saunders Company, 1966.

Periodicals

Research Quarterly. American Association of Health, Physical Education and Recreation, 1201 16th St., N. W., Washington, D. C. 20036.

CHAPTER TWENTY-ONE

Testing and Measurement

The use of various tests and measurements in programs of physical activity has a long and at times a glorious history. The early Greeks evaluated their athletes on performance as well as upon how close their body builds approached the proportions sculptured by their artists. This same emphasis upon the measurement of physique, bodily proportions, and the like can be seen in the early efforts of college physical educators in this country during the 1860s. For example, Dudley Sargent, at that time, measured the freshmen students in his charge, and then attempted to prescribe exercise programs designed to remedy deficiencies he perceived in their muscular conformities, postures, and the like.

Toward the middle of the 1920s, physical educators in several colleges and universities in the country began to broaden the scope of physical testing, and included performance tests of various kinds in the batteries they used. Tests of strength and running speed seemed to predominate; but at the University of Texas, shortly after that time, Dr. David Brace formulated tests which contained various balance and agility items.

Appearing in the 1930s and 1940s were tests of personality, attitude, and similar attributes, reflecting a trend in educational measurement started in the department of education at Columbia University and at the department of psychology at Harvard around the turn of the century. During those two decades, these measures were being employed by physical educators with varying degrees of success.

In the 1950s an important development in testing physical attributes took place when the factor analytic techniques were applied to the identification of the manner in which the totality of human performance is apparently undergirded by what were found to be a number of separate ability traits. Tests were developed to represent these traits, which as a group would apparently represent the entire spectrum of performance capacities that can be evidenced by humans engaged in movement tasks which involved activity of both the larger and smaller skeletal muscles.

During the past ten years, highly individualized testing programs have been developed, suited to the needs of various groups of children and youth. There seems to be a decreasing trend to measure in exact ways the posture and body build of children and college-age students; rather, emphasis has increasingly been placed upon motor function in both groups. During this same period of time the elementary classroom teacher and pediatrician have begun to look, with some success, toward physical educators to aid them in a search for helpful tools with which to measure motor competencies among school-age and preschool children. A project sponsored and carried out by the Research Council of the American Association of Health, Physical Education and Recreation in the 1960s culminated in the formulation of reasonably sound norms for a variety of sports-skill tests.

Sometime during your undergraduate days you should be exposed to information dealing with the important subjects of tests and measurements in physical education. This type of content may reach you within several courses; for example, in a course dealing with the manner of instructing various types of sports activities, or perhaps in a more coherent manner by being contained in a single course.

Content of this type should bring out several points. You should be made aware of the various types of tests which may be employed in evaluating various proficiencies in physical education and athletics. Furthermore, the manner in which tests and measurements may be employed should also be discussed in such a course. The ways of applying these kinds of measures should also be explained to you. As a thread running through all this information should be some basis upon which you might acquire and formulate a type of testing philosophy; or at least data which permits you to incorporate into your total philosophy what you learn about evaluation when dealing with youngsters.

Several questions should be asked when one considers instituting a program of tests and measurements within any given situation. For example, a basic query is whether that which is to be measured is indeed measurable. Such attributes as attitudes, self-concept, and the like are not only difficult to evaluate, but also measurement tools with which they can be adequately assessed are often difficult to locate.

Another question which should be posed is if what is to be measured is *worth* measuring; and if it is, how much time should be devoted to evaluation. At times too much time within a program of physical education may be devoted to testing physical qualities, with not enough time spent upon activities which purportedly improve the attributes assessed.

If an inordinate amount of time is taken for testing, as contrasted with time devoted to the program of activities purporting to change the attributes tested, student apathy toward both test and program may occur. Generally, 10 percent or less of class or practice time should be occupied by efforts at evaluation.

Further points should be considered when attempting to formulate a sound measurement philosophy. For example, many physical educators working with children point their activities directly toward the items in the tests which they later administer. This strategy, of course, will elicit the hoped-for changes in the scores later obtained. When the instructors participating in a given physical development program are too sensitive toward a test battery which will purportedly evaluate their efforts by measuring the success of their children, they may also tend to teach toward the tests. The evaluation of the success of fitness programs is usually "bent" by this type of "corrupting" condition.

In general, despite some of the pitfalls described, instituting sound programs of testing based upon scientifically well-established measures may have several beneficial effects within physical activity programs of various kinds.

1. Testing, if well-applied, can provide an important motivating influence upon the children and youth evaluated. If the scores collected over a reasonably long time period are made available to children, they may strive harder to improve. Testing with this objective in mind should be relatively easy to administer, and the resultant scores should be made available in understandable form to the children tested.

   Another important consideration at this point is whether the test scores obtained should be used to motivate an individual to compete against himself, and to attempt to achieve progressively better and higher scores; and/or whether the child should be compared either favorably or unfavorably against some type of existing norms. At times this latter use of the test scores may have a detrimental effect upon children whose initial or final scores are not meeting acceptable standards. To circumvent this type of possibly undesirable inter-child competition, or competition between the individual child and some type of purportedly desirable average, two methods of testing can be employed: (a) Each individual may be offered a reasonably unique testing program. Thus, each child pursuing his own program of improvement produces scores which can only be contrasted to his previous scores, and which are not comparable to those of his class-mates. (b) The percentage of improvement evidenced by an individual child, rather than the actual scores produced, may be recorded.

2. Another important objective which may be met with some type of evaluation program is to make instructors and coaches more sensitive to their own teaching effectiveness. The results of performance tests may, for example, reveal that indeed little or no progress is being made, when at the same time the instructor had felt that he was doing his job. The collection of scores from subjective measures obtained from students may provide the instructor with more information about himself than will objective data about the performance of the students in his charge. For example, I once gave a questionnaire to college students in several swimming classes I was teaching, to ascertain just how important they believed 15 practices used in classes were in motivating them to work harder. The result of this research, when I evaluated the data, was that the students attributed far less importance to competition between individuals than I would have guessed. After I inspected these results I began to place more emphasis upon the goal of self-improvement rather than upon inter-individual competition.[1]

3. Testing can also be employed in physical education classes and on athletic teams by determining whether goals for improvement and desirable change are truly met. Generally, this is done by comparing test scores prior to the introduction of some kind of physical program, to those collected at the completion of the program. Usually within school situations the results of this type of comparison will produce positive findings. The final test scores will indeed be higher and better at the second administration than they were initially; therefore, interpretation of the scores should be carried out with care. A great many factors other than the actual content of the program can contribute to the change in scores, including the effects of the personality of the instructor and the fact that the children may be maturing and thus improving naturally in the attributes tested. Taking a test also results in learning how to take that test, so that successive administrations of the same test invariably lead toward higher scores.

Despite these problems, however, inspection and comparison of pre-program and post-program test results can lead toward more effective teaching methods, and also toward more meaningful content. There are

[1]It is usually found that individuals tend to attribute their own values to others, and since I perceived myself as competitive, I had believed that those in my charge were similarly motivated.

other technical and practical considerations to be kept in mind, some of which are covered in the final sections of this chapter.
4. A fourth valuable outcome which may be derived from the institution of testing procedures, is that the act of testing children often makes the tester a more careful and accurate observer of the behaviors he is assessing. Increased sensitivity to motor characteristics of children of various ages, or to the unique movement tendencies of individual athletes, are often revealed to the tester who is acute enough in his observations to really see his testees.

Technical Problems When Selecting
and Administering Tests

Not all tests and testing programs are equally good. In fact, if poorly conceived, administered, and interpreted to students, a potentially helpful assessment can result in an experience which may be harmful to all concerned.

A thorough discussion of the matter in which tests are constructed, administered, and evaluated cannot be undertaken here because of limitations of space. At the same time, the warnings contained in the paragraphs which follow may lead the more enterprising student to explore some of the texts listed in the final pages, and to be as productive and scientific as is possible when actually assessing children and youth.

Some of the guidelines which one should follow when using tests of various kinds are as follows:
1. The test or test battery should be directed toward the exact attributes it is desired to change. The tester should use his time and that of his students efficiently by giving only tests which sample different abilities; and not giving, for example, several strength tests whose scores may correlate highly with one another. If the scores from two physical performance tests generally rank a group of children in the same manner, from the most proficient to the least able, they are probably sampling the same basic quality in the children; and administration of both of them may be a waste of time and money.
2. The tester should be aware of the broad range of tests available to physical educators—measurement tools which sample a wide range of attributes which in some way impinge upon programs of physical activity. He should select from among these the ones which suit his needs. Tests pertinent to physical educators may be classified in several ways. For example:
    (a) There are tests which measure various bodily conformations:

limb girth, weight, body build (ponderal index), bony girth, and thickness of subcutaneous fat deposits (measures of this last type are taken by evaluating skin fold thicknesses).

(b) Tests exist which measure basic performance attributes: physiological capacities, heart rate adaptations to exercise, recovery time following exercise, and strength (moving strength as tested when assessing push-ups, as well as static strength tested when hand-grip pressure in pounds per square inch is taken). Tests of balance (moving along balance beams, and more dynamic balance tests such as stable posturing positions balancing on one foot) may be employed in this category. Tests of reaction time and movement speed are also measures of basic movement capacities.

(c) There are tests of complex individual motor acts, as in tasks involving accurate movements of the limbs, hands, or the total body. Tests of this nature may include a shuttle, a zigzag run, a standing broadjump, and the like.

(d) Tests of sports skills are also available to physical educators, or they may be formulated within the facilities available at a school. As was mentioned, there are norms available in a number of individual skills against which individual and group performances may be contrasted.

(e) Tests of overall game proficiency may be formulated, and various observational data may be combined into some kinds of general ratings. As will be pointed out again in this chapter, these more subjective ratings should usually be collected independently by more than one observer, and then compared to determine whether in truth they are reliable measures.

(f) There are a number of personality, attitude, and self-concept tests available to physical educators which, with careful administration or supervision by a qualified psychologist, may be useful in a number of ways. Such tests, for example, may ascertain just who within a physical education class brings negative feelings with him each day; and if correctly administered and interpreted personality tests are given to a large turnout of football players, important information about the personal makeup of each one may be surveyed by interested coaches and incorporated into other performance information.

(g) There are other more subtle performance measures which may be obtained about groups of children and youth, measures involving some type of motor act which may reveal information about other facets of their personalities. For example, measures of self-control gained from asking elementary school children to "move as slowly as you can" in various motor tasks (line drawing, arising from a back-lying position, etc.) may be helpful in assessing self-control while in classrooms. Persistence, ability to withstand pain, and general fortitude in athletes may be measurable by asking children to engage in various relatively uncomfortable tasks for "as long as you wish." In past research studies, these tests have included holding half-maximum grip strength on a hand dynamometer, holding out a leg with knee straight while seated on a chair, and similar tasks.

Thus, the spectrum of tasks which may be employed is broad indeed. The physical educator should select from these the ones which are congruent with his objectives, and which are appropriate for the types of children or youth with whom he is dealing.

3. Another important consideration when instituting tests and adopting specific ones, is whether or not the test is reliable. If the test is one which has appeared in the research literature, and which has been standardized on populations of youth similar to those you are serving, there is usually little problem.

On the other hand, one of the important qualities of any test, whether motor or intellectual, is whether the scores gained from a group of children are consistent; whether the ranking of the children on one day, based upon these scores, would be similar to that formulated if the scores on the same test administered on a different day were employed to rank the same students. If the scores of groups of children or youth fluctuate markedly from day to day, the test is of little worth. If, on the other hand, the test scores remain relatively stable from day to day, the test is said to be reliable.

Other indications of test reliability should also be considered. For example, if the measures gained are based upon someone's personal observations, as when scoring general game proficiency, it is scientifically sound for two observers to observe the same performance at the same time, and to record their scores independently. These scores should then be compared, by contrasting the ranking of the participants based upon the two sets of observations obtained. If the rankings are dissimilar, it should be concluded that the reliability of the observations obtained are questionable.

4. Validity of a test refers to whether it is in fact evaluating the quality it is purporting to measure. Validity is usually established by comparing the scores obtained on a test with scores from a similar established test which has been viewed by the scientific community as accurately evaluating the attribute under consideration.

Again the concept of correlation or ranking is important. Does the test you are developing or using tend to rank a group of people (best to worst) in the same manner as would an established test? If yours does, then it is usually said to be a valid measure of some type. At times, establishing the validity of a test becomes an exercise in historical interpretation. If, for example, you try to validate a certain intelligence test, you may correlate it against another, which in turn has been correlated with another; and so on until you arrive at the fact that Benet, a developer of one of the first tests of I.Q., selected the items for his test by searching within his own mind for items which, if successfully completed, probably contributed to the success of the French schoolboy of the last century! The same kind of historical examination may be undertaken to establish the validity of various performance tests.

On the other hand, a test may be said to have "face" validity. For example, it appears that, based upon an acceptable definition of strength, squeezing a handgrip does indeed evaluate at least one portion of what might be said to be strength (e.g., force in pounds of muscle contractions in the palm).

5. When formulating tests or selecting appropriate instruments from the literature, it is important to utilize those which will encompass the abilities of the youth evaluated. Tests which are too easy or too difficult will not adequately discriminate among the various children or youth being tested. A too-easy test results in the collection of uniformly high scores, while one too difficult for a particular population of children will produce scores that are similar and low. The attempt should be to obtain scores with any given testing instrument which evidence a reasonably wide spread from the highest to the lowest score.

6. The conditions surrounding the testing environment should be similar for all individuals tested, and reasonably well controlled. If it is decided to give some type of verbal encouragement to those tested, then all should be encouraged in a similar manner. If the children are tested in groups, usually a convenient method in physical education classes, then the quality and type of group interaction should be similar in all groups tested (e.g., how many are present and what they say to each other). However, for best results in physical performance tests, individual administration without the presence of others is usually best. Study after study indicate the highly significant differences in scores from boys and girls in late childhood and early adolescence who are subjected before testing to some kind of motivating "pep" talk, or who are otherwise influenced by those around them. These effects may especially alter fitness scores.

Testing is carried out constantly on an informal or formal basis during the teaching and coaching of physical activity. The coach observing his football players during the early days of the spring workout evaluates them constantly, as he talks to his aides and to himself regarding the capabilities and characteristics of each which may enable the potential player to make a contribution to the later success of a team. The same occurs in a physical education class. These relatively informal observations, however, may be more formally carried out with the multitude of tests available for measuring performance, fitness, body build, personality, and attitudes. In general, it is becoming increasingly good practice to carry out these more exact observations via tests, instead of relying solely upon observational evidence. It is hoped that the content of this chapter will prompt the student to learn more about the kinds of tests and measurements available to those working with physical activity as a teaching modality, as well as to gain information concerning how these tests may be employed effectively.

Summary

An effective, well-conceived program of tests and measurements can aid in the initial screening of youth for classification purposes, can verify the extent to which teacher-pupil goals are reached, can motivate students, and can aid the tester to become a more careful observer of youth and children in action. A well-designed testing program should match the nature of the tests with the capacities of the students tested, as well as with the objectives sought within the activity carried out.

Tests can evaluate basic performance capacities; ascertain the physical conformities of children and youth, and their proficiencies in various sports skills; or delve into more subtle personality traits, attitudes, and performance preferences. Tests selected for administration should be reasonably difficult, should be reliable and valid, and at the same time should be administered under reasonably well-controlled conditions.

Information concerning tests and measurements should lead toward the formulation of an educationally and scientifically sound testing philosophy. Such a philosophy should lead the tester toward principles concerning what tests to select, how often and in what ways they should be administered; as well as toward sound ways of communicating test findings to the children and youth who have been subjected to evaluation.

Student Activities and Discussion Questions

1. Select a test from the literature, which evaluates a quality which interests you. Ascertain its reliability, validity, and toward what types of children (i.e., age, sex, etc.) the instrument may be directed.
2. Formulate your own physical performance test. Administer it to ten children twice, one time each on consecutive days, at about the same time each day. Compare the manners in which the scores on the two days rank the children. Determine whether the test is a reliable one or

not. (You might compute in rather exact ways what is called a rank order correlation; your instructor may help you obtain the mathematical formula for this.)

3. Test a group of children or youth with a test of physical performance. After one month's time, retest them. Compare the average performance scores of the group collected at each testing. How can you account for the changes (if any) seen when the comparison is carried out? This comparison also may be carried out with rather exact statistical procedures, in which your instructor might aid you.

4. Develop an attitude test containing ten questions which will purportedly evaluate how people feel about physical activity, athletics, a particular sport, physical educators, or coaches. What are some of the considerations which should be kept in mind when formulating questions for your inquiry form? What must you do to establish the reliability and validity of the testing instrument you develop? How and with whom might such a questionnaire be used? What cautions would you have to observe in its use, and in the dissemination of your potential findings?

References

Barrow, H. M., and McGee, R., *A Practical Approach to Measurement in Physical Education*. Philadelphia: Lea & Febiger, 1964.

Campbell, W. R., and Tucker, N. M., *An Introduction to Tests and Measurement in Physical Education*. London: G. Bell and Sons, Ltd., 1967.

Clarke, H. Harrison, and Clarke, David H., *Research Processes in Physical Education, Recreation and Health*. Englewood Cliffs, New Jersey: Prentice-Hall, Inc., 1970.

Cratty, Bryant J., and Hutton, Robert, *Experiments in Motor Performance and Motor Learning*. Philadelphia: Lea & Febiger, 1969.

Larson, L. A., *Measurement and Evaluation in Physical, Health and Recreation Education*. St. Louis: C. V. Mosby Company, 1951.

Scott, M. G., ed., *Research Methods in Health, Physical Education and Recreation*. Washington, D. C.: American Association of Health, Physical Education, and Recreation, 1959.

CHAPTER TWENTY-TWO

Motor Development

One of the critical "blocks" of information to which you have some exposure as an undergraduate deals with the manner in which the motor characteristics of children and youth undergo change due to aging. Data of this type may be found in separate courses titled "motor development" or some similar label, or in the classes dealing with more general aspects of child development sometimes given in departments of education.

To truly accommodate individual differences in children when planning and carrying out programs of physical activity, age and sex differences should be considered. It is within this general subject area that information critical to the assessment of children's and youth's capacities and inclinations for movement should be acquired. Armed with knowledge of this type, the instructor should not only be better able to direct efforts in more constructive ways when working with children of various ages, but also should be able to plan programs with more meaningful content.

A course dealing with motor development should begin, just as the child begins, with content directed toward understanding the movement characteristics of infants shortly after and shortly before birth. A sound grasp of the nature of infant reflexes, and the manner in which they at times either support or oppose the later voluntary movement patterns, should aid prospective physical education teachers to understand the best ways to teach skills to elementary and secondary school youth.

Classes dealing with motor development may take several primary approaches to exposing the student to information. On one hand, the emerging characteristics of the infant, child, and adolescent are outlined within a time scale; and, for example, motor ability traits of children of ages two, four, eight, ten, and 12 can be compared. A second related course of action is to spend some time examining several motor ability traits and/or skills, and deciding how they differ among children of increasing age. Sex differences should also be dealt with in a course of this nature.

However, undergirding basic information of the type mentioned in the previous paragraph should be data which sketches various theories of child development which in some way treat the emerging "motor component" of the child's personality. A student armed with some kind of basic theoretical viewpoint can better integrate new information into a coherent fabric, from which he may make further generalizations and helpful translations into practice.

Two primary types of theories have in some way attempted to integrate the manner in which children develop in rather total ways, with the way in which movement characteristics emerge and manifest themselves. For the sake of simplicity, one kind shall be referred to as a "layer cake" theory, while the second will be termed a "latticework" theory.

One of the most prominent theories of child development has been advanced by Jean Piaget. This "layer cake" theory incorporates ideas and concepts which attempt to explain how motor attributes of infants evolve into higher-level thought processes seen in children, youth, and adults.

Piaget's observations of his own three children led him to formulate several primary tenets of his theory, only some of which will be reviewed here. A general assumption made by Piaget, however, is that the sensory-motor period of infancy underlies, and gradually evolves into, various perceptual and thought processes (or as Piaget terms them, "schematas.")

The theory is a detailed one, and one which has led toward a great deal of further thought on the part of others and to research both in the United States and abroad. For example, the early sensory-motor period of infancy has been divided by Piaget into several parts, from the initial phase in which only reflexive (automatic) motor behaviors are seen, through other stages which evolve out of this first one. Other advanced components of the sensory-motor period include a second stage, during which the child voluntarily initiates simple behavior in reaction to various objects; things seen become something to reach for and to grasp. The third stage involves the emergence, according to Piaget, of acts which are initiated by the child, rather than the child simply responding to events and objects. The infant between four and nine months begins to realize that his own movements can cause things to happen; and that he can make these movements himself, without waiting for some event or other person to initiate them.

The phases which evolve out of this third one begin to evidence a growing mental competence on the part of the maturing infant. For example, he may evidence awareness of the existence of an object and search for it as it drops from view, even though he can no longer perceive it directly through his senses (termed "object permanence" by Piaget).

The theory espoused by Piaget is a profound and deep one, and a book several times the size of this one is needed to illuminate all of its points effectively. The primary focus of Piaget's theory is upon the development of thought processes, and motor activity is believed to form the base from which these emerge.

I have outlined in a recent text another approach to explaining the manner in which children develop their movement capacities, as well as other facets of their personalities.[1] In general, rather than suggesting that the development of a child may be diagrammed as a pyramid with the movement at the base (as shown), a type of grid or latticework model was espoused.[2]

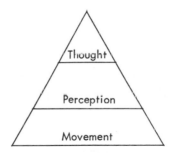

Figure 22-1.   Pyramid "Movement, Perception, and Thought"

In general, some of the primary axioms of this latticework theory are as follows:

1. It is believed that the infant evidences nearly simultaneous emergence of abilities dependent upon visual impressions, hearing, simple thought

[1]Bryant J. Cratty, *Perceptual and Motor Development of Infants and Children* (New York: The Macmillan Company, 1970).

[2]A *model* is a theory which has not become fully developed and for which there is as yet not a great deal of experimental evidence.

Maturity

Birth

Figure 22-2

processes, vocalization, and movement. Diagrammed, these emerging components of infant behavior may be depicted as shown in Figure 22-2.

2. As he matures, it is held, these general "trunks" of abilities fragment into numerous specific abilities and components. For example, the simple movements of the trunk quickly become divisible into those involving forward movement (crawling), and those in which the movement is upward (sitting, and later standing). These again divide as, for example, the infant acquires a number of ways of moving both upward (jumping, hopping, etc.), as well as moving forward (running, skipping, and similar behaviors). Manual activities also tend to fragment as the child matures. For example, at about eighteen months the infants begin to evidence the ability and desire to do a number of things to objects, including throwing them (blocks and balls), drawing with them (pencils), and continuing manipulative behavior. This fragmenting process is outlined in Figure 22-3.

3. A major premise upon which this model is based involves the suggestion that as maturation proceeds, various bonds are formed between abilities which previously functioned independently.

    By middle childhood, for example, the child's ability to watch moving objects, which is seen in infants as young as six months, becomes paired with his ability to move his body and to catch balls. The "bonding" of manual abilities with verbal abilities occurs by the age of six when the child becomes able to write letters and words. Numerous other examples could be described. The emergence and formation of these bonds may be depicted as shown in Figure 22-4.

4. Not only are some necessary bonds formed with maturity, but also the child may evidence a dissolution of useless bonds as he grows older. The capable child of seven or eight years of age, for example, no longer needs to read aloud; and the well-coordinated child of three years no longer needs to watch his feet when walking, just as the adult no longer needs to observe his hand inscribing his name during the entire course of the signature.

    Several axioms pertinent to the education of children have been formulated upon consideration of this model for child development. For example, it has been suggested that educators have several primary jobs when attempting to improve the motor attributes of infants, children, and youth, including:

1. Educators should aid some children to form helpful bonds between various visual, perceptual, cognitive, and movement abilities, to develop new attributes needed to accommodate to and cope with the environment.

2. At times the child must be helped to dissolve bonds between motor and other traits which may impede his performance in various skills. For

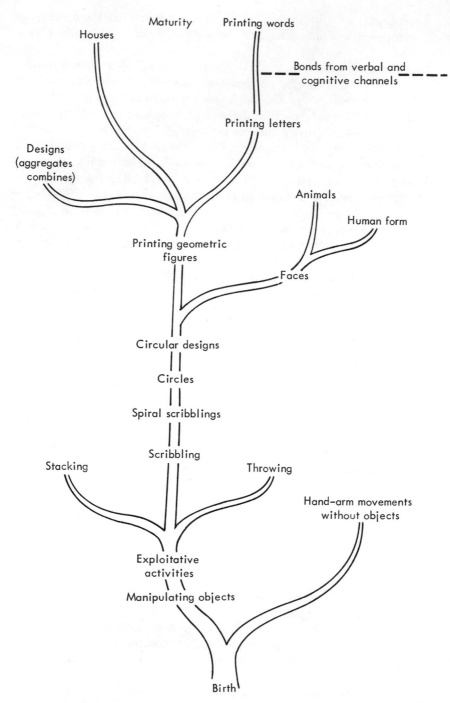

Figure 22-3

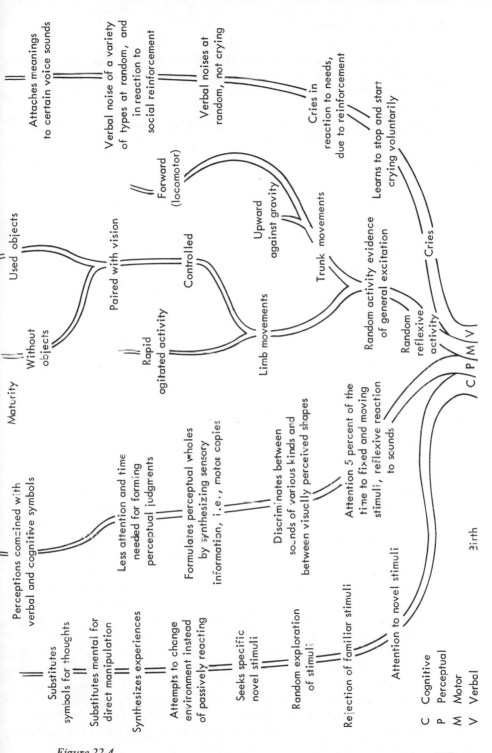

Figure 22-4

229

example, the less attention given to his own body parts as he performs a skill, the more he may organize the movement of teammates and of balls within the complex game situation.

3. At other times the educator may aid in the formation of what are termed "synthetic bonds" between various attributes which are not normally paired, particularly when attempting to work with atypical children. For example, a program of movement games, in which spelling is elicited as children jump in grids containing letters, pairs locomotor abilities (jumping and hopping) with cognitive processes (spelling) in a manner not usually found in the typical school environment.

The model contains other facets, the elaboration of which would consume more space than can be allotted to their exposition here. For example, the model explains the manner in which "blunting" of various attribute channels may occur, and the uneven manner in which various groups of abilities appear to emerge in the child. It is believed that this type of multi-dimensional model may be helpful when considering the ways in which the infant generally matures; as well as the manner in which various discrete behaviors function independently, and at other times are interrelated in complex and subtle ways.

A more operational look may be taken at the maturing child in action. One may, for example, consider the ways in which the child's structure changes as he grows and, more important, how various parts of the child's body are modified relative to each other. The infant's over-sized head, upon becoming smaller relative to his body size in childhood, probably contributes to the assumption of better balance by children of five and six years of age than was evidenced at two years of age. The structural changes in the male adolescent in shoulder width, to cite another example, probably contributes to increased strength during these years.

The motor attributes of children of various ages should also come under scrutiny within a course in motor development. Students should become familiar, both through their reading and via direct observations, with just what a five-, seven-, and nine-year-old child looks like when he is asked to perform various motor skills. A number of motor capacities should be considered within such an evaluation, including drawing, balancing, locomotor abilities (hopping, skipping, walking, and other variations), ball handling skills, broad jumping, running speed, agility of the limbs and of the total body, as well as various manipulative skills.

A thorough grounding in the information available, relative to the motor characteristics of children of various ages and of both sexes, should serve to make the physical education graduate an important member of a professional team dealing with general and specific developmental problems in the schools. For example, the child at five evidences various capacities, while at the same time is unable to perform accurately a number of tasks whose successful execution will be seen in later childhood. The five-year-old will usually be able to hop (using one foot) and to jump (two feet at a time) for short distances without too much trouble; but if asked to do so with accuracy, into small squares for example, he may have some trouble. The five-year-old can usually execute a standing broadjump of about three feet; and can jump over a bar about one foot high or slightly higher, using a two foot takeoff and landing. He will be able to draw reasonably good squares and circles, but the drawing of a triangle will usually prove difficult.

During these early years of childhood, developmental problems may be evidenced which will cause considerable stress to children both in classrooms and on the athletic field. Clumsy children are ridiculed by their peers on the playground, and often pressured for rapid handwriting by their classroom teachers. A thorough knowledge of the child's capacities, particularly during the years he enters school, can be an immeasurable assistance to the total school community.

During early childhood, as in later childhood, the girls will usually excel the boys (because of a slightly more mature nervous system) in tasks requiring accuracy and control. Girls will jump more accurately, draw more precisely, and evidence more total control when asked to balance in various ways. On the other hand, even during these early years, the boys will usually manifest more force in their movements (both in appearance as well as in actual performance measures). The boy, for example, will usually run faster, jump higher and farther, throw farther, and throw and jump with better total body involvement than will his female classmates.

Later in childhood, children become highly specialized in the abilities they evidence, depending upon the opportunities they have had to learn skills and to play vigorously. Their parents' attitudes and the equipment available, in various degrees, contribute to or detract from what they can do with their bodies.

Their performance "curves" plotted for each year in childhood often level off at various ages, indicating a time of little or no improvement. Balance scores often evidence this plateau effect, and generally cease to show improvement by the age of 12 to 14 years. In other cases, particularly in the area of strength, there is a regular improvement usually seen at each year of life.

By seven, a child can balance on one foot with his eyes closed, can hop and jump accurately, and can begin to throw a ball for a considerable distance. His manual abilities begin to mature, and he becomes able, for example, to touch the tip of each finger quickly to the thumb of the same hand. He can draw and print accurately, his letters become more recognizable and smaller, and he can manage the lateral lines required when drawing a triangle. The seven-year-old can usually skip, and is seen to shift his body weight properly forward when throwing. He becomes able to jump using his arms for lift and/or distance by extending them upward and forward as his legs extend.

In late childhood, various components of his visual and motor systems begin to work together. He can watch small balls coming from some distance and not only predict where they are likely to land, but can also position himself there and catch them with his outstretched hands. He requires games of more complexity to keep his interest, while at the same time he seeks a variety of activities in which to participate.[3]

Several fallacies abound in the literature relative to the motor abilities of children in late childhood and early adolescence. For example, it is usually written that children in this age range evidence increased clumsiness. This statement, however, is not usually made with a great deal of precision, nor is it supported with any valid evidence. For, in truth, children in late childhood and early adolescence evidence better performance scores in virtually everything they do, than do children in middle childhood and younger. Children in early adolescence often are as large as those in their late teens, to whom they are compared, and who indeed post higher performance scores than do their younger peers. In general, it is seen that children and youth continue to improve in most motor skills, and in measures of basic performance capacities, in a step-by-step manner each year as they grow older. The results of research studies do not indicate any marked retrogression of ability during late childhood and early adolescence.

A number of factors impinge upon the motor ability and skill manifested by the adolescent boy and girl. It is this age range toward which many physical educators in training will later be directing their efforts, and thus a thorough attempt should be made to understand how adolescents function. Social expectations, structural changes, and biochemical modifications during adolescence serve to raise considerably basic motor capacities of both girls and boys, although it is usually found that the actual performances of males are more likely to reflect basic capacities than are the performances of the females of the species.

---

[3]One recent study in Scandinavia found that, while the more fit children in early childhood seemed the less capable academically, with perhaps the less fit during these years spending their time in study rather than action, by late childhood the intellectually more able students were the most fit; indicating, according to the researcher involved, that as childhood games became more challenging they attracted the brighter children, and thus promoted their fitness.

Boys in schools are still given every social incentive to excel in athletics, while receiving varying amounts of societal censure for not moving their muscles well. Adolescent girls do not have to contend with this type of pressure; but, at the same time, may align themselves socially with male athletics in various ways for additional prestige.

Girls in adolescence receive, in general, approval for excellence in areas other than athletics. Their appearance, "personality," and even their intellectual attributes frequently occupy center stage. At the same time there is data which suggest that the social censure which was often attached to female athletic competition and participation in the past in the United States has, to some degree, started to dissipate, and in some sports in certain parts of the country has disappeared entirely.

The strength and endurance of both boys and girls in adolescence are about twice what they could manifest a few years earlier in late childhood. During early and middle adolescence, the boys begin to surpass the girls to an even greater degree than they did in childhood in tasks requiring power, while at the same time catching up with and passing their female companions in activities requiring accurate movements, perhaps because of the increased practice they engage in.

Adolescent girls' physical performance scores, when collected in organized ways, are likely to evidence irregularities, as their moods and monthly cycles may affect just how hard they try in various tasks. Physical education teachers often encounter great difficulties motivating both girls and boys in physical activities during the adolescent years, as during this time of life youth become highly selective of what they are doing. The youth in America, to an increasing degree, are not likely to "buy" some of the meaningless "arm-waving" exercises and games which offer little physical or intellectual challenge. Physical educators presenting activities which are less than meaningful to these youth will likely become disappointed with the efforts they are able to elicit, and indeed may encounter resistance evidenced by the disinclination on the part of the youth to even begin the tasks presented.

The study of motor development may and should contain information which will enable the prospective physical educator to understand and to deal with individuals in adulthood, and even those classified as aged. Adult recreational programs within the community and in industry demand leaders who can formulate activities compatible with the needs and capacities of the senior citizens. Older people may at times be threatened "psychologically" by the introduction of new physical and recreational activities; and encouraging the aged even to begin a motor task will often task the best teaching the recreational leader or physical educator can provide.

People within this age group, from 40 to 80, begin in various ways to lose the capacity to perform vigorous and forceful acts. At the same time they bring an extensive background of experience to the playfield and recreational center, experience which can often be exploited and utilized when attempting to "build in" new skills. Programs for those individuals, if handled properly and based upon sound principles derived from a thorough background containing information dealing with the nature of physical performance of the adult and aged, can make important personal contributions to its participants.

Summary

One of the essential "blocks" of information to be obtained by physical educators as undergraduates should deal with the manner in which the physical capacities and performance characteristics of infants, children, youth, and adults change with age. Additionally, particularly concerning childhood and adolescence, differences between the sexes in various motor capacities should be explored and understood.

A general knowledge of child development, containing both theoretical as well as applied information, should underlie a deeper grasp of various facets of motor development. Accompanying this theoretical and practical base should be an attempt on the part of the student to relate the manner in which various motor attributes reflect, contribute to, and at times accompany other facets of the child's personality, including his cognitive, perceptual, verbal, and emotional characteristics. Armed with this information, the physical educator should be able to work with teams of specialists from other disciplines concerned with assessing the total development and developmental problems of the child entering school for the first time.

More highly motivating programs for adolescent boys and girls should be forthcoming if physical educators obtain a thorough grounding in the available data dealing with adolescent development. The manner in which the two sexes may at times be placed together for meaningful activities, as well as when it is appropriate to separate the sexes during childhood and adolescence, should become reasonably clear after a scholarly consideration of the available information. In a similar manner, recreational and fitness programs for adults and for the aged should evidence improvement if their instigators become able to predict accurately the problems in motivation and performance which may arise within this population.

Student Activities and Discussion Questions

1. Observe a five-year-old boy at play. Contrast him with a girl of the same age, relative to the vigor of activities and to the type of activities selected.

2. Evaluate via various performance tests the abilities of the five-year-old boy, and compare the scores obtained to those gained from assessing the same competencies of a seven-year-old boy. What tests might you place in such a battery? What differences do you see or might you expect to observe?

3. Inspect a recreational program for the aged at your local park. What principles of program planning seem to coincide with what you know about the interests and performance capacities of this age group? What do you observe that might indicate some discrepancy between the program and maturational characteristics of the aged?

4. Compare a group of boys and girls, from 12 to 16 years of age, in various capacity measures: strength, endurance, running speed, etc. Not only note performance differences, which are to be expected, but also carefully note the attitudes of each group (reflected in resistance to or acceptance of the testing program). What do they say when being tested? What effect might onlookers of either sex have upon the performance of both sexes as they are tested?

References

Books

Cratty, Bryant J., Martin, S. M. M., Jennett, C., and Morris, M., *Movement Activities, Motor Ability and the Education of Children.* Springfield, Illinois: Charles C. Thomas, Publisher, 1970.

_____, *Perceptual Motor Behavior and Educational Processes.* Springfield, Illinois: Charles C. Thomas, Publisher, 1969.

_____, and Martin, S. M. M., *Perceptual-Motor Efficiency in Children.* Philadelphia: Lea & Febiger, 1969.

_____, *Perceptual and Motor Development of Infants and Children.* New York: The Macmillan Company, 1970.

Espenschade, Anna, and Eckert, Helen, *Motor Development.* Columbus, Ohio: Charles E. Merrill, Inc., 1967.

Falkner, Frank, *Human Development.* Philadelphia: W. B. Saunders Company, 1966.

Kellogg, Rhoda, *Analyzing Children's Art.* Palo Alto: National Press Books, 1969.

Stott, Leland, *Child Development.* New York: Holt, Rinehart and Winston, Inc., 1967.

Wickstrom, Ralph L., *Fundamental Motor Patterns.* Philadelphia: Lea & Febiger, 1970.

Periodical

Physical Educator. 4000 Meadows Dr., Indianapolis, Indiana 46205.

CHAPTER TWENTY-THREE

Teaching Methods

During your undergraduate years you may be exposed to information pertaining to teaching methodology in a variety of contexts. You may, for example, find that separate courses are being offered in the upper division physical education major. Parts of courses dealing with the coaching and teaching of various sports are likely to be devoted to knowledge about teaching methods. Courses you may take within the department of education may likewise contain content concerned with educational psychology, the psychology of teaching, or the like.

Generally, as a physical educator and coach you should be seeking information of two types during your undergraduate years at the college or university. (a) A large part of the knowledge you acquire concerning teaching methodology will involve general principles which you may apply to most of the classes and teams you will later deal with, regardless of the sport or type of physical activity involved. (b) A second area of knowledge you should be seeking deals with specific techniques for teaching and coaching, appropriate only for various sports.

Within the first category is found, for example, content dealing with the general manner in which people learn, the use of demonstration, the spacing of practice, and perhaps the manner in which people may be motivated to learn best. The second classification (b) contains such things as proper methods for spotting performers when attempting to execute specific gymnastic stunts, how to arrange tennis classes for the teaching of the serve, class organization necessary when teaching soccer skills, and other techniques for effectively transmitting specific skills in various sports.

If you complete your college training armed only with general methods for presenting a variety of material (physical and mental content), you are not going to be completely equipped as a physical education teacher or coach. At the same time, if you deal only with specific methodologies pertinent to various sports skills, you are not going to be able to evaluate new methodologies, and you may not be able to correctly integrate into meaningful lessons the teaching methods you have in your possession. A second danger you will incur if you dwell only upon teaching techniques in specific skills is that you will be less flexible in your teaching, and will not be able to modify your teaching approach to accommodate to individual differences in the psychological, maturational, and physical makeups of children and youth.

In a chapter the size of this one, a detailed examination of the specifics concerning the teaching of various physical education and recreational skills is obviously not possible. Several of the texts listed at the completion of the chapter contain detailed teaching methodologies about specific skill areas. The pages which follow delineate several broad categories of considerations relative to the teaching of activities commonly found in physical education and recreational programs. Tying in these general guidelines with the teaching or coaching of the many sports and recreational skills is possible only if the student (a) is perceptive and able to translate theory to practice, and (b) if he also obtains practice in teaching specific skills, keeping in mind a variety of general considerations and observing what actually happens to his students. A formula for this process is offered below.

General Considerations and
Teaching Techniques:
Skill Improvement in Children

For example, in teaching the somersault the instructor may generally consider the nature of the social context (who is watching), whether he will attempt to teach all or a part of the skill, how much he will permit the child to seek the movement for himself, etc. He will then select those factors which he feels are relevant, combine them with how to assist the head and shoulders of a child attempting a front somersault for the first time, and then apply his knowledge to the child—that is, assist his head to turn under the body by kneeling to the side, etc. A similar process goes on, with or without the conscious awareness of the instructor or coach, every time a skill is taught. By considering some of the general methodological principles outlined in the paragraphs which follow, you later will have a broader list of considerations from which to choose; and thus will be able to more readily adapt your approach in teaching to the situation and to the child with whom you will be dealing.

What are Instructions?

When considering the broad subject of teaching methodology, one of the first problems to come to mind is: "How shall I instruct?" Generally, when one thinks of instructions, one thinks about something that someone is showing or telling another person about a skill. However, in addition to this obvious type of instruction is another more subtle category. People instruct *themselves* when approaching a skill. Most performers over the age of four or five probably engage in a great deal of sub-vocal (you can't hear it) encouragement, discouragement, or specific formulas for doing a particular type of skill.

It may be your job later as a coach to interfere with this type of self-instruction as little as possible, particularly if the quality of the directions they seem to be giving themselves appear to be as helpful or even more useful than the directions you are extending to them. Unthinkable that a trained graduate in physical education could be of less help than those he is to teach! Yet in a study completed at the end of the 1960s it was found that a group of college students who were left free to instruct themselves in badminton ended up playing better than a second group who were given a rather structured program of instruction.

Would this same thing be found when dealing with less mature, and hypothetically not as bright, children in junior high school? Perhaps so, and perhaps not. In any case, it might be hypothesized from the study which is outlined above, that the mature college-age students were better able to analyze their skill in the light of their own individual differences than was the instructor of the second group, who apparently adapted a single structured teaching method to the entire group.

Physical educators who control students too rigidly may be impeding the level of activity and fitness they would have gained if they had been left alone merely to ramble on the grass. All physical educators should at all times attempt to determine just how much formal instruction and control is needed by various groups of people, who exhibit skill levels of various magnitudes. One of your first jobs as an instructor of physical activities may be to prevent yourself from over-teaching your pupils. This idea is expanded in the section which follows. The literature on instruction suggests that instructions may emanate from at least three sources: from a teacher who may communicate in a number of ways how the skill may be accomplished, from the performer himself who gives himself various unheard orders and directions, and finally from the nature of the task itself. It would seem to be the job of the physical educator to mix these three types of instructions in the proper way, and to be available to the student when and if he is needed.

Trial and Error Versus Formal Instruction

The above paragraphs suggest that practicing a given skill at a given time may be based to some degree upon either trial and error (plus self-analysis by the performer), or upon some kind of formal instructions emanating from another person. Just when trial-and-error learning should be permitted, as opposed to formal instruction, depends upon a variety of variables:

1. Trial-and-error learning is more effective if the learners are mature, intelligent, and have had some exposure to tasks similar to the ones being practiced.
2. Trial-and-error learning may be effective either during the initial stages of learning a skill (during which the learner may be comparing how to do the new skill with the execution of other similar ones), as well as during the later stages of learning (during which time the learner may be accommodating to unique attributes which he possesses, and about which the instructor cannot be expected to be aware).
3. Some combination of trial and error with formal instruction is likely to prove best, particularly if the instructions are well-placed in the learning process, consist of information understood by the learner, are relevant to the task at hand, and are offered under conditions and in ways which are not considered stressful by the learner.

In conclusion, these axioms suggest that a coach or physical education teacher should not always feel that it is his job to offer *his* instructions; rather, he may at times simply know when to keep silent, permitting the learner to teach himself.

Perception and Teaching

Research during the past 20 years indicates that to teach effectively one must accommodate to individual differences in the manner in which people put together what they hear, see, and feel. In general, the kinds of cues from which an individual will learn best are not very predictable. Some, for example, may learn best by seeing a demonstration of a skill, others by hearing it explained, and still others by having the opportunity to practice it (i.e., to feel the movement through their muscle senses). Moreover, most children and youth depend upon a variety of cues, some of which may be inherent in the teaching-learning situation, and others which the instructor may make available to them.

The research findings make it seem axiomatic that to teach physical skills best, the instructor must be able to communicate to the learner through a *number* of the learner's senses. In each class there are individuals who may learn best in a variety of ways. For the instructor to reach all these students he must be able to explain the skill well, to demonstrate it (or show a film, or have a class member demonstrate), and to permit practice of the skill. If any of these ways of instruction are not available to the instructor or coach, or if he is ineffective in the use of one or another, it is likely he will lose some of the team or class members.

There are some signs, however, that young children are most likely to learn well if their limbs are moved, or if they are permitted to imitate a child of similar size. Verbal instructions are most effective when teaching adults, by inserting them during the initial stages of learning. Viewing a demonstration must be immediately followed by opportunities to practice. However, most exact principles need further research, and are specifically applicable to the teaching of various individual skills.

Several things should be kept in mind when demonstrating, when permitting the performer to view his own actions, when manipulating the limbs of another person, and when guiding him in the execution of a given skill. For example, to use a demonstration best, the learner must be able to identify with the demonstrator. Using an expert to show beginners how to perform a skill may not be as effective as permitting them to see an individual whose skill level is nearer their own.

The use of a videotape to permit a performer to view his own actions immediately after executing a skill would seem to be sound practice. The feedback is immediate, nonverbal, and usually uncontroversial (i.e., the performer will not usually argue with the appearance of his own movements as quickly as he may with the words of an instructor or coach). On the other hand, it has been found that beginning performers in several activities, including gymnastics and dance, have been visibly upset by vividly seeing themselves perform in a clumsy manner on the videotape. At the same time, many sports skills are easy for the performer to see himself perform, so the use of expensive equipment may not be necessary. In general, the immediate feedback offered by the videotape machine is most likely to be helpful in the teaching of skills which, when executed, involve a good deal of spatial disorganization (tumbling, diving, trampolining, pole-vaulting, high-jumping, etc.); and is more likely to be effective with those of moderate and high levels of skill in the various activities.

Other interesting research findings suggest that when guiding the movements of another person, one should be careful not to overcontrol the performer. If this occurs it is likely that the learner may unduly "fight" the directions of the teacher, and combine the wrong muscular reactions in an incorrect sequence while apparently performing the skill. In one study on this subject, for example, it was found that while quick performance was forthcoming when a group of individuals were guided in a reasonably complex movement task, more retention occurred in a group of subjects who had to control their own movements when initially learning the skill.

Thought and Movement

Physical educators, among others, sometimes forget that the learner has a brain and thinks when attempting to learn a skill. While it was earlier explained that performers give verbal instructions to themselves, it may also be true that you will find children and youth extremely good at giving themselves sound instructions, and that the processes of thinking through the skill will be extremely helpful to them.

For the past 30 years, studies have been carried out concerning the manner in which mental practice contributes to the learning of a motor skill. In one recent investigation it was found that during the *initial* stages of learning, thinking about the task was *as* effective as actual practice in performing the task! Most of the information in this area, however, suggests that there is an optimum amount of physical and mental practice productive of best performance and retention; and that either physical or mental practice by itself is not as effective as both taken together.

Several other types of investigations have demonstrated the importance of having your students think about a task while they learn it, and while watching others perform. For example, in one study it was found that skill in a one-handed task was developed as quickly in a group of subjects by watching others perform, as it was by a second group which was asked to practice it first with their other hand. Investigations of cats have shown that they too can observe another cat executing a complex motor task and learn from mere observation; let's hope that you will permit the children and youth who will later be in your charge to do the same.

Muska Mosston has developed a teaching methodology which relies primarily upon the development of cognitive processes through movement experiences. One adaptation of this theory was described briefly in Chapter Seven on elementary education. Several threads run through this theory which have been accorded the attention of teachers in fields other than physical education. For example, it is assumed that no true learning will take place unless the learner makes, or is offered, some choices within the learning context. It is further assumed that, when judged practical, the instructor should gradually transfer to his pupils decisions concerning the manner in which a task may be modified, the way in which it should be evaluated, as well as the reasons for selecting a given group of tasks in the first place. Most important is the phrase "when it is judged practical," for the proponent of this theory does not advocate simply "throwing open" the doors of creativity and problem-solving without first gradually extending to the learner the opportunities to make a minimum amount of decisions himself, and then evaluating the result of these initial ventures into self-determination.

This theory has as a basic ingredient the suggestion that teachers should consider what is termed "a spectrum of styles" when teaching; and adapt the amount of teacher-authority, versus decisions made by youth, according to the skill the learners evidence when first permitted to make their own decisions, as well as to other goals and conditions within the learning environment.

The proponent of this conceptual framework suggests that more physical effort will be evidenced by children and youth when they are permitted to make the activity selected "their own thing," rather than having it dictated and monitored from a higher authority (the teacher). But most important, children and youth will evidence development of emotional, social, and intellectual attributes when the teacher permits them to engage in qualitative social reactions with each other, to carry out intellectual endeavors in various movement activities, and to demonstrate emotional stability and control.

To consider this broad theory, one which is having far-reaching effects upon physical education in this country, a thorough perusal of the writings of the educational methodologist Mosston should be carried out. At the same time, to practice the tenets the theory suggests, you must perhaps give up some of your needs to control others. You must also be concerned more with the processes children and youth go through when learning, than with quick success evidenced by performance scores. When you become able to do this, you may find that the children in your charge become more fit to modify their skills effectively, and to select appropriate actions when complex game situations demand the performance of a variety of quick, well-executed, and appropriate responses.

Overview

There are a number of basic considerations relative to teaching methodology which your instructors in physical education classes might present for your careful consideration. Some of these were discussed in Chapter Seventeen, dealing with the psychology of physical activity and motor learning.

Additionally, however, you might be presented information which explains how children and youth may be aided to retain skill best. In general, it is found that instructions to retain seem to result in better retention; people seem to learn better when they are aware that they must repeat some skill. Therefore, the teacher might explain to all learners just when and how they must redemonstrate their proficiency.

Easiest to retain, whether movement or verbal abilities, are skills which are rhythmic and integrated in nature: poetry rather than prose, or nonsense syllables and rhythmic movements rather than those which do not go together smoothly. Similarly, information embedded into the middle of other information is more difficult to retain, than are information or movements nearer the beginning and the end of a series. The practice should be to either emphasize material which may be contained in the middle of a semester or of a class period; or to place material you wish to be remembered best into the end or beginning of your lessons.

Discontinuing a lesson without giving all the answers may also create what is termed a "need strain," which will result in better retention over a period of time than if each lesson is complete unto itself. Some researchers have found that practicing a movement incorrectly may bring vividly to the learner's mind just what movements or submovements should be avoided, and thus create better final learning. Others have found that spacing practice may create better initial learning than if practice sessions are placed too closely together in time.

The axiom "practice makes perfect" might be substituted by the suggestions that "rest may help more than practice," and that "at times, imperfect practice may elicit best learning."

Another principle which is frequently aired in various tests in physical education is that initial practice should be given at full speed, so that the true nature of the movement later to be performed is somehow imprinted into the nervous system. When searching for the data supporting such a suggestion, however, I found that indeed only one poorly-conducted study contributed any findings which in any way supported this contention. In my later research, I found that mother gorillas in Africa were found to teach their offspring the more hazardous turning tasks by starting them in a slow, careful manner. Of course, some might accuse the mother gorillas of not consulting the proper research journals. However, the teaching principle they seem to have discovered may be a valid one for a human learner who is exposed to the complex spatial relationships inherent in some of the more difficult gymnastic stunts.

Summary

In the preceding pages some of the more controversial "principles" of teaching skills have been presented. Their airing may serve to give the student of teaching methodology an appreciation of the complexity of the problem of instructing others in athletic and physical education activities. In general, several primary considerations should be kept in mind: teaching should be applied in a manner which will permit the learner to take part in the learning process; he should be given time to think about the task; and he should take time between practice trials during which the movement may "set in" his nervous system.

The efficient instructor should be capable of utilizing visual demonstrations, of explaining the desired skills verbally, as well as of teaching his class in ways permitting exploration of the skill by the pupils in his charge. It is hoped that the information in this chapter, coupled with information you may obtain concerning the ways in which skills in specific sports may be taught, will enable you to work more effectively as a physical education teacher and athletic coach.

Student Activities and Discussion Questions

1. Observe a physical education teacher instructing a class or an individual in a given skill. Upon what sensory cues is he depending primarily? How might his efforts be speeded up, and made more effective? How would you have instructed the skill differently?
2. List, with the help of a gymnast, some of the specific skills needed when spotting tumblers. What spotting devices do you need?
3. With the help of a tennis teacher, indicate what apparatus and what specific teaching methodologies are helpful in the teaching of tennis.
4. Are some of the instructional methods used in the various field sports (soccer, field hockey, speed ball, rugby, football) common to several sports within this general classification? Which types of methods might be used in most or all of the sports listed?
5. Study a good swimming coach or an experienced swimming teacher. What percentage of the time do they devote to formal instruction, versus trial-and-error learning? Does this percentage vary according to the level of skill exhibited by the class; or according to the stroke or aquatic skill being presented?

6. Discuss with a technician, or with a coach who has used them, the costs and other problems and advantages accompanying the use of the videotape feedback system (including a television monitor, videotape machine, and camera). In which sports or skills is it likely to be effective? In which is it least effective? What considerations should be followed when using it in a lesson? How does this apparatus differ, relative to its effects upon learning, from the standard teaching film?

References

Books

Cratty, Bryant J., *Movement, Perception and Thought*. Palo Alto: Peek Publications, 1969.

———, and Martin, S. M. M., *Perceptual-Motor Efficiency in Children*. Philadelphia: Lea & Febiger, 1969.

———, *Psychology and Physical Activity*. Englewood Cliffs, New Jerey: Prentice-Hall, Inc., 1968.

Davis, E. C., *Successful Teaching in Physical Education*. Englewood Cliffs, New Jersey: Prentice-Hall, Inc., 1948.

Fait, H. F., *A Manual of Physical Education Activities*. Philadelphia: W. B. Saunders, 1967.

Flanigan, T. E., *Teaching Aids for Health, Physical Education and Recreation*. New Lenox: Department of Physical Education, Lincoln Way Community High School, 1962.

Groves, W. A., *Class Guide for Physical Education*. Danville, Illinois: School Aid Company, 1968.

Kozman, H. C., *Methods in Physical Education*. Dubuque, Iowa: W. C. Brown Company, 1967.

Langton, Clair Van Norman, *Principles of Health, Physical Education and Recreation*. New York: The Ronald Press Company, 1962.

Mosston, Muska, *Teaching Physical Education*. Columbus, Ohio: Charles E. Merrill, Inc., 1966.

Singer, R. N., *Motor Learning and Human Performance: An Application to Physical Education Skills*. New York: The Macmillan Company, 1968.

Periodical

Journal of Physical Education. Physical Directors Society of YMCA, North American; 347 Madison Avenue, New York, New York.

PART FOUR

Graduation and Afterward

CHAPTER TWENTY-FOUR

Graduate Education

Many teaching and coaching positions in the United States require the student to engage in postgraduate training of some type. Many states require, for a secondary teaching credential, practice-teaching and courses in education above and beyond the bachelor's degree. After securing a position in teaching, with or without graduate training, the instructor is usually required yearly to present evidence of professional improvement; this evidence often takes the form of graduate credits from the local college or university.

Work past the bachelor's degree may also be undertaken by an individual who wishes to obtain an advanced degree: the master's or doctorate. At times students spend their fifth year in college working for both a master's degree as well as a teaching credential of some type. Work in special education and physical education, as described in Chapter Eleven, usually requires special credentials earned after graduation. Often graduates with the B.S. or B.A. degree are given temporary appointments within school districts, with the understanding that they will embark upon a graduate program at the same time they are engaging in their first year of instruction.

The decision of whether or not to enter graduate school is often made for the prospective graduate student. Entrance to postgraduate work requires a number of academic qualifications, which an individual may or may not possess upon receiving his B.S. degree. A grade point average of near 3.0 (B) on a 4-point system is usually required; and if yours is much below that, you may have to search for a university which will accept you. Often, however, these requirements are lowered if you perform well on one or more of a number of admissions tests, such as the Graduate Record Examination. At the same time, your upper-division grade point average, if indicative of an upward trend, may serve to admit you even if you stumbled a little during your first two years at college.

As is true of your undergraduate preparation, your graduate program will be as meaningful as you are willing to make it for yourself. The professional growth you experience will be directly related to the amount of effort you are willing to expend. Most departments of physical education in colleges and universities have reasonably adequate libraries, and the immediate and long-term worth of your program may to a large degree depend upon how much and how well you use these library facilities.

There are several important considerations in selecting a graduate program, some of which are more practical than academic. For example, if you are planning to work on a teaching credential during your fifth year, it is important that you find a program located in the same state in which you later hope to teach. Graduate requirements leading toward credentials for teaching differ between states, so graduate preparation of this nature in one part of the country is not likely to aid you a great deal when obtaining a secondary or elementary school position in another state.

If you are seeking a graduate degree so that you may enter college or university teaching, or for some other reason you do not desire to enter public school instruction immediately after receiving your advanced degree, the list of colleges or universities you may wish to enter is somewhat more extensive.

There are at least seven relatively academic factors worth your thought prior to deciding upon an appropriate graduate program. At the same time, someone who knows you well should provide counsel when this critical time in your career is reached. Perhaps a member of the staff in your department could advise you.

1. Evaluate the quality of the staff as well as you can. Attempt to determine whether the competencies of one or more coincide with your interests and goals. Graduate programs will generally force you into a close relationship with a member of the faculty. One member of the faculty may supervise your thesis toward the latter part of your program, while others will get to know you and your competencies in the small graduate seminars in which you will take part. There are several ways in which you as an emerging student may judge the quality of various faculties under which you might be considering doing work.

For example, you may attend national and state conventions, hear faculty members speak, and then make appointments to speak to them; your present staff members may be able to give you some "line" on their abilities and interests; or some of those you are evaluating may have written books which may give you an idea of their competencies and weaknesses. In order to determine whether a group of professors really attend to the needs of their students and are frequently available for student conferences, you may contact some of their former students and ask their opinions on these matters. Still another way to see if you wish to attend a given college or university, and to do graduate work under various professors, is to visit the campuses, talk to these people, and perhaps attend one or more of their classes as a guest.

Finding a large number of competent faculty members at a given institution may not be as important as finding one or two who can direct your program and, most important, who will permit you to take courses in other departments within the university during your graduate year(s). Some of the stronger doctoral programs in the country permit, indeed encourage, their students to do just that. For example, they may have students enrolled in courses in physiology and anatomy at the medical school on campus, or in other ways have formal or informal cooperative arrangements with other disciplines related to physical education.

2. Find out whether faculty members seem to over-direct their students' efforts by pressuring them into carrying out doctoral or master's theses within rather narrow areas; or whether more individual creativity is permitted. You may need, and thus may seek, close direction; on the other hand, you may feel you need certain professional and technical competencies, but at the same time will want "to do your own thing" when engaged in graduate studies.

3. If you expect to carry out meaningful research as a graduate student, you will want to determine not only if there are active researchers on the faculty you are considering, but also whether there are reasonably good facilities for your research interests. Look carefully, do not be overly impressed with shiny and sometimes unused laboratory equipment, but consider carefully the quality of people you find and of the ideas being worked on *within* such laboratories. Are the laboratories busy working only on the professor's pet projects, or are graduate students engaged in their individual research efforts? A most revealing question which you might pose, if it seems judicious, is: "Just what are you doing here?" The embarrassment and hesitation which such a question may bring about in those to whom it is posed is a small discomfort, as compared to the professional deadend you may experience if you find yourself in a relatively sterile and unproductive situation.

4. Seek ways of supporting yourself financially within the graduate program you are considering. Most universities permit half-time work when a student attends full-time as a graduate student. This work can consist of teaching activity classes or working as a laboratory assistant, both of which can prove professionally rewarding. The staff members you visit, as well as those at your present school, should be able to direct you toward sources of possible support within and outside the university you are considering. Often there are research grants being carried out which require part-time assistants, and government support to graduate students may also be available. Often small grants can be obtained from private or public agencies, with which you can carry out the latter portion of your graduate work.

5. Attempt to gain information concerning the quality of the library facilities available. Visit the library at the school of your choice; determine particularly the range of the research journals and texts available in your field of interest. If you find that the library is inadequate, do not hesitate to look elsewhere for your graduate education. I believe that the single most important factor undergirding the quality of a graduate program is the nature of the literature easily available to the student.

6. Assess the graduate programs you are considering in the light of your future professional goals. If you plan to spend a year working on a master's degree, and then enter teaching and/or coaching, you may want to select a program which expands your background in a more general way than would be desirable if your ultimate objective is a doctorate. If you seek a doctorate, a staff and program which will enable you to grow in the depth of your understanding of a particular area of knowledge would probably be more appropriate.

7. If you plan to work toward a doctorate, it is important to obtain at the completion of your first postgraduate year, from an individual who is familiar with you and whose judgment you respect, a candid assessment of your potential and of the strengths and weaknesses you have evidenced during your early efforts. If this evaluation of your abilities is very negative, it may be desirable to readjust your professional goals. Listen well when you are told that "you may not make it"; the advice is usually honestly offered, and should be considered carefully. There is nothing more tragic than to observe an enterprising student, often at considerable financial sacrifice, spend three to seven or more years working toward a doctorate only to find his goals unattainable. On the other hand, if this first year's evaluation results in the receipt of less ominous news, you should take heart, attempt to rectify the weaknesses which are observed in you, and proceed toward your educational goals with renewed vigor.

Summary

After evaluating your own needs, interests, and professional goals, you should carefully consider the staffs, libraries, and laboratories of various programs you might enter. The breadth, versus the depth, of the program's offerings should also be considered in relationship to your own future aspirations.

The time you spend in graduate work following your first four collegiate years is likely to be a most productive and exciting time. If you are able to bring about a happy "wedding" between your capabilities, abilities, and goals, with the conditions you find within a specific program, your effectiveness as a professional worker is likely to undergo marked changes; while your personal development is also likely to evidence a desirable metamorphosis.

References

Books

American Association for Health, Physical Education and Recreation, *Conference on Graduate Education.* Washington, D. C.: American Association for Health, Physical Education and Recreation, 1967.

Snyder, R. A., *Professional Preparation in Health, Physical Education and Recreation.* New York: McGraw-Hill, 1954.

Periodicals

Associated College Admissions Counselors Journal ACAC Journal, 801 Davis St., Evanston, Illinois 60201.

College and University. American Association of College Registrars and Admissions Officers, Curtis Reed Plaza, Menasha, Wisconsin.

CHAPTER TWENTY-FIVE

Gaining Experience
and Your First Position
After Graduation

Individuals wishing to work with people in various types of physical activity programs should receive, as early as possible in their careers, the opportunity to work with children and youth in positions resembling those for which they are preparing. This experience may have come before you entered college, as there are many opportunities to take leadership roles within various youth programs while still in secondary school. The Boy Scouts, YMCA, Campfire Girls, Woodcraft Rangers, Boys' Clubs, and private recreation and camping programs offer both voluntary and paid jobs which boys and girls in high school may fill.

First experiences with children may have come to you in your family; perhaps it was during this period of your life when you first began to believe that you might work in athletics or physical education. Some research has indicated that an individual who attempts to serve others is likely to be from a family in which there is more than one child.

Various voluntary, private, and publicly-supported agencies, dealing with the physically handicapped, the retarded, the aged, the culturally deprived, and the blind, also provide a place where experience might be gained during your early years of college. At other times a family might be seeking help with a problem child of some type, and may post notices in student placement bureaus on your campus requesting a college student to come into their home on a regular basis.

Part-Time Experience During College

There are several guidelines which you might consider when seeking and working in part-time jobs while still an undergraduate. Some of these suggestions may not be appropriate to your situation; however, others are of more general applicability to a variety of environments.

1. Seek part-time positions which really test your capabilities, or will tend to develop the talents you may later need as a teacher, coach, or therapist. You may, if a girl, during your freshman or sophomore years find baby-sitting positions; however, later you should try to find work with groups of children in various school situations, as well as in private and recreational clubs. Taking care of a single child with physical, mental, and/or emotional handicaps will later provide more of a growth experience for you than will the baby-sitting job with a normal child.

2. Once you take a job, regardless of how menial, simple, or demeaning you may feel it to be, do a good job. You are attempting to become a professional person, so you should not expect to "burn too many job bridges." Your first positions are primarily for experience, but the most important outcome of these jobs can be in the form of recommendation you may need very much when seeking your first full-time position upon graduation. You should not quickly float from part-time job to part-time job. If you once decide to take a job, despite the poor pay and perhaps poorer working conditions, apply yourself, give your services for a reasonable period of time. Obtain a clear picture of any part-time position before committing yourself; but once you accept the job keep it and work at it.

3. There may be positions available in athletics, recreation, or physical education which do not involve the routine—seek these! I was fortunate, for example, in obtaining a position in the City Hall in Los Angeles when a sophomore at the university. I spent two days a week assisting in the administration of an extensive adult sports program. My first duties included assigning officials, scheduling facilities, organizing leagues over the phone, formulating publicity, and similar functions. It was a valuable experience for me at that point in my life. There may be similar positions available in your community.

4. It is not unprofessional to ask for, and to expect, a reasonable wage for the services you render. If you approach a voluntary agency, you are volunteering yourself free of charge. It is my personal belief, however, that college youth are often exploited when they are encouraged "to take a job for the experience" without regard to the remuneration they may need and deserve. Toward the terminus of your college career you should truly possess a background which is worth a respectable wage to your employers, whether they are interested in you part-time or full-

time. Listen carefully when you are being "sold" on a job solely for the experience you may receive. No one is likely to place a higher price on you and your services than the one you set yourself; be aware of your true value to yourself and to others. Ask for a reasonable wage when working as a college student in agencies which have budgets, for private individuals who wish your services in some way, and for commercial companies you may contact for employment.

5. Employ a variety of channels when seeking part-time employment. Friends and their parents are a most valuable source. Your college placement office is another source, while newspaper ads can also provide you with job leads.

6. At times, gain part-time or full-time experience in situations other than those related to your future profession. Newspaper office experience, for example, may be important to you in a number of ways. Administrative or clerical experience can also aid you to organize yourself better, to carry out your own schoolwork more efficiently, to meet and work with a variety of people, and also perhaps to communicate verbally and in writing with more clarity. A summer or two could be spent in a job such as this.

7. If you are thinking of entering one of the para-medical specialties— physical therapy, occupational therapy, or the like—by all means affiliate in some way with a hospital during your undergraduate years. Work as an orderly, a nurses' aide, a volunteer in an ambulance, or in some other way become associated with the medical profession and find out "how it really is."

8. When seeking a part-time position, remember that you must sell yourself. Emphasize what you can do for the individual seeking help in a given position; however, do not oversell your background, claiming experience or qualifications which in truth you do not possess. Admit to a lack of background if indeed you lack background. Your candor may be rewarded.

Be interested in getting what you can from every new experience you enter. Most prospective employers after your graduation will look carefully at the range of job experiences you have obtained, and will inspect closely the recommendations you are able to obtain from your past bosses. Choose your part-time college jobs carefully, and after embarking upon them perform well, honestly, and energetically.

Full-Time Employment

Seeking a position is sometimes pleasant, sometimes unpleasant, and almost always physically and emotionally fatiguing. Upon graduation, and perhaps following a year of graduate work, you may have several feelings about yourself, all of which may be magnified out of proportion: (a) on one hand you realize better than anyone else the various deficiencies of background, personality, and skills you bring to your prospective employers and to the jobs they have to offer; and (b) you may believe, with some arrogance, that you are highly trained, fully qualified, well educated, and physically attractive; and indeed may feel a little surprised and hurt when the personnel supervisor of the first school district you approach does not immediately seek your services. Don't worry; both types of feelings are common and may recur at various intervals during your weeks and months of searching for the right position. In truth, you are probably not as well qualified as you might at times feel you are; while at the same time your appearance, scholastic record, and letters of recommendation present a reasonably attractive picture of you which does not reveal the "holes" in your background and personality.

Your preparation for the weeks and months of interviews, however, begins with your first days and weeks in your college major. The impressions you make on your instructors, your fellow students, and your part-time employers are critical. Your performance in classrooms, and on athletic fields or in gymnasiums, reveals a great deal of information about your capabilities and personality that all who come in contact with you will consciously and unconsciously read and file away for future reference.

It is sometimes said that one of the best ways to evaluate character is by assessing the manner in which an individual deals with those who are somehow inferior to him in status. How do you treat your fellow classmates? How do you react toward the young boys or girls at the YMCA you may work with a day or two a week? If you are a first-string varsity athlete, how do you relate to those on the fourth and fifth strings? These reactions of yours, if inappropriate in a number of situations, may later catch up with you during the critical time of life when you are searching for your first professional, full-time position.

Prior to looking for your first position in teaching and coaching, there are several principles worth your consideration.

1. While an undergraduate, seek broad experience related to your prospective full-time job position. From employers whom you satisfy in these situations, you may gain letters of recommendation.
2. Seek letters of recommendation only from those individuals who: (a) are able to write good ones about you, (b) whose positions and titles are likely to have some influence upon those hiring you, and (c) who tell you they can write a *good* letter about you and your qualifications. Your letters of recommendation often will be sent directly to a placement file at your college, without the opportunity on your part to

inspect their contents. They will then be available to prospective employers; and their contents, if inappropriate or even less than enthusiastic about you, can be truly damaging to your chances of obtaining a position of your choice. Attempt to get letters from individuals in the community, as well as from those with whom you have had courses. Most students have favorite professors who will write laudatory letters. Indicate the range of your experiences by the letters you place in your file.

3. Do not wait for your college or university placement office to arrange all the job interviews for you. Sell yourself by personally contacting administrators responsible for hiring personnel in various school districts. You are essentially picking your community. When you arrive at a particular school, if there seems to be some acceptance of you, you may see the facilities and talk to the principal and staff of the school.

   Find a community or communities which you like. Find out about their financial backing of educational programs, the nature of their curriculum, and the quality of their administrators; then arrange an appointment to talk with appropriate hiring officials. When you arrive, tell them you like their community as a place to spend the first part of your professional life.

   Most cities of reasonable size have a number of positions which physical educators might fill each year; the question is whether hiring officials feel you have the personal and professional qualifications to fill one of them. If you believe you do, and wish a position there, impress personnel officers by the appearance of your well-prepared placement file, by professional conduct when seeking an interview, by the manner in which you follow up your visit with appropriate correspondence, and by the personal appearance and behavior you exhibit when interviewed.

4. Attempting in every way possible to find out about the basic philosophies held by your prospective administrators and colleagues is most important. By observation and interview, try to find out how it really is to work in the position you are seeking. Talk to others in the district with positions similar to the one you are seeking. How do they feel about their superiors (allow for a certain amount of healthy griping), about their working conditions, the facilities and equipment they have available to them, and the type of children or youth whom they are serving?

   While you are not likely to find a situation which is perfectly congruent with your expectations and the abilities you possess, if there is too great a disparity between what you are and the situation you are entering, your first and critical years of teaching are likely to range from uncomfortable through unpleasant to disastrous. Unsuccessful first years can plague you later. If you do not receive permanency (tenure) in the first district you enter, subsequent employers will want to know why. They may want to know whether the situation was really as intolerable as you suggest, or whether you are simply a malcontent who will cause problems wherever you may alight.

If you are a prospective coach, you should take a particularly close look at the community philosophy about, and interest in, their athletic program. Are you willing to place your job "on the line" every season when your athletes enter competition? Are community pressures relative to the sport you hope to coach ridiculous or minimal? How will you react under the various demands made upon your time and energies by supporter groups, by your administration, and by the community at large? What do the coaches currently within the district say about these problems? With which of these men are you likely to work; and how do your philosophies seem to coincide or diverge? Will discrepancies between the manner in which you and your prospective colleagues feel about athletics, educational objectives, the role of sport in the development of youth, winning, etc., be likely to cause problems severe enough to result in your dismissal after a year or so? Think these things over before signing your contract.[1]

5. Look carefully at the salary scale, at opportunities for earning extra remuneration in various roles, and at the apparent promotion policies of the district you are considering entering. Do they seem to promote their counselors, administrators, and supervisors from within the district; or do they go outside their community frequently when seeking supervisory help? What chances are there for you to advance, taking into consideration the size of the district, the age of others with whom you might later compete for positions, and your own goals and capabilities? Does the district you are considering tend to dismiss teachers after two or three years, rather than extending them tenure? Too many districts in the country, particularly some smaller ones, engage in this practice; not (as might be expected) to upgrade the quality of the teachers they retain, but to absolve themselves from having to pay increasingly higher salaries to teachers as they reach the upper levels of the salary scale. Two young teachers may together earn a salary equal to that of one teacher who has been in the district ten to 12 years; the district budget director may be well aware of this fact.

What is the nature of the total community: its ethnic makeup, political leanings, and general outlook toward the schools and education? Are bond issues being supported? Is there community involvement of a constructive nature in the programs initiated by the schools; conversely, are the schools sensitive to community needs when instituting new

[1]It is also an excellent idea to have your lawyer look over any coaching or teaching contract prior to signing.

courses and enrichment experiences? What is the community's size? Will you be too frequently noticed by students and their parents as you conduct your private and public life within the city, or will its size render you relatively inconspicuous? Will the type of inspection you might receive in a small community irritate you? And finally, of course, will you be happy living in such a community? Some school districts prefer to have their teachers live in the community they serve, since teachers will then spend their money with the merchants whose taxes purportedly pay their salaries.

If you decide that a position is right for you after considering some of the factors discussed above, and if the district believes that you are right for them, then ask for your contract; and, after carefully reading it with the help of your lawyer, sign it. You are in, at least temporarily.

Several other sections of the text (the chapter dealing with physical education at the secondary school, and the section discussing athletic coaching) discuss the conduct you should exhibit when working in your first position. You should, after obtaining your first job, be ready to spend a full day doing what at first will seem an exhausting job. Your student-teaching days will seem mild compared to the five or six periods you must put in, together with perhaps an after-school activity of some kind. The tensions you experience as the result of new adjustments to a variety of students, and when getting to know your colleagues and administrators, may be considerable. But somehow you will wend your way through your first year or two of teaching and coaching. I hope the satisfactions will outweigh the disappointments, and that the personal successes you experience will override the failures you may also be confronted with. It is helpful to remember, particularly if you are an eager, young, idealistic (a great thing to be!) college graduate, that in truth you may not exert a startling, magical, immediate change in the attitudes, skills, and lives of your students. Many people have influenced the lives of the youth you will serve in more dramatic ways than you can hope to duplicate, and may have had negative influences upon their characters in a manner too penetrating for you to overcome within a few weeks of half-hour physical education periods.

At the same time you may find, toward the end of your first year, that you have been truly important in molding the outlooks of more youngsters than you might have felt you were reaching. You will be informed in subtle ways when you may be succeeding: for instance, when the quiet senior asks you what one has to do to become a physical education teacher; or when a parent shakes your hand with thanks during an open house; or when, perhaps, a student just looks at you one day with respect and admiration in his or her eyes.

References

Books

Endicott, F. S., *A College Student's Guide to Career Planning.* Chicago: Rand McNally & Company, 1967.

Hoppock, R., *Occupational Information: Where to Get It and How to Use It in Counseling and in Teaching.* New York: McGraw-Hill Book Company, 1963.

Knapp, C. G., *Physical Education: Student Teaching Guide.* Champaign, Illinois: Stripes Publishing Company, 1962.

Periodicals

American Vocational Journal. 1025 15th St., N. W., Washington, D. C. 20005.

Journal of College Placement. College Placement Council, Inc., 35 E. Elizabeth Ave., Bethlehem, Pa. 18018.

Vocational Aspects of Secondary and Further Education. Pergamon Press Ltd., Headington Hill Hall, Oxford, England.

Vocational Guidance Quarterly. National Vocational Guidance Association, 1605 New Hampshire Ave., N.W., Washington, D. C. 20009.

CHAPTER TWENTY-SIX

An Overview
and a Look Ahead

Several writers, during the final years of the 1960s, attempted to formulate just what one might expect of physical education and of physical educators in the twenty-first century. I will not try to look so far into the future within these pages, but rather will make a relatively conservative effort to discern just what trends may occur in physical education and associated careers during the decades of the 1970s and 1980s.

This type of soothsayer-like writing is an undertaking which is perilous to the extreme. For example, it is difficult, if not impossible, to separate the things one *wants* to happen from the things one actually *believes* are likely to occur. Secondly, predictions of this nature are invariably influenced by narrow personal experiences, biases, and outlooks of their authors. However, despite these and other pitfalls in such an undertaking, I shall push bravely ahead.

At the completion of Chapter Nineteen, some of the trends which may soon emerge were described. Examined below are other variables which may influence the directions movement programs and movement specialists will take in the years just ahead.

Career Channels

One of the primary purposes of the text was to acquaint students considering a major in physical education with the variety of careers which

might lead out of such a course of study. Chapters Six to Fourteen outlined only some of the many positions which young men and women
might enter upon graduation.

For example, to an increasing degree during the 1960s the athletic
trainer attached to both college and high school teams began to obtain
academic credentials and a professional background which enabled
him to offer better service to youth. Generally, the preparation of the
more capable trainers has included not only a B.S. degree in physical
education, but also a certificate in physical therapy, obtained after an
additional year of study and clinical experience. Athletic trainers often
take part in workshops to sharpen their skills and, like therapists, are
able to employ a number of types of equipment in order to reduce or
prevent athletic injuries. Trainers in progressive athletic programs
today work closely with the team physicians. Training room experience
while an undergraduate is available to most who contemplate becoming trainers after graduation. Modern emphasis in athletic training
includes not only the remediation of athletic injuries, but also, through
judiciously applied exercise, the prevention of such problems before
they occur.

Another interesting field has been entered by a number of professional people whose backgrounds had been in departments of physical
education. The human factors expert is an individual usually combining
a background in psychology-physiology with work in engineering and
mathematics during his undergraduate or graduate years. The job of
these men is to explore and attempt to solve problems dealing with the
integration of humans within some of the simple, as well as the more
complex, man-machine "systems" found within our space effort, industry, defense establishment, and daily life. At times these combination
human performance experts-engineers have studied the effort needed
when wielding a hammer, with an eye to designing a more efficient
hand tool with which to pound nails. At another level, several physical
educators were attached to the Apollo space program, attempting to
devise exercise programs and to deal with other problems encountered
by our astronauts.

Generally, the human factors expert works on teams composed of
professionals in other disciplines, including engineering, physiology,
psychology, metallurgy, and similar fields of study. The physical educators attached to the Apollo program have good backgrounds in physiology; while one of the founders of the Human Factors Society in the
United States was a professor of physical education. Some universities
in the United States have distinct undergraduate and graduate majors
titled "biotechnology" or some similar label.

It is possible in the 1970s that some of the career titles dealt with in
the previous chapters may merge together in various ways; while it is

also probable that several new types of jobs will appear on the scene. For example, at this time there is a rather fine line between the jobs carried out by the physical and occupational therapists. In future years the various therapies discussed in Chapter Fourteen may merge into a single field called, perhaps, "movement therapy." The focus of such a general professional merger would be to improve the motor attributes of the atypical child and adult, using movement as the primary method of help.

Increasing fragmentation of the various therapies may also occur; and more states may begin to establish educational criteria for the separate occupations of dance therapist, occupational therapist, corrective therapist, and the like. In any case, it appears that some helpful kind of reorganization and refocusing of these and similar occupations would be a constructive change.

Elementary Physical Education

One of the more significant trends in elementary physical education in the 1960s was the emergence of, and interest generated by, the "movement" movements, perceptual-motor training, sensory-motor education, and similar programs. Generally, their proponents purported to somehow change attributes other than those directly involving motor activity, by exposing children to various types of tasks resembling quite closely tasks usually found in physical education programs.

Some writers, including this one, expressed marked skepticism about these programs during the latter part of the 1960s, particularly in the light of a great deal of research evidence which failed to support some of the more elaborate claims. At the same time, the 1960s saw a large number of people in education begin to pay more attention to how children move, to the importance attached by children to their bodies, to their playground skills, to the clumsy child in the classroom and playground, and to the concomitant emotional and learning problems which sometimes accompany clumsiness.

This interest in movement by individuals who were previously oblivious to the obvious attributes which children evidence, and which physical educators have held dear for hundreds of years, was in many ways a breath of fresh air which many competent physical educators were able to channel into new and constructive programs for children in elementary school. Psychologists began to see the social punishment an inept child received at play reflected in a low self-concept, which in turn influenced his motivation to engage in classroom work. Educators began to perceive anew the importance of recess and physical education within the school day; and more and more teachers in special education, remedial reading, and similar components of the educational program sought the assistance of physical educators to help the physically-withdrawn child improve his self-image. Some of the requests by these educators for help could be met; while at other times no one with the proper background or attitude was available within departments of physical education. Hopefully, in the 1970s and 1980s more physical educators will begin to contribute in positive ways to the early motor education and movement remediation of children entering elementary schools.

If the principle discussed in Chapter Seven is a valid one, it is possible that during the decades ahead the country will see an interest in, and programs for, children of preschool age. Several professors during the final years of the 1960s were busily at work on texts outlining helpful techniques and environments through which to improve the physical abilities of babies! Perceptive physicians can usually diagnose even moderate motor problems in infants shortly after birth. Perhaps physical educators can have a hand in devising and carrying out programs through which these infants can be aided to gain optimum development, while it also may be possible to develop techniques, applied perhaps by parents or educators, through which the normal infant can be aided to experience the maximum possible amount of physical development.

Democratic Teaching in a Democracy

Even the most hard-of-hearing educator or physical educator could, if he listened carefully, note the fact that students during the 1960s somehow wanted to have more of a say about what was handed to them, forced upon them, and what they were "motivated" to do by teachers. One physical educator in the United States (Muska Mosston), upon arriving from his native Israel in the 1950s, was both surprised and shocked to find youth within a "democratic" society in close-lock step in physical education classes, performing meaningless and poorly motivated exercises "by the numbers," and engaging in close-order drill as they moved from roll-taking to the athletic field or gymnasium.

His reaction was to propose a more democratic method of teaching, through which youth of all ages could be encouraged, if they were not already too subservient, to begin to think for themselves about ways to execute various sports skills and game strategies, and about how they might even evolve their own program of physical improvement. In 1970 an Institute for the Study of Teaching Behavior was established by Mosston in Pennsylvania. Hopefully this trend will continue, and others in both our field and other disciplines will not only verbalize and write about new practices, but will also innovate ways of carrying out educational processes which are more productive and less abrasive to both learner and instructor than were those in vogue during the first 60 years of the twentieth century.

Theory and Practice in Teacher Education

Several trends might be predicted in the area of teacher education during the decades ahead. Some of these appear presently to be budding.

There seems to be a trend, for example, to expose undergraduate students early in their schooling to the types of teaching situations in which they propose to spend the rest of their lives. Freshmen and sophomore courses in several colleges during the latter part of the 1960s incorporated practice-teaching experiences into the classwork. In this way students could begin to see some of the problems they might have met and overcome within both their classes and themselves. The increased social awareness exhibited by college-age youth in the 1960s led many, including physical education majors, to seek and obtain opportunities to work with physically handicapped and culturally disadvantaged youth, both in the United States and abroad. These early experiences in programs of this nature resulted in students who were more aware of the realities of life, and who at times tended to be more skeptical of the platitudes issuing forth from some of their less-aware instructors.

It is becoming increasingly apparent that two opposite types of trends in sight during the 1960s will probably come in balance during the next two decades. Many of the smaller undergraduate major programs, which formerly contained only a course or two in exercise physiology and kinesiology, with the majority of the work concentrated upon how to coach various sports, began during the middle and late 1960s to include more and more theory courses. Particular emphasis was placed upon content containing reference to the psychology of physical activity.

On the other hand, some of the more "high-powered," theoretically-oriented curriculums initiated at some of the universities in the country began to undergo reexamination during the latter part of the last decade. The result of this reexamination in some cases has been a shift of the curriculum in the direction opposite to what has occurred in some of the smaller state colleges and universities. More and more leaders of these "academic" programs are beginning to discover that most of their graduates sought, and were accepted into, teaching jobs at the secondary levels; and an increased number of practical, method-coaching courses are beginning to reappear in programs of this nature.

The effect of these two opposite trends, during the next several years, should be the achievement of a reasonable balance in teacher education curriculums throughout the country.

Graduate Education

Several types of trends can be discerned in graduate physical education programs throughout the country. At the same time, there have been many weaknesses apparent to those who have surveyed such programs in America during the 1960s and early 1970s.

In general, graduate programs in physical education during the 1960s became increasingly research-oriented. Students spent more time consulting basic research journals in physical education and in related fields. Their graduate research projects were likely to be respectable basic or applied investigations, rather than "how-to-do-it" projects such as those frequently done in libraries in previous years. Some graduate faculties seemed to select staff members with specific interests, to direct the energies of their graduate students into rather narrow and deep courses of study. One large eastern university, for example, instituted and perpetuated a doctorate with an emphasis in motor learning; and it is well known that extremely competent Ph.D.s with backgrounds in the biochemistry of exercise are "produced" by another university in the midwest.

Graduate programs, particularly those with relatively small staffs, evidence the inclination to "farm their graduates out" to other graduate programs on the same campus for some of their doctoral work. Graduates with this type of experience are often highly competent. Taking work in the medical school, and in departments of physiology and psychology, has given and will give most master's and doctoral candidates a penetrating look at the basics of physical activity.

Still present on many campuses, however, are several disturbing factors which hopefully will be eradicated in the more "enlightened" years ahead. The fact that on some campuses men and women students at the graduate level are educated by separate faculties seems preposterous.[1] One does not gain a male or a female degree in biochemistry or mathematics. Surely physical educators in the decade ahead will begin to see how they weaken their graduate and undergraduate programs by exhibiting such a cleavage, by dividing the available talent in this antiquated manner.

[1]One erudite observer recently termed the practice "freaky."

It has been my observation that the graduate programs in physical education in the United States, particularly those awarding a doctorate, are markedly uneven in quality. Some are what one would term "strong," containing faculty members who engage in creative research and who are acknowledged scholars in their subject-matter specialties. These same programs have well-equipped research laboratories and libraries, which enable graduate students to conduct worthwhile investigations.

At the time of this printing, however, there are physical education departments in the United States awarding the Ph.D. degree (a research degree) which do not have a research laboratory among their facilities. Their faculty membership includes individuals evidencing dubious levels of academic achievement, and their libraries do not approach adequacy. Hopefully, at some level within the next few years, coercive standards committees will evaluate the programs available within which a student may pursue a higher degree in physical education. The results of this type of evaluation, plus some serious internal evaluation by departments of physical education which offer graduate courses, should lead toward programs of better quality within the decades ahead.

There are just beginning to emerge the skeletons of several research institutes which may, when expanded, provide fruitful facilities in which post-doctoral programs may be founded. Hopefully, those presently constituted will be expanded, and others will be established; so that scholars with their doctorates in physical education may continue to improve themselves at all stages of their careers, and thus improve the quality of the effort they extend to the profession and to people.

Coaching

In Chapter Ten I have expressed that athletics may be worthwhile in the life of a youth, and that the role of the coach is an important one within the educational environment. A hopeful trend was the tendency of many coaches during the 1960s to seek penetrating answers to questions related to the leadership of athletic teams. Hopefully, during the years ahead, coaches will progress from gimmicks[2] to a realistic, scientific, and humanistic approach to leading the youth in their charge. Some Europeans with whom I have come in contact have expressed to

[2]Recently one swimming coach at a major university, after scoring an upset and winning a conference championship, was deluged with phone calls from nearby high school coaches wondering what they could do to their teams to insure similar success in the week they had left prior to their own state meet!

me their feelings about even the high-level coaches from our country who visit theirs. They say that while American coaches seem to be "good guys" possessing pleasing personalities, and that all within the foreign country generally turn out to hear them speak as they pass through, it quickly becomes apparent to the foreign listeners that Americans are not really well-grounded in the basic sciences underlying physical activity. They seem to know training techniques reasonably well, but have little idea concerning the physiological, sociological and psychological mechanisms underlying some of the things they "try out" on their teams.

Many national coaches of teams from other countries possess good academic backgrounds, which enable them to institute practices likely to optimize the performances of their athletes, despite the fact that the countries they represent may not have a large population from which to draw. The leader of an Olympic gymnastic team in Mexico City was known to be one of the best kinesiologists in the world, while the coach of the Russian track team at the same competition held a Ph.D. in physiology.

While it may be unrealistic to expect coaches in our major sports to obtain a similar background, hopefully in the years ahead efforts at self-improvement will be undertaken, which will result in some of the unfortunate stereotypes which the public holds of coaches being eradicated. Additional knowledge about the basic mechanisms underlying physical activity may have a more important influence upon the win-and-loss record of a coach than does attendance at interminable clinics. At clinics, many of the same drills are repeated endlessly by one or more of the more successful coaches within their sport, who in turn are usually merely guessing as to why certain things "seem to work."

Further, training in some aspects of the behavioral sciences by the coaching fraternity should similarly result in improvement in their performance as human beings. They may begin to accommodate better to individual personality differences among the athletes they lead; and at the same time they may be able to get the most out of an athlete with some type of personality problem, or may become able to aid athletes to seek their own solutions to performance "blocks" which may be plaguing them. The outcome of acquiring this type of background, whether as an undergraduate or in workshops following graduation, should be manifested in integrating the athletic program within the total educational program in colleges and in high schools in more helpful ways than has often been the case during the first 60 years of the twentieth century.

Communication in Physical Education

There were signs as the 1960s ended that more fruitful communication is likely to take place in the decades ahead between theoreticians, researchers, and the physical education teachers and coaches who contact children and youth each day.

Some writers from university and college faculties are beginning to write texts which are comprehensible to others in addition to workers within their own research laboratories! Programs in workshops and conventions will likely contain sessions dealing with interpretations of research literature for the benefit of attending teachers; while, conversely, many researchers are instituting programs within the universities and colleges, or in neighboring schools, through which they can investigate practical and applied problems relative to teaching and learning processes.

All of these trends, hopefully, in the years ahead will result in better communication between various components of the profession of physical education, communication which at times was lacking in the past. University scholars are given the time, and have the library facilities, through which they may make important contributions to the literature; and through their investigative efforts can explore and evaluate new practices. Teachers in the schools, on the other hand, are closely in contact with children and youth. Intramural bickering within the profession has generally been demonstrated to lead nowhere.

From the Laboratories

The opportunities seem limitless for physical educators who wish to make a significant contribution in some aspect of either applied or basic research dealing with human motor activity. Work still needs to be done, for example, in just what levels of exercise are needed and can be tolerated by people within various age groups, who evidence various individual physiological characteristics. At least as important is to ascertain just what motivates, or fails to motivate, people to work vigorously in physical activities. A fruitful area of study, related to these, concerns the nature of psychological changes which may accompany the achievement of increased levels of fitness by adolescent and adult populations.

More basic than these questions are problems dealing with the manner in which various cellular-level changes occur, both during exercise and as the human action's capacity for work is improved through some kind of fitness regimen. This type of research is presently being done using humans, other primates, and rats, in laboratories in physical education departments.

At the end of the 1960s, there was a proliferation of investigations, including some small-group studies, dealing with the social psychology of physical activity. Hopefully this trend will continue. The interactions between small-group members vigorously engaged in activity, and of others in the competitive situation, are important and vital in the formation of the motive structure of people at work, play, and in athletic competition. When some of these powerful social forces are better understood, more effective performance environments should be forthcoming—environments which will not only produce better individual and group performance but, as important, will produce situations which will be emotionally more "healthy" to those participating and to those directing such participation.

Further work in the social-psychological area should examine the teen subcultures within high schools and within the total community. A thorough evaluation of the values and attitudes of contemporary youngsters hold about physical activity, and participation as spectators in athletic events, may prove embarrassing or encouraging; but at the very least it may stimulate physical educators to take a more thorough look at the nature of their offerings, and how they are "packaged" for consumption.[3]

A broader look at various social and ethnic influences upon free activity choices among youngsters in various parts of the larger cities might result in individually "tailored" programs of games, fitness activities, rhythmics, and folk dances for each secondary school. The movement propensities, activity choices, and values about athletics of various kinds, appear even to the casual observer to be markedly different among various cultural factions within the larger cities of the United States. It appears that the 1970s and 1980s might be a time to transform these subjective observations into more exact sociological surveys.

It is to be expected that emphasis upon various psychological variables will continue to interest researchers in physical education. Hopefully, not only will studies be carried out which seem to pile pebbles upon pebbles as they "uncover" minutiae, but at the same time rather deep "shafts" of inquiry will be dug into relatively unexposed problems.

---

[3]A recent survey by a former Olympic champion assigned to write a series of fitness articles for the Los Angeles *Times* revealed that only about 25 percent of the high school youngsters she surveyed reported liking their physical education classes! The remainder were either neutral on the subject, or expressed dissatisfaction with the content of their programs or the way in which they were taught.

The topic areas which researchers have begun to explore as this book is printed will doubtless be elaborated upon further. For example, it is likely that more work will be carried out to widen our knowledge about how physical activity may contribute to, or detract from, the acquisition of academic skills by younger and older children. These types of investigations, which have appeared for years in the German and Russian literature, and more recently in the Scandinavian and American research journals, if pursued far enough, may result in individually designed curriculums for children evidencing various propensities for movement. Such curriculums could consist of school days containing various percentages of both active and passive learning experiences, designed to meet the unique needs for activity of various groups of a school population.

Disciplines and subject-matter areas which in the previous decades seemed to have contributed little to our understanding of physical activity programs may, within the coming years, begin to exert a considerable influence over researchers and scholars in our field. For example, there is likely to be a closer alignment between politics and physical education in the years ahead. The political climate in the United States at the end of the sixties and beginning of the seventies cannot be ignored by anyone planning programs of any type in, or related to, the school systems. Planners of activities as vital and important to the community as athletics and physical education will ignore the political context at their peril.

A perusal of the cultural and physical anthropology literature should also inspire younger scholars in our field to take a more enlightened look at the basics of motor activity, in individuals and within various subcultures in the United States. The evolution of game choices by adults and children may be studied more constructively by individuals with a broad background of cultural anthropology. Those formulating exercise programs intended to stress the structure of modern man may learn important lessons from a consideration of the manner in which the human "animal" evolved to his present form, and the factors in his constitutional makeup which still seem to be in a state of flux.

The national awareness of ecology during the early 1970s should continue to make itself felt in society during the years ahead. Again, to ignore the pollution of air, sky, water, and most of all of people, is to court extinction. I am unaware of any sound studies that have been carried out, for example, concerning the influence of air pollution upon the physical performance of young school children. And yet I, as many others, have been a shocked and concerned observer of the great duress in which athletes find themselves when trying to work hard under conditions which prevent efficient oxygen utilization by their cardio-respiratory systems as they attempt to process polluted air. Hopefully, studies of this nature will be carried out shortly, and their results made public.

The investigations and areas of concern superficially enumerated on these pages represent only a small percentage of the topics upon which evidence is needed in order to make wiser decisions about physical activity programs for people of all ages and conditions. Hopefully, some of the readers of this text may make a contribution to our knowledge about some of these topics; but all of those who peruse these pages may become able to interpret and to incorporate what is useful from the research literature in the years ahead, by careful and penetrating scholarship during their undergraduate careers.

Tomorrow the World!

There were many signs in the decade of the sixties that the world is getting smaller. This same trend has been reflected in professional physical education circles. International groups to study and exchange ideas concerning problems in physical education common to all countries, as well as those concerned with specific components of physical education, have met regularly during the years following World War II. The United Nations, as well as governmental agencies in the United States and in foreign countries, have facilitated the exchange of scholars and the formulation of conferences dealing with problems in health education, recreation, athletics, and physical education. It is likely that this trend will continue and expand in the decades which terminate the twentieth century.

Even more helpful will be meetings resulting in international cooperation, which in turn will lead toward productive programs of physical education and athletics in the so-called developing countries in Africa and other parts of the world. During the past 20 years, individuals have been encouraged and financed to take trips to various smaller countries in the world, as informal ambassadors of athletics and physical education. Their impact at times has been a helpful one. Perhaps in the future, more cohesive and organized efforts will be made in the direction of international cooperation, which in turn may lead to sets of standards being formulated, teams of "experts" being constituted, and aspects of physical education, health education, and recreation being compiled. In this manner, the final years of the twentieth century will witness more productive international cooperation, and more positive programs of action, as a result of these common efforts between nations.

Appendix

Course and Faculty
Evaluation Sheets

Evaluation of Instructor

1. Were the goals of the course clear from the beginning?
   Comment _____

2. Does the instructor stimulate intellectual curiosity sufficiently to inspire you to read further in the field?
   Yes____No____ If yes, in what ways? _____

3. Should he be more available at office hours for consultation and discussion? Yes____No____

4. Does he show an interest in teaching? Yes____No____
   How? _____

5. Would you like to see an increase in any particular teaching method?
   Comment and recommendations _____

6. Is the course well-organized? The lectures? _____

7. Is there adequate explanation and/or discussion in lecture and/or quiz section for comprehension of the material offered?

8. Give your personal evaluation of the instructor. _____

Evaluation of Course

1. Were all the assignments purposeful, or were some just "busy work"? Be specific _____

2. Are the assigned readings sufficiently helpful to merit reading them? _____

3. Are the course exercises other than examinations (i.e., papers) worthwhile and helpful? _____
   Do you think outside exercises should be incorporated in the class? _____

4. What is the relationship of the lecture to the text material? (That is, are the lecture and text material unrelated, or repetitious, or do they supplement each other?)
   _____
   _____
   Do they represent a bias of the professor? Yes____No____

5. Was too much time or emphasis placed on some part of the material? If so, on what part? _____

6. Was too little time or emphasis placed on some part of the material? If so, on what part? _____

7. Do the examinations pertain to material covered in class? Yes____ No____ If no, why? _____

8. Should a grading scale be based on prior classes or on the scores in your class? _____

9. Examinations are (check as many as apply):
   Fair _____
   Too hard _____
   Too easy _____
   Tricky (in an unfair way) _____
   Too infrequent _____
   Too frequent _____
   Comment _____

10. Grading was (check one):
    Too hard _____
    Too easy _____
    About right _____

11. Do you feel course evaluations are beneficial and necessary? Comment _____

12. How might the course be changed or reevaluated by the instructor for future presentation of the material? _____
    _____
    _____
    _____
    _____

Index